The Helldivers' Rodeo

The Helldivers' Rodeo

A Deadly, EXTREME, SPEAR FISHING
Adventure Amid the Offshore Oil Platforms
in the Murky Waters of the Gulf of Mexico

Humberto Fontova

M. Evans and Company, Inc.

New York

M. Evans and Company, Inc.
216 East 49th Street
New York, New York 10017

Library of Congress Cataloguing-in-Publication Data

Fontova, Humberto
    The Helldiver's Rodeo / Humberto Fontova
    p. cm.
    ISBN 0-87131-936-5
    1. Scuba diving—Mexico, Gulf of. 2. Spear Fishing—Mexico, Gulf of.
3. Drilling Platforms—Mexico, Gulf of. I. Title.
    GV840.673.M62 F65 2001
    799.1'4—dc21   00-58702

Book design and typesetting by Evan H. Johnston

Printed in the United States of America

9   8   7   6   5   4   3   2

Contents

Acknowledgments

Without my wife this book would not have happened. This book is dedicated to her. The feeding, maintenance, and disciplining of three teenagers (who skew father-ward in temperament) was a gruesome ordeal with the "head" of the family constantly holed up in his office seeking inspiration. That was bad enough. I also relied heavily on Shirley's (full-time) accountant's mind for the technical details so crucial to a book that deals with scuba diving to immense depths, computers and assorted gadgets, and when trying to remember the words to "Disco Inferno". Somehow we made it. And not just through this book. The contract for this book was signed on our twentieth anniversary. Maybe that means something. You'll have to ask her, she's better at finding the hidden significance in such things.

Hearty kudos to my editor, Marc Baller, who somehow assembled the jigsaw puzzle that became this book.

Special thanks also to the guys who shared their rig-diving stories. Book or no book, sharing lunch or beers with this crew was a kick, a good antidote to listening to the whiny males on Seinfeld or Friends—Terry "Poppa Smurf" Migaud especially. "Mr. Helldiver" himself, he opened his house, his mind, his closets, his records—everything to me.

The roll call also includes Terry's fellow Helldivers, Stan "The Man" Smith and Louis Rossignol, Sea Tigers Darren Bourgeois and father Gerry, their long-time dive mates, Val Rudolfich, Mitch Cancienne, and Allen "King Spear Fisherman" Walker.

Bob Larche and Randy Evans merit special thanks for opening up about dive incidents not exactly pleasant to recall—the loss of buddies. Charlie Romano added a little Sicilian spice.

From over in Baton Rouge, Clay Coleman, Max Smiley, Bobby Geanelloni, Terry Brousseau, Nancy Cohagen, Mary Beth Isaacs all helped immensely. Frank "The Knife" Olah, kept me in stitches with his stories.

The history of this sport came not from some musty newspaper clippings but from the musty mind of Johnny Bonck. Musty? I jest of course. May we all be as lucid, spry and downright exuberant as septuagenarians.

Again, a lot of people contributed to this thing. But it would have come to naught without a supportive family.

Introduction

The area off the coast of Cojimar, just east of Havana, is known by some for the best marlin fishing on Earth. About five miles from shore, the bottom of the ocean drops to 3,000 feet. Geologists call this the "continental slope." Among its admirers was "Papa" Ernest Hemingway. Here he made his longest residence, at Finca Vigia, fishing daily. Here his "Old Man" fought his epic battle with the monster marlin. And here, right off the beach in 1961, my cousin Pelayo and I prowled the shallow reefs with goggles and straightened coat hangers, impaling fish.

The coat hangers were flattened and sharpened on one end. The other end went through a hole drilled through a six-inch section of broomstick, which had a sliver of old inner tube looped and nailed to the back; bow and arrow style. You held the broomstick section with one hand, gripped the coat hanger and inner tube with the other, pulled back . . . aimed, and—FLINK!

All the while, stern *milicianos* stood watch on the sand, glaring and fingering their Czech machine guns, like any teenaged boys with their first guns, actually. They had orders to shoot any boat that entered the water. Already people were going "fishing" and turning up in Key West.

We were seven at the time. We'd have loved a marlin but settled for yellow grunts (*ronquitos*), ten-inches long, twirling in a flurry of sand on the coat hanger. Then we carried them triumphantly to our parents on the beach. That night Tata, my nanny, fried them up whole, Cuban style, the skin salty, garlicky, limey, and crispy. The meat underneath: white, juicy, and flavorful. The head: on.

Tata looked nothing like Mami in Gone With The Wind. She looked more like Condaleeza Rice or Whitney Houston—a young elegant mulatress. She would put out stale bread in the backyard for the pigeons and sparrows every afternoon, then watch them from the back window. Pelayo and I knew the routine. So we'd sneak through the banana trees with our Daisy BB guns, get in range, and pop them (the BB's bounced off their wings). Tata hated that. She'd fuss at us every time. *"Malditos!"* (roughly, "punks!") she'd screech, chasing us with a switch.

This was 1961, early in the Revolution. Stale bread was still expendable. Later it became a delicacy, along with sparrows and pigeons. Also, the Reds hadn't gotten around to confiscating BB guns just yet. In due time.

Those Czech machine guns were all over 1961 Cuba. Pelayo and I saw them again up close two months later, when they came for his father. We were in his backyard with our BB guns, annoying the pigeons, but safe from Tata, who was deep into her siesta that day.

Some milicianos came from behind a wall, scowling as always, but nervous, jerky. The pigeons scattered and the Reds looked over—"Ah!" their faces brightened. "Munchkin counter-revolutionaries!" And they threw up the checkas and slammed the bolts, the little holes at the end of the barrels pointed straight at us.

We froze. It's been almost forty years but I still remember those little holes. Then—"ahhh!" Their faces softened—slightly. "Just BB guns." One came over and yanked our prized Daisys (we'd just gotten them for Christmas) from our trembling hands. *"Para la Revolucion!"* he exclaimed as they made for the house's back entrance. Other milicianos had come around the front.

That was a famous phrase back then. Every time the Reds stole something, confiscated something, every time they abolished another right, it was: "Para la Revolucion!"

Pelayo's father looked doomed. An official of the *ancien regime*—a military man, in fact. As colonel in the Cuban navy he'd been naval attache in Washington during World War II.

Didn't look good. He looked *paredon* (the wall opposite the firing squad) bound, if anyone did. Everyone had advised him to flee north. But he refused. "I have nothing to be ashamed of," he countered. "I've done nothing wrong! And this is our homeland, *carajo!*" As if that mattered to the communists.

Well, they finally came for him. Now, we assumed there would be a show trial, a volley at the wall, and a hidden grave. It was happening all over Cuba.

Tata saved his life. Yes, she went to the prison herself. "This man is a *santo!*" she shouted at the Reds. "*Muy honrado!* He's never mistreated me or any others." Here was a humble mullatress speaking, the kind of person the Revolution was supposedly all about. "Why him? You are a bunch of *sin-verguenzas* [shameless ones, scoundrels]! Release him!"

Amazingly, it worked. He was released to exile—for him, still an agonizing punishment.

Hell, those milicianos took our BB guns home for their kids. And that raid was odd, actually. They usually came at dawn.

I saw the checkas up close again a month later, the very day we left Cuba. Four were pointing at my dad on the very tarmac of the airport. We'd been walking to the plane that would take us to the United States and freedom. At last! Out of that hellhole!

"*Señor Fontova!*" What the? He looked around. We all looked around. "*Señor Fontova—gusano!*" ("worm", what the Reds called their opponents). Four milicianos, scowling, bearded, armed, grabbed Dad from each side by the arms. They'd gotten a full-grown counter-revolutionary this time.

"Go ahead," he told my mom, who found herself in the white-knuckle clutches of six little hands; my brother, my sister, and me. "Whatever happens to me, I don't want ya'll growing up here."

Tears, hysteria . . . but we left. Next day, from a cousin's house in Miami, Mom called Cuba and fainted while on the phone, fell on the floor. People rushed over. My aunt grabbed the phone. "Ayy, NO!" she shrieked. Dad was in La Cabaña.

Yes, La Cabaña, firing-squad central. They went off every dawn. The gallant Che Guevara took over the old Spanish fortress in 1959, crammed its dungeons with "counter-revolutionaries" jerked from their homes in dawn raids, and started signing death warrants—three hundred a week—for two years. The men (and boys) were yanked from their cells every dawn, bound and blindfolded . . .

. . . *"Fuego!"* and the bodies collapsed against the blood-spattered paredon. A soldier walks over with a pistol for the coup de grace—pow! This one's still twitching over here—POW! Families shrieking and wailing outside the walls of the fortress to no avail, the bodies were bulldozed into mass, unmarked graves. No, folks, this wasn't Eastern Europe sixty years ago. This was the fate of 21,000 men (and boys) ninety miles off our coast, with the Beatles on Ed Sullivan, with Ozzie Nelson and Beaver Cleaver on our TVs, and with the *New York Times* rhapsodizing about the Cuban Revolution.

Armando Valladares listened from his cell. In *Against All Hope*, he wrote that the cries of "long live Christ the King!" and *"Viva Cuba libre!"* would make the pits of that centennial fortress tremble, right before the shots rang out.

Che was hell on smiting his enemies, all right. But only when these enemies were bound, gagged, and blindfolded. His academic groupies and Beltway press agents beat the drum about some valiant guerilla fighter, but any actual battles in his "war" against Batista escapes the memory of those who lived in Cuba, especially those who supposedly fought against him. When he finally did find himself in bona-fide battles, finally up against men who could shoot back in the Congo and Bolivia (Cuban exiles working for the CIA, as it turned out), Che was outfoxed, outfought, routed, and got a taste of his own medicine.

"Don't shoot!" yelled the gallant Che, when they finally cornered him in Bolivia. "I'm Che! I'm worth more to you alive than dead!"

Dad had heard the *"Viva Cuba libre"*, too, from his very cellmates. He says that some of them even gave the "fuego" order themselves. He'd been in La Cabana for three months after his aiport arrest. Then he caught up with us here in New Orleans. They released him—don't ask us (or him) why.

That was thirty years ago. Now Pelayo and I find ourselves a few hundred miles north of Cuba and speaking a different language. We're brushing that "continental slope" again, diving again, spearing fish again. We arrived a gaggle of penniless and terrified Cuban refugees—didn't even speak the language. But our terror was short-lived. Louisiana has always embraced immigrants and even visitors. She greets them joyfully at the gangplank or tarmac like a lost grandmother, beaming and waving frantically. She rushes out, lifts and twirls them. She mashes them into her ample bosom and riddles their head and face with kisses, her stubbled chin poking them and her garlicky breath suffocating them. But no matter, she makes her point: *"Welcome!* You're family now!"

If you are American, maybe some corporation transfers you or your partner down from the East Coast or Midwest. You get here with your fly rods, your goofy hats and vests, your dinky little creels, your granola bars and mineral water in cute little squirt-bottles. You arrive with trim bodies, clean minds, restrained appetites, dormant libidos, and a canoe on neat little racks atop a shiny SUV with a PRACTICE RANDOM ACTS OF KINDNESS bumper-sticker. You always ask me where you can go "canoeing"—whatever that means.

Six months later an outboard flecked with dried shrimp-heads and fish scales juts out of your garage. Empty beercans rattle in your SUV. Empty wine bottles cram your garbage cans. Those Jimmy Carter smiles have vanished, replaced by the lecherous smirks of Groucho Marx or Mae West. High fiber and fitness have given way to hot fudge and fun. No more grim faces and drudgery at the health club. Now it's radiant faces and revelry at the carnival club. Your conversation, once curt, to the point, and meant to convey actual facts or uplifting advice has become a free-wheeling and spicy ramble, wonderfully free of sanctimony and utterly devoid of facts. Its purpose is now the proper one: to provide a backbeat and exercise the jaw muscles between gulps of beer, sips of wine, the sucking of heads or the slurping of gumbo.

An old Cajun who ran a roadside seafood and poultry dispensary near Galliano put it a little more bluntly one day. We'd pulled over to buy some shrimp after a dive trip and were shootin' the shit with him. "Lemme told you why," he said, pointing a gnarled finger at my cousin Pelayo. "If you can't eat 'em or fuck 'em, they're worthless."

We'd asked him why he'd gotten rid of some peacocks that had been parading around in front of his stand.

Same as the area off the coast of the *Cojimar* river, the mouth of the Mississippi River lies near the very edge of the continental shelf. Here, northward-flowing Caribbean currents clash with westward-flowing Gulf currents and the southward flow of the Mississippi itself. Gulf water meets river water here. Even without the river nutrients such an undersea precipice and vortex of clashing currents would pack in schools of big pelagics.

Maps show how Louisiana juts out into the Gulf below the coasts of Texas and Mississippi. A little sliver of a peninsula bordering the river below New Orleans juts out even further. That was the river's doing—at least until the levees shackled it. For ten thousand years this "father of all waters," as the Indians called it, whipped back and forth across the landscape like a huge (but somewhat lethargic) water wiggle, depositing its fertile cargo of sediment. Most of Louisiana below Interstate 12 thus sprouted in the open gulf. In geological terms something "sprouts" in ten thousand years.

That's why we're so close to the continental shelf yet only twelve miles offshore. We trailer the boat halfway to it, on a four-lane highway. Those one hundred miles of road south of New Orleans would be a hundred miles of open water off the Texas, Mississippi, or Florida coasts. The river robs Peter to pay Paul in a sense. Iowa's loss is our gain—until the levees went up, that is.

Clamped down by the levees, running fast, the river now dumps Iowa's loss into the deep Gulf. The silt doesn't spread out and build land nowadays. It's channeled through the constantly-dredged river passes into the deep open water, eventually building huge mud cliffs that keep toppling over—massive undersea mudslides, avalanches of sunken silt that keep lurching towards the shelf. Too bad you can't see down there. Geologists tell me it probably looks like southern Utah; deep brown gorges, towering cliffs, plunging buttes—the whole "Badlands" bit.

It's a weird place. Mud on the bottom and mud on the top. But in between, cobalt blue Gulf water, just like Belize. And you talk about *fish*. In this respect it's *nothing* like Belize, or Cayman, or Cozumel. Mud is much better for growing things than sand, ask any farmer. Well, it's the same in the sea.

This nutrient-rich, organic crud jumpstarts the food chain. It starts at the bottom of the chain with phytoplankton, "the base of the sun-driven food web" according to marine biologists. The little buggers swarm in these waters. The book *The Oceans* shows an infrared photo of the world's oceans, showing the relative densities of phytoplankton by color. Yellow and orange denote the areas richest in this microscopic fish-chow. And damned if the waters off the Louisiana coast don't beam like a bonfire on that map. That phytoplankton blooms at the base, then everything on top moves in for the feast—all the way up to the "apex predators:" the sharks, tuna, amberjack, cobia . . . or in this case, us.

Add the adjacent estuaries—a huge marine incubator and nursery that comprises 40 percent of America's coastal wetlands—throw in deep water and a vortex of clashing currents, drop in thousands of massive steel reefs—any *one* of these ingredients produce abundant fisheries. Combine them and you get marine habitat unparalleled on the globe.

"I'd never seen anything like it." That's dive instructor Brad Barouse of Seven Seas Dive Shop in Baton Rouge. And he's in a good position to judge. "I traveled around the world while in the Navy, diving everyplace we stopped: the Red Sea, Truk Lagoon, Indonesia, Micronesia, *all* over the Caribbean . . . and I'll tell ya, there's *no* place that'll even approach the numbers and size of fish around these oil platforms."

Indeed. That's why we go out there. But there's that *murk* . . . the Mississippi drains 40 percent of the United States, and it seems like every grain of the fertile cargo that took the voyage swirls through the waters around us when we jerk against the rig hook at Main Pass 191.

In 1952, a National Marine Fisheries Service trawler, seeking to promote U.S. commercial fisheries, dropped a small test long-line in this area off the mouth of the Mississippi. They started cranking it up and immediately realized the ship's hold would never suffice for the number of huge tuna, billfish, and sharks that jerked around on the other end. Word got out, quick.

Trawlers and longliners from Taiwan and Japan started fishing these waters thirty years ago. The Jap longlines were held afloat by big glass orbs that local big-game fishermen took only as irresistible targets. We'd always pack pistols or shotguns on fishing trips to this area anyway. Sharks swarm in these waters and often hit the bait before a tuna, wahoo, or marlin. One blast with a .38 slug through the head has a wonderful calming effect on these brutes. Twelve-gauge buckshot pellets work even better. But these weapons served poorly for long-range shots at longline floats.

Soon we were packing the scoped hunting rifles on every offshore fishing trip. The floats bob in the waves and the shooter rocks on the deck or bridge, even with a rest on the railing. So it was keen sport to shatter one from anything over 100 yards . . . Did I say shatter? More like *explode*. A 150-grain soft-point traveling at 2,500 feet per second makes an exhilarating impact when it smacks thick glass on the water. Wagers were often placed and whoops erupted as the "pe-TAAOWW!" echoed over the waves and the floats were blown to smithereens, one after the other in fine sequence. Like I said: it was irresistible, especially on a slow fishing day and midway through the gin.

"Man what a kick to be shooting at dem bastids again!" Nick had earned five battle stars in the Pacific in WWII. He always rode on the bridge and his eyes lit up with every shot, roaring with mirth at every hit. "Like hitting a downed pilot!" He beamed, reminding us that, "Hell, they wasn't *all* kamikazes!"

Not that foreigners were the only commercial fishing boats in this area. Snapper boats from Florida and the Carolinas hook up to the offshore oil platforms, drop their lines, and crank aboard more red snapper in two hours than in two weeks of fishing along the Atlantic. Longliners from Maine and Massachusetts also made the scene, forsaking the famed Grand and Georges Banks.

Point is—the area swarms with fish.

One

DOWN AND TANGLED

"The WAY-AY-ting is the HARD-est part," squawks Tom Petty
from his hit record. But he doesn't know the half of it. Aboard
their twenty-eight-foot Wellcraft, Mark and Jimmy had been
waiting for their dive mates to surface—and it was getting hard
indeed. Rig-dives don't usually take this long.

Thirty minutes ago Ronnie and Steve had plunged through the
surface murk with their six-foot spear guns and aimed for the
bottom 400 feet below. Not that they'd reach it—*voluntarily* or
alive, anyway. They'd probably turn around at 230 feet or so if
nothing big showed up. Why push it?

Some would say they were already pushing it. Dive manuals
say the nitrogen (80 percent of what you're breathing) buzz starts
at 100 feet. "Rapture of the deep" Cousteau called it fifty years
ago. "Deep-sea intoxication" according to his contemporary,
Hans Haas. "Death catches the diver in a butterfly net whose
mesh is so soft it closes in on him unnoticed . . . one loses all mis-
givings and inhibitions and then, suddenly, comes the end."

"Martini's Law" we call it nowadays—every fifty feet of depth
equals the effects of one dry martini on the human brain. Bad

enough by itself, but they also say that the oxygen (the remaining twenty percent of what's in the tank) becomes *toxic* to the human central nervous system at 218 feet—blackouts, hysteria, derangement, convulsions, seizures. Grim things if you're in your living room; much grimmer 200 feet under the Gulf. These authorities advise recreational divers to haul back at 130 feet.

Ronnie and Steve were on a hunt, a hunt where you close to within feet of the prey before slapping the trigger. So if something big *did* show up down deep during the dive—and Ronnie or Steve stuck him . . . and the fish got a couple of loops of spear gun cable around them . . . well, that's what I meant by *voluntarily* and *alive*.

Swells get big out here, and each one jerked the boat violently against its mooring. The boat was twenty miles off the Louisiana coast tethered by a rope and "rig hook" to an oil production platform. This steel monstrosity had a deck towering a hundred feet above them and a three-acre maze of legs and crossbeams that plunged four hundred feet to the Gulf's floor. Below that, pipes poke down for two miles and suck out the oil like huge straws. The whole thing gives "eco" types the willies. But Mother Nature—that bumbler—has yet to design a reef even *half* as prolific.

Ronnie and Steve were both thirty-one years old. They'd been diving together for years, as a team. They'd both go down with guns but whoever shot first would expect the other to come lend a hand during the ensuing melee. Jimmy and Mark had a similar set-up. All on the trip that morning were experienced rig divers in peak physical condition. Ronnie himself was a dive instructor.

So his dive mates suspected trouble. *Something* had to be wrong. *Steve and Ronnie should have surfaced ten minutes ago.*

This "rig-hopping" or "bounce-diving," as we call it, doesn't take long. You hunt your way down through the steel labyrinth as massive schools of spadefish, bluefish, and assorted jacks part grudgingly to make way. Covered with barnacles, sponges, coral, and anemones, this metal maze seems a world apart from the unsightly structure above. You forget they're connected. Fish surround you the entire dive. But you ignore them. You're after the huge ones—the one-to-three-hundred-pound monstrosities that lumber through the murky gloom that forms on the muddy floor of the Gulf. You're not a voyeur down here either; you're a full-fledged participant in nature's relentless cycle of fang and claw. If you find a big fish, you stalk him and spear him. Then the fun *really* starts—depending, of course, on the size of the fish and the accuracy of the shot.

If the six-foot shaft doesn't kill or paralyze the fish by hitting the spine or cranium, you've got to get to him somehow, then straddle and paralyze him. Rodeo cowboys make good rig divers. You stick your arms through the spear gun bands, run it up on your shoulder and start yanking him in, as you fin towards him. Then you either reach in with a gloved hand and start ripping out his gills or grab your ice-pick and go to work on his head.

We used to employ dive knives for the coup de grace. But that takes too long and involves too much effort. Any economizing on bottom time and exertion figures big when you're 200 feet under the Gulf, immersed in the murk and buffeted by a three-knot current. And, oh, there's that two-hundred-pound fish on the end of your spear gun—the brute dragging you around and battering you against the beams, and he shows no signs of fatigue.

Done right, the ice-pick plunges into the cranium on the first or second jab. You twist it around and jab again, then again and hopefully the beast stops lunging and starts quivering. Now it's time to start up—but not too fast. Remember, you're at two hundred fifty feet now.

But not too slow either. You've only got five hundred pounds of air left. And it's getting damned hard to suck it out this deep. It'll get easier on the way up. So if you can't straddle and paralyze the fish, there's no choice but to eventually let go of the gun—unless you're not thinking clearly because the fish went on a rampage through the rig and bounced you into the barnacled beams like a human pinball (back in the '50s the guys wore football helmets for this type of rollicking fun). But even without a rig-pummeling, your brain's hopelessly fogged—"narked out" as we say. There's no escaping nitrogen narcosis at this depth.

So if nothing big—big *enough*, I should say—showed up down

there, Ronnie and Steve should have ascended. Five minutes on the way down, three minutes looking around, another five minutes coming up. Nothing to it. There's not much bottom time at these depths, five minutes tops; therefore: *Steve and Ronnie should have surfaced ten minutes ago.*

These "rigs," as locals call the offshore oil platforms that dot the Gulf off Louisiana's coast, claim several divers each year—not the rig itself, of course, but the waters under them. And these particular ones always claimed a disproportionate share, three divers in the summer of '99 alone.

Not all accidents occur in the depths. A few years back a diver watched his buddy stick a smallish (thirty pound) cobia at some rigs a few miles west of here. Cobia favor the top portion of the water column in the summer. The diver speared this one at around 30-foot depths— nothing to it. "A breeze," figured his buddies as they watched him tussling with the fish. They were running low on air and saw that the fish seemed under control, so they gave the "O.K." signal, saw it returned, and made for the surface. They clambered aboard the boat where another buddy was waiting and fishing.

Twenty minutes later, their buddy hadn't surfaced. Worse, no bubbles seemed to be rising from the depths. They both suited back up, plunged in and quickly spotted him, casually sitting on a beam no more than thirty feet down, the fish still darting around him. What the . . . ? No bubbles rose from his regulator and he seemed to be in an awkward position, ensnared in spear gun cable.

They swam over, and while one struggled with the flesh-shot fish the other began the grim task of unraveling the steel cable from around the diver's neck, where it had crushed his trachea and strangled him as efficiently as the *garrote* of medieval torture chambers. And that was a small fish. Even a thirty-pound fish can pull a diver around.

It's best not to dwell on these things. "Stay calm" is the cardinal rule of diving—rig-diving especially. But when your buddies have been down thirty minutes and no bubbles seem to be ascending through the murky water . . . *aha*—there's some! But that could be anything—some pipe on the rig breaking wind, some air pocket let loose by one of these monstrous swells.

The water's deep out here. The current's vicious, and the murk layer (silty freshwater floating over the heavier saltwater) is always around. Sometimes it's thin, often thick, and occasionally impenetrable, depending on river levels. The visibility can range from the hundred feet of Belize to the ten inches of Mississippi river on the same dive. But the fish are plentiful and huge. Most of Louisiana's spear fishing records (which are also the nation's) are wrestled to the surface and winched aboard around these rigs.

Still no bubbles seemed to be rising and Jimmy watched as a glum Mark, the only one with bottom time left, started suiting back up for another 200-foot plunge, this time without his gun. There was nothing on Mark's face to reflect the giddy thrill in his gut that accompanied his first dive an hour ago. He'd be hunting again, but for his buddies this time, afraid of what he'd find. They'd been too deep too long.

Then Steve suddenly popped to the surface, unadvertised by any bubbles, just as Mark was buckling his weight belt.

"Steve!" Jimmy yelled as he leaned on the gunwhale, then, turning to Mark, "There he is!" They were jubilant—until they noticed that Steve wasn't moving. He was bobbing in the swells face down.

Steve was unconscious. He'd been unconscious for several seconds—very crucial seconds as it turned out—the seconds when he was ascending the last hundred feet to the surface. Because of the change in pressure, the volume of gas in a scuba diver's lungs *quadruples* from 90 feet to the surface. Something has to give. When a diver exhales, the extra air is released through the windpipe. If he's holding his breath, what gives is lung tissue, which ruptures, or releases bubbles into the blood. The danger of an arterial gas embolism—a bubble forced out of the lung tissue by the decreasing pressure—is greatest here. The bubble travels through the arteries till it lodges in the heart, triggering a heart attack, or in the brain, triggering a fatal stroke.

Steve was still unconscious when they hauled him aboard, but he came to quickly and started coughing up blood. Not a good sign. "Ronnie's still down there," he gasped. "He's tangled with a huge grouper. I couldn't help him . . . I ran out of air."

Mark plunged in and descended 200 feet, his gut in an icy knot, his brain partly numb, partly aflame with ghastly visions. He reached the murk, but found nothing. No Ronnie. No huge grouper. He ascended a bit and started circling the rig, looking for bubbles—praying, pleading, *straining* to detect that tell-tale little line of silver globules that meant his friend was still breathing somewhere down there. But there was nothing but a murky void below him, with fish finning lazily around. How can they be so damn *calm?* Mark thought to himself, when I'm sucking air like a maniac and my goggles are filling with tears! Don't they *realize* what's going on? It seemed strange. *Everything* seemed strange at that point. Finally his own air ran low and he finned up.

The next day the *New Orleans Times Picayune* ran the headline: SCUBA DIVER SPEARS 300-POUND FISH, DISAPPEARS.

Oddly, Steve's passing out is credited by some with saving him. This opened his glottis and allowed air to escape from his expanding lungs as he ascended, preventing a pulmonary baro-trauma, or a ruptured lung—preventing a fatal one anyway. He coughed up blood for weeks.

He'd seen Ronnie spear the 300-pound fish below him and head-ed down to help. The shaft had missed the big grouper's spine and brain, so the fish was going crazy. It already had the cable wrapped around Ronnie a couple of times. Steve plunged into the melee, grabbing cable, spear, fish, whatever, and got himself wrapped in the process. In the madness and confusion the regulator was some-how yanked from his mouth. He was reaching frantically for it when another hard yank from the fish actually cut his regulator hose and bubbles started spewing everywhere. Now he's 200 feet underwater, wrapped in the cable, with no air. He fumbled for the hose thinking to stick it in his mouth but soon it expired. Somehow he untangled himself and started up. Somewhere on the way up—

his dive mates estimate about halfway—he blacked out from lack of oxygen. That's all he remembers until he was in the boat.

He recovered completely and moved to Belize for a year . . . had to get away.

The Helldivers' Rodeo lands on the first week of June. Too early, say some divers—the ones more into the aesthetics than the hunting. The Mississippi is usually still high in early June. This makes for a guaranteed murk layer. It also makes for excellent spear fishing. Fish feel safer in the murk. There are more of them around and they let you get closer. But that doesn't make *you* feel safer, that's for sure.

The first Helldivers' Rodeos were actually snorkeling affairs held off the seawall in Lake Pontchartrain—almost in downtown New Orleans. The lake's maximum depth is about eight feet. River murk wasn't an issue then. Much has changed.

The very first was in 1963, according to Helldiver club historian Terry "Poppa Smurf" Migaud. "We'd always go for picnics at the lakefront," he says, "a bunch of families, and we started snorkeling along the lakefront seawall out there, spearing sheepshead then bringing 'em up and barbecuing them. Can't get much fresher than that. Well, the wives started measuring to see who had the biggest—the biggest sheepshead that is! Yeah, the biggest fish. Then they started giving awards, presents (I won't say what) for the biggest one. This went on for a couple summers. Well, one thing led to another and in 1963, we formalized the thing and called it the 'Helldivers' Sheepshead Spear Fishing Rodeo.'"

"A few years later we expanded it to include the Gulf and the rigs. A few of us had already started into that. Plenty dive clubs had started up by then. So we started competing against the guys who'd been diving the Grand Isle Tarpon Rodeo for years. Things really got interesting then."

Call it coincidence, but the first book on scuba diving, *The Silent World* by Jacques Cousteau; came out, the first underwater film, *Red Sea Adventure* by Hans Hass, came out; and the first offshore oil platforms went up off Grand Isle Louisiana, all practically simultaneously.

"It all seemed to happen at once," says New Orleanian Johnny Bonck, now 72. "These guys like Cousteau and Hass—to us they were like Lindbergh, Lewis and Clark, Columbus, Cortez, Buffalo Bill, all rolled into one. They were pioneers, adventurers, explorers—and most importantly—hunters."

The year was 1953. "Hell man," Johnny snorts. "You'd never know it from the stuff they were saying thirty years later, but half of Cousteau's book and Hass' film were about spearing fish! To us it seemed like the only reason for going diving. Here in New Orleans and south Louisiana we were all hunters and fishermen, grew up that way. Now we had a sport that seemed to combine the best of both. And even better, we had unexplored territory to go hunting in. Nobody had been down there yet. We couldn't wait to get down there . . . see what the hell it looked like . . . see what the hell was down there. From fishing we had a pretty good idea though."

The first offshore oil platform actually went up in 1947, twelve miles off the Louisiana coast near Morgan City (thirty miles west of Grand Isle). Hollywood dramatized the event with the 1953 movie *Thunder Bay* starring Jimmy Stewart.

Jimmy played the wildcatter engineer who designed and installed the first offshore platform. An inspiring story for any red-blooded American. Here's Jimmy as the pioneering oil engineer, the innovator, the trail-blazer, the risk-taking hero, putting it all on the line—his capital, his reputation—for the future of the internal-combustion engine.

The thing went up, and say what you want about these numb-skull, unlettered Cajuns; they saw the light immediately. They discovered more fish than ever. They found work on the platforms themselves, paying in two months what they'd earn in a year's fishing. They started renting their fishing boats out to ferry supplies for the oil companies—again, earning in one trip what ten fishing trips cleared. They caught on.

Fishing boats started hooking up to the new platforms almost immediately. And almost immediately their fears vanished. Sometimes it took as long as ten seconds though; the ten seconds the bait was traveling to the bottom. Then *wham! Hang on!*

Grunt, crank . . . groan . . . crank . . . and finally a huge snapper or grouper or jack surfaced.

But about half the time the fish wouldn't come up. Indeed, the fishermen might go overboard and down himself—unless the line mercifully snapped.

"We knew some monster fish lurked down there," Johnny recalls.

Johnny's father was a founding member of the nation's first fishing rodeo, the Grand Isle Tarpon Rodeo, which kicked off in 1929. By 1953 most entrants were fishing around the oil platforms that had sprouted just offshore of this Louisiana barrier island. "You wanted to come into the weigh-in with the mostest and the biggest." Johnny says. "So you fished next to a platform. Simple as that."

"We'd hook some monstrosities alright." Johnny laughs. "But couldn't get the damn things on board! Remember, this was *way* before catch 'n release became trendy. We'd hook something that felt like a freight train. If the line held we might finally haul him up—some monster jewfish, or jack, or shark. Okay? Now what?"

Easy. This was Louisiana. They were all hunters. So . . .

"*Blam—blam—blam!* We shot the damn thing! We'd carry shotguns, rifles, and handguns out there and blast the hell outta them. Then winch 'em aboard."

But a sporting and conservationist ethic prevailed even then. "You couldn't shoot tarpon, tuna or marlin." Johnny clarifies, "only jewfish, sharks, and manta rays."

Manta rays? Come on Johnny! Manta rays are plankton eaters, like whales for heavens sake! You'd never catch one on bait. These are beautiful harmless creatures. Women and kids ride on their backs. They're the main attraction at dive sites across the temperate seas.

"Oh no," He answers. "You're right. We couldn't catch the things. They never bit on anything. You'd see them gliding along close to the surface and we'd pull alongside and cast everything we had at them. They wouldn't touch a thing. They were driving us crazy. So we had no choice. We had to harpoon them."

The movie version of Moby Dick showed the rollicking thrill of a "Nantucket Sleighride" which is what they called it after a whale was harpooned and rode off with the boat in tow. A "Cajun Sleighride" wasn't quite as long or fast. But what the hell. It was a social thing down here like everything else. The wives, girl-friends, aunts, and mothers didn't want a roller-coaster ride any-way. A 15 foot manta ray with a homemade harpoon in his back and a thick nylon rope as a leash provided more genteel enter-tainment. Mantas rarely caused the on-board *barbeque* pit to be spilled during the cruise. "We had a ball," says Johnny, "drinking, laughing, saving fuel. Hell I remember a big manta pulling around a thirty foot boat for two hours once."

"Sure, by today's standards it's awful", says Johnny. "But these were the early fifties. People didn't look at it as wasteful or bad or anything. You were spearing an ugly deep-sea monster, that's all. A 'devilfish.' When he tired out you blasted him in the head—wherever that was, we finally found it—and towed him to shore and to the scales. Everyone crowded around, ooh-ing and aah-ing and taking pictures. The guy who harpooned it got a trophy and his picture in every paper in Louisiana, usually standing between two rodeo beauties in swimsuits, smiling away."

So blasting hooked or harpooned fish at boat-side was approved by the Rules Committee of the Rodeo. "Okay fine," says Johnny. "So I tell my Dad, 'hey, if you can shoot fish to bring them aboard, how 'bout letting us shoot them underwater with spear guns and enter them in the Rodeo?'"

And thus the Grand Isle Tarpon Rodeo introduced its spear fishing division in 1953. Almost immediately they started getting divers from all over the world. Spear fishing tournaments were already being held off California, in Europe in the Mediterranean, and in Australia. So when word got out—only took one year—they started getting the top divers from all these places in Grand Isle. When outsiders first went down and saw what was under those platforms, they couldn't believe it . . . and here's guys who were diving the Great Barrier Reef and the like. They'd hit the surface just gasping and jabbering away. All night long over dinner and drinks that's all they talked about. They'd *never* seen so many fish, and so many *huge* ones, in one place in their lives.

At least these guys had dived before. No one had in Louisiana prior to 1952. Our coast wasn't right for it. Too muddy. No reefs. The platforms solved the reef problem. Even better, located well offshore, the water around them was clear Gulf water.

Johnny recalls that the first rig dive was by himself and friends Roy Smith and Roland Riviere. Roland owned a local sporting goods store on Canal Street in downtown New Orleans named, imaginatively, *Roland's*. And he'd just received a shipment of some underwater breathing contraptions called "aqualungs," the first in the state.

"We think maybe the first in America," says Johnny. "Among the very first, anyway. We couldn't wait to try them out."

And so they did. It was in June of 1952. They went out in a twenty-foot boat and hooked up to a—by today's standards— shallow rig. The platform stood in 60 feet of water and was located six miles off Grand Isle. The water was pretty clear that day. No BC, no wetsuits, none of that stuff. They were dressed in old cotton jumpsuits, double hose regulators. They just grabbed their spear guns and jumped in. Sure, they were a little scared— sharks and all.

The water was a little murky near the surface, but fish surrounded them immediately. Sheepshead, spadefish, jacks. Further down it got clear, then even clearer as they descended. Then they saw them . . . they kept blinking and refocusing, didn't seem possible . . . they all huddled close to each other down there, still a little nervous, while pointing and looking at each other, their eyes and gestures asking, "Can you believe this shit?"

Call me melodramatic, but I see Johnny, Roy, Roland, and their chums in the same role as the first men who crossed the Bering Land Bridge and found virgin hunting lands teeming with unsuspecting prey on a new continent. Like our Paleolithic ancestors, these New Orleanians were all compulsive, instinctive, fanatical hunters. They were seized by the same rush that buzzed Alley Oop, when he topped the ridge over the Rockies and beheld that herd of giant bison.

"Looked like a herd of cows," Johnny says. "Didn't seem possible. Musta been twenty or thirty huge jewfish—all well over three hundred pounds—just herded up on the bottom, right above the bottom murk, in fact, half obscured by it. That's why I say they looked like a herd of cows. You saw those big dark lumps over the bottom haze—incredible. I'll never forget it—not as long as I live. Not after logging hundreds of dives over the next forty years. What a sight!"

It sounded fishy to me too, when interviewing Johnny. "Don't believe me hunh?" He asked. "Okay." Then he pulled out an old underwater film—and I mean old. Remember, Hans Hass's *Red Sea Adventure* dates from 1953. Johnny's was taken in 1955. "No underwater cameras back then, Hom-boy-da ["Humberto" in New Orleanian]. This was a regular home movie camera of the time and I made a waterproof casing for it." The film shows Johnny under a rig with *seven* jewfish around him, each well over three hundred pounds. He was waving a five-pound mangrove snapper in front of one. The snapper was impaled on a huge shark hook, which was attached to a heavy nylon rope, which was tied around the rig's beam. Johnny wiggles it in front of a monster jewfish, who looms out of the murk and edges closer to him . . . closer, closer, the damn thing could have easily swallowed the 5 '7" Johnny. He senses it too. So Johnny lets go of the hook and holds the rope about six feet over the bait, waving it, jerking it . . . the jewfish lunges out—*whoom!* Inhales the mangrove, turns to lunge back and—*aack!* He starts battling the rig.

The *Encyclopedia Britannica* lists jewfish as "any of several large fishes of the sea bass family (Serranidae), especially *Epinephelus itajara*, found on the Atlantic coast of tropical America. This species sometimes attains a length of 2.5 metres (8 feet) and a weight of about 320 kilograms (700 pounds). The adult is dull olive-brown with faint spots and bands."

Incredible, no?

Slowly Johnny and his dive mates eased down towards them and shot one—*whoom*, off it went, snapping his spear gun cord like thread. Roland shot one, same thing. Roy, same thing. They were using the only spear guns available then. They were from France and came with a little nylon cord on the shaft. Fine for those Mediterranean fish, but no one at the time had a gun that could hold the size fish they had under the rigs, because no other diving site in the world had such fish.

It took them a while to get the hang of the thing. But where could they turn? Who else was doing this type of diving? No one, of course. They were on their own. So they replaced the nylon cord with steel cable, bought new shafts and went back down a few days later. Sure enough, there was another huge school of jewfish down there, or maybe the same one. *Wham!* Johnny hit one right behind the head and it zoomed off—taking the spear gun with it.

Hey, they were making progress. No longer losing just the shafts and the cord, they were now losing the whole gun! Finally, they asked themselves, "Why does the shaft have to stay attached to the gun?" So they attached the shaft to a heavy nylon rope and the rope to an inflatable life preserver. The plan was for one of them to shoot the jewfish, then all three would straddle the life preserver and either have a tug of war with the fish or go for a ride, then finally wrestle him up. It sounded like a cinch.

The following weekend they went back down, feeling like old pros by now. Soon another jewfish loomed from the bottom murk. Roland whacked him, the rest grabbed the life preserver, and off they went, plowing through the bottom murk, the rope between their legs. It was a blast! Now, a jewfish is a bottom fish. So he heads down, no stopping him. And all the platforms at that time had a main crossbeam, about five feet from the bottom. Unfortunately, they didn't know that at the time. The beams were hidden in the bottom murk, and they wouldn't have been able to see down there. But they sure *felt* it—BONG!

The jewfish zoomed under it and they got their bells rung. Don't ask me how they didn't get killed. Banged up, cut, shredded, bruised—yes—all that. But nothing serious.

So, the following week, they showed up at the dock on Grand Isle with football helmets and shoulder pads. Everybody who saw them thought they looked nuts but, to make a long story short, the padding helped, and finally they boated a couple.

Johnny will never forget the day they boated the first one because it was also the first day that he and the others had ever seen women in a new bathing suit called a "bikini." It was Roland, Dick Alba, and Johnny diving that day. They were hooked up to the rig with the monster jewfish hanging at the side of the boat—so actually they hadn't quite boated it. But they had landed him, anyway. The thing was huge—that much they knew. But they had nothing to compare it against. Nobody had ever boated one around there. They were excited, jubilant—they had finally done it! So they started celebrating, with booze, of course.

As they were getting into it, screaming, whooping (nobody high-fived back then), carrying on, taking pictures, they saw this big yacht pulling up to the rig, to fish. They had seen it at the marina on Grand Isle the night before. It hooked up to the rig, and some women got out on the bow to sunbathe—"and man!" Johnny recalls. "We like to go nuts! They were wearing these two-piece bathing suits! And it was unbelievable—their navels were showing. To us it almost seemed like they were naked. Remember this was 1952. No *Playboy* or anything."

After they recovered, Johnny and the boys started waving, whistling, showing off. Soon they were diving off the bow of their boat, like Johnny Weismuller from the Brooklyn Bridge. They were carrying on—and, of course, still dipping into the booze. Roland got up on the bow and began waving at the girls. Then he stuck his huge dive-knife in his mouth crossways, biting it, just like Tarzan when he's diving in to fight a crocodile. He made a big show, waving around to the rest, back to the girls. Then he wound up like an Olympic diver and plunged in.

The girls cheered and clapped. Dick and Johnny couldn't let Roland get all the attention! So they grabbed their dive knives, bit them, and followed Roland, the women cheering and clapping away.

Johnny hit the water—and knew he was in trouble. "Owww! I had a double-edged knife." Johnny remembers. "When I hit that wawda—that sucker sliced into the corners of my mouth and almost to my gums." He came up, the water red all around him. Then Roland surfaced, grabbing his mouth, which was pouring blood too. Dick was the only one intact. His knife had a dull side. And he'd bitten it right.

Their mouths and lips had swollen hideously by now. They could barely talk, mumbling and slobbering bloody drool all over the deck. Only one cure for this dreadful affliction: more whiskey. And there was plenty more on deck. Ah yes. Their mood brightened. Now they had no choice. The bikini-broads were still looking over attentively. They'd *have* to redeem themselves.

So Roland went out, suited up, grabbed a speargun and started waving to the broads again. He'd be the first down and the first up, with a big fish to impress them.

But his boat had drifted close to the rig now and there was a crossbeam maybe ten feet underwater. Johnny had noticed it on the way down during the first dive. "That thing was covered with sea urchins!" he recalls. "Big black spiny things—I mean *covered* with 'em."

Roland had just finished spitting into his mask. He was on the edge of the bow, *right over* that crossbeam. "Hey Rol!" Johnny shrieked but splish—too late. There goes Roland. He'd jumped in with arms spread, still waving at the girls—and landed on his butt.

Johnny rushed to the rail only to see a roiling mass of bubbles, more bubbles, and more. Then Roland surfaced. "Sure enough" Johnny laughs, "that crazy sucker had landed on that mass of urchins, butt first. And he was hurtin' for certain." Johnny and Roy hauled the howling, thrashing Roland aboard.

The bikini broads knew something was wrong so they pulled their boat alongside. Turns out, one was a nurse. She came on board, bent down and gave the diagnosis. The urchin spines had to come out, she said. If not, they'd keep burrowing and cause infection, like porcupine quills.

They carried Roland onto the girls' boat for the procedure. "Man, I'll never forget that," Johnny chuckles. That gorgeous woman—still in her bikini—was down there, poking around with her fingers, rubbing, inspecting, and yanking them out. Shoot man, I almost went and jumped on those urchins myself!

Yes, they'd boated a big jewfish—finally. But they were still losing three or four for every one they boated, and were battered mercilessly in the process. There had to be a better way.

And, the cry was heard. "We had a spear fishing clinic at Roland's store by an expert at fish slaughter." Johnny recalls. "It was 1957, I think."

"Zee trick," the man who ran the workshop said, "eez to aim for zee brain and kill zee fish instantly. Zees is how: you form an equilateral triangle from eye to eye and then to a point above and between zee eyes. Zhat's vere you aim. Zee spear sinks into his brain right there and he eez stunned, immediately immobilized."

This expert fish assassin spoke with a thick French accent because he was a skinny frog named Jacques Cousteau. His aqualungs had proven to be a big hit down here in New Orleans. It was time for a promotional visit to *Roland's*, his major distributor, in this most French of American cities.

"We'd taken him to lunch to A&G Cafeteria," remembers Johnny. "Can you believe that? A Frenchman! An' here we're in New Orleans, America's culinary capitol!"

Turns out, he loved it. He had meat loaf or Salisbury steak with macaroni and cheese or something like that. They laughed at that, but he'd snorked it up. He was great."

The issue was killing huge fish, however. And Costeau got right down to business. He gave a demonstration—a clinic, of sorts,—to a bunch of local divers on how to kill these monstrous jewfish. He showed where to aim to smack the brain, same lesson big-game hunters get from the white hunter on their first elephant hunt.

And it worked. They started aiming for the brain and stoning them. *Flunk!* and they'd keel over dead. Then the divers would just swim up to the boat with them.

"Yep, we learned to kill jewfish from Jacques Cousteau," Johnny says. "Then they started getting scarce."

Then they almost disappeared. Shit happens. Happened to the mammoths, mastodons, and giant sloths of North America when some predators holding spears moved in from Asia and shoved the sabertooths and cave bears off their apex perch.

"Move over tiger, you chump," said these scrawny, upright creatures. "Step aside bear . . . now watch how real predators work."

Some scientists say that was the end for the late Pleistocene's mammals in North America. Johnny and his diving chums found the same thing under the Gulf in 1952. Big, stupid game, subject—for the first time in their history—to the human predatory instinct.

And the jewfish looked fated to share the fate of the mammoth.

But who knew?—except the divers themselves, that is. This relative handful of people were the only ones who saw what was going on down there. They saw jewfish disappearing, so they stopped shooting them. Yes, amazingly, well before the State or the Feds moved to protect jewfish, the Louisiana Council of Dive Clubs had removed them from all competitive diving. Now, they're back.

Two

HEADING OUT

On rodeo kick-off morning, the elements seemed to have joined in a conspiracy against us. The ugliness started as soon as we cleared the jetties. Drizzle stung our bare torsos. Up ahead, two waterspouts snaked from the dark clouds *directly* in our path to the Main Pass rigs. We were huddling behind the console for shelter when a bolt of lighting crackled out and we jerked spastically into each other. I started to laugh nervously when the thunder boomed and we jerked again, my arms shooting out over my head and hitting my friend Tom's. We looked at each other and tried to chuckle—*ha-ha!* But our eyes gave it away.

Tom looks like a young Rock Hudson, if Rock was a little on the short side—5-foot-six, to be exact. He's worried that he's getting up there in years, too. "Tom!" I consoled him at a birthday lunch shortly after we met. "What's all the fuss about? You're younger than Mick Jagger, by a year!" That cheered him up.

It took Tom a while to break into our group. We met after he'd been kicked down from the regional headquarters in Dallas to my backwater New Orleans office. Of the guys on this boat, Tom's still the FNG (Fucking New Guy)—I've only known him for ten years. The other two guys are my cousins, Pelayo and his younger brother Paul. "Pablito," as we used to call him, was the first of our family born in the U.S., in 1962, right here in New Orleans. When Castro took over, my Aunt and Uncle came to New Orleans. Paul's nickname—"On-the-Ball"—came much later, when as a teenager he started following his older brother and his friends on hunting and fishing trips.

In Louisiana's shallow salt marshes we fish with "popping corks," to keep the bait a little off the bottom. You "pop" it to mimic the sound of a shrimp or baitfish on the surface and this attracts the trout and reds. Paul was always great at popping but was easily distracted for some reason.

"Your cork, Paul!" We kept yelling when it plunged.

"What? Unh? OH!" And he'd finally rare back and set the hook. This went on for a morning and a case of beer. "Man, you're really on-the-ball today, Paul!" our friend Chris blurted after netting a gorgeous redfish for Paul. And the name stuck.

Later that evening we figured it out. Chris, Pelayo and I had been fishing from the elevated bow. Paul was below us on the deck. The water was rippled that day and from his angle Paul had trouble seeing when his cork had plunged. And he always had ten feet of slack in the line, so he couldn't feel the tug.

Paul attended LSU six years after us. We couldn't distract him from his studies with our usual nonsense because, oddly, Paul was serious about college. He actually *knew* what he wanted to study. He had ambitions for when he got out. He majored in computer science and rakes it in as a programmer today. We make him spring for the beer. He can afford it.

This was a far cry from Tom's last dive with us. That had been in Cozumel. Four of us, including my childhood friend, Chris, plus wives. To the little Mayan dive masters we probably looked like part of the group. Just another bunch of gringo tourists unable to understand the salacious comments they were making about the dripping gringas they were helping aboard after the day's first dive, four of whom happened to be our wives. Little did they suspect that my cousin Pelayo and I understood every word.

I noticed Pelayo's jaw muscles harden and his eyes narrow after a particularly lewd comment by the little Mexican with a shark tooth earring on our left. *"Good Lord,"* I thought. "Here we go."

I could already see the news release: WILD FRACAS ON COZUMEL DIVE BOAT LANDS TWO LOUISIANA MEN IN NOTORIOUS MEXICAN JAIL. LOCAL POLICE CHIEF, EMILIANO "EL GUAPO" SANCHEZ, GIVES LITTLE HOPE TO THOSE WORKING FOR THEIR EARLY RELEASE, WHO APPEAR TO BE VERY FEW.

The hideous vision rattled me deeply and I nudged Pelayo. "Come on man," I stammered. "Let it slide. It's no big deal. We're on vacation. The girls don't even understand."

"But I do!" he snarled. "Heard what that little bastard just said about Gina?"

I didn't think Pelayo had much justification. We'd been doing the exact same thing all morning. It was hard enough to resist commenting when the skimpy swimsuits were dry and strategically positioned before the dive. When wet and haphazardly positioned after the dive . . . well. I'd need a hundred more pages to list all the advantages of speaking a second language that your wife doesn't.

But Pelayo wouldn't listen to reason. He shook me loose and started walking over to the giggling dive masters. "Chris, Shirley, Toni, Tom, Cindy!" I suddenly yelled. "Let's walk around to the other side of the boat for a minute. I think they sighted a manta ray over there." An ugly scene was bound to unfold. I wanted them shielded.

"Be ready for trouble." I whispered to Chris and Tom.

Chris made a fist and bashed it against the railing. "Don't worry," he snarled. "We'll stomp 'em."

I pretended to scan the emerald waters around us for the mythical manta ray, but nothing happened. No wild yells, moans, grunts, thumps, or splashes from the other side of the boat. Hhmmm. A few minutes later Pelayo walked around with a big smile on his face. "He said he'll take us out tomorrow morning." He beamed. "Spear fishing, on the northern side of the island."

"I thought that was illegal down here," Tom said with a bewildered look.

"Nothing's illegal down here." Pelayo smirked. "For the right price."

On the boat ride out, the girls had befriended a New Jersey couple who'd spent most of the first dive feeding and petting a huge black grouper that hovered around us. They were on their fourth trip to Cozumel in as many years. "Did you see the beautiful grouper?" The wife beamed at our wives.

"Sure did." Pelayo interrupted. "Looked just like the one I speared last week at the oil platforms."

The couple both grimaced and shook their heads. Our wives rolled their eyes, curled their lips and jerked their heads in the unmistakable gesture of: *butt* out!

"*Blam!*" Pelayo motioned with his fist. "Shot the big sucker right through the gill plates!" Pelayo's eyes blazed with blood lust. He licked drool from his lower lip. "But I still went to the mat with him. Good thing Chris showed up and finished him off with the ice pick." Chris made muscular jabbing motions in the air to demonstrate.

"You're . . . you're *awful!*" the wife cried with her voice cracking. She and the husband walked off. The girls followed, apparently unimpressed with our subtle approach to explaining our sport.

We mended fences over dinner that night at the well-known tourist trap, Carlos 'n Charlie's. Tequila does it every time. The day's events take on a special charm: You forget the sunburn. Sitting on that sea urchin now seems amusing. The cure involving uric acid even more so. The moray that clamped its teeth around your wife's hand until you diced it with a dive knife now elicits guffaws from people into their third round of half-gallon margaritas. In minutes your wife raises her bandaged hand to beckon the waiter for the fourth. After the fifth you give in and show everyone the urchin wound, about a foot below the fire coral burns that cover your lower back.

But now, quite a distance from Cozumel, Tom, Pelayo, "On-the-Ball" Paul, and I were wallowing through four-foot seas in a blinding, horizontal rain that stung our chests like ice needles. In the confusion we overlooked the shrimp trawler directly ahead.

"Look out!" Paul screeched, while grabbing the wheel from Pelayo. But it was too late. We were already over the trawl. The big shrimper's fantail was covered with Vietnamese flapping their arms and screaming some rapid-fire gibberish that was unintelligible to everyone but Tom, who'd gotten a government-sponsored tour of their homeland and its rice paddies some years before.

Tom cupped his hands around his mouth and let fly with another string of gibberish that baffled us but seemed to greatly intensify the shrimpers' emotions. One of them jerked a gaff from a wall and started waving it like an ax. He was about four feet tall with a huge hat and was hopping up and down like Yosemite Sam.

Tom smiled, and screamed some more gibberish; a few of Yosemite's oriental colleagues started laughing. But Yosemite himself continued his hoarse screeching and jerky pantomime. Then another peal of thunder jerked our gaze skyward. We finally cleared the trawl and lumbered off through the swells and drizzle, a crew of little brown men shaking their fists in our wake.

We missed the worst of the squall with a three-mile detour. The marine forecast had called for "two to three foot seas."

"As usual," Pelayo snorted as he spit into his mask after we'd hooked up. "We oughta know by now. What they mean is two *times* three-foot seas. Hell, it's gotta be five foot seas out here."

The twelve miles of open Gulf had pounded Pelayo's twenty-foot Aquasport mercilessly—and us within it. Our brains were turning to jelly and our butts to putty. Then, trying to snag the oil rig's beam with the rig-hook while the boat was bouncing around like a cork in the heaving swells had been a real treat.

Twice I nearly went over, bashing my shins and elbows on the railing as the hull came down off the crest of a wave. Tom, naturally, tried to help. He slipped as we came down from a swell, smacked his head against the rig hook, tripped over an ice chest and gouged his arm with a spear gun point when he hit the floor. The spear gun had been stored carelessly, the shaft pointing up and the point uncovered.

I'd made a mental note to arrange it on the way out but was distracted by the "clang—clang! CLANG—CLANG!" of the air tanks as we pounded our way out. You'd think we'd get this right by now, but *noooooo*. So, every mile or so Pelayo would haul back on the throttle. Paul and I would yank the bungee cords into place, jam a few boat cushions here, a towel there, trying to get the tanks arranged nice and snug, nice and sturdy.

Then we'd hit the first wave—*clang! Clang! Clang!* The hell with it. Let 'em clang. They don't call us the Dog and Pony Dive Club for nothing. That's when I forgot about the gun. It was actually Tom's own. He'd spent half the night sharpening it, then neglected the little plastic cap. Now his arm was gushing blood.

"Here," I said, and chucked him a towel from the storage chest. "How bad is it?"

"Ah, it's nothing." He tried to smile.

I've known Tom a long time. He'd say it was "nothing" if his freaking arm was dangling from his shoulder by two tendons and bone shards from his scapula were sticking out of his cheek, which is exactly what happened to him in 'Nam, while he was hosing down some VC with a machine-gun from a chopper. Thirty years later the scars still cover half his arm.

"They shot back," he shrugs, whenever anyone asks him about the scars. I know that tone. It's the same tone my father-in-law used when I'd asked him about Anzio or the Bulge. "I was always in the right spot at the wrong time . . . or the wrong spot at the right time," he'd always quip. And that was it. But I knew it took a little more than bad timing to get the two silver stars with oak leaf clusters and the purple hearts my mother-in-law showed me one day while rummaging through his things.

I never press the issue. The tone is unmistakably, "change the subject, please," the tone of a man who has actually *seen* combat. They never seem to notice all that thrill and romance that rivets us to the seat at the movie or excites the narrator on the History Channel. Even after six Buds or half a bottle of Crown, I could never get the whole story . . . with Tom either. Anyway, this spear gun gouge was a minor matter. He'd been through worse—much worse.

The water was rough and filthy, the sky gray and dreary. No sun to enliven our moods. Now an early injury, before we even hit the water. What a start. Our disco wetsuits never fail to provoke a burst of mirth with guests. Not today. Tom just shook his head with that bent smile. Nothing seemed to help—not even the Village People's classic: "Macho-Macho Man! I got-ta be—a Macho Man!" Pelayo had shoved it into the boom box.

"It's the perfect theme for a rig dive, huh guys?" Pelayo looked around, starting to bob to the beat.

Especially our rig dives, where old disco clothes serve as wet-suits. Pelayo looked over at Tom. "Hey Tom," he blurted. "These suits are actually an improvement. Should'a seen us a few years ago. We'd come out here looking like a bunch'a winos."

"Oh yeah?" Tom looked up and tried to smile, trying to be polite. "Winos hunh? Yeah, great." He wasn't listening. He was busy tending his arm.

A normal "cajun wetsuit" consists of an old flannel shirt and blue jeans. Those brass zippers don't rust. And the heavy denim protects the flesh—crucial when that muscle-bound torpedo called an amberjack is bouncing you around the barnacle and coral encrusted beams like a pinball. At a recent party Paul held up a stick of cheddar in front of Tom. "This is your arm," he said solemnly. Then he ran it against a grater three times. "This is your unprotected arm against a rig's beam when an AJ or cobia is taking you on his merry ride." Tom caught on immediately.

I've seen fishermen with heavy tackle surrender to large amberjack. "Here!" they'll gasp. "Take over for a while!" as they hand the rod to the first mate. " My arms are giving out! Whew!" and they start rubbing their biceps.

I saw a Saints linebacker do this, and the amberjack was bare-ly forty pounds. Imagine an eighty-pounder on the end of your spear gun. You're down there with him, in his element, sur-rounded by these shredding devices. Sure, you can let go. But few rig-divers give in that easily. Point is, you're gonna get beat up pretty badly. You want a heavy layer of fabric between you and those beams.

Paul was already suiting up on the bow, vainly sucking in his gut while working the plastic zipper on his polyester pants. He'd shaken his booty in them seventeen years ago—we all had. But that was a much skimpier booty. Cramming his current booty into the same casing was proving arduous. Not that I had much room to talk. My love handles drooped over the tight polyester cummerbund like a huge roll of boudin.

"Man, it's been three months since the end of hunting season," I said defensively, while patting my gut. I could see Pelayo snickering while pointing it out to Tom, trying to coax him out of his funk. "I always put on a few pounds between the hunting season and the underwater hunting season. That fishing doesn't require much moving around. We get fat and lazy in the spring. You'll see, by next month I'll be trim again . . . throw me a beer."

Tom was mum. He paced the bow and pressed the towel against his arm. He frowned when he saw me chugging the Bud.

"Martini's Law, right?" I said, toasting him. "*Right?* . . . you've heard of it?"

"Sure," he replied. "Nitrogen narcosis . . . hits you down deep."

"Well?" I shrugged. "Why not drink the martini itself? Effects are gonna hit you anyway, right?"

Tom snorted, nodding in disgust.

"In fact," Paul said. "When your bloodstream's crammed with alcohol, it has less room to absorb the nitrogen . . . or it absorbs it more slowly."

"Damn right." Pelayo quipped after a hearty gulp."We heard it from a doctor who dove with us."

"Oh *COME ON!*" Tom snorted. He finally came alive. "That's the *craziest* thing I ever heard! Alcohol *dehydrates* ya. That makes it worse . . . where did that guy get his license? A doctor like *that*, he oughta be in jail. He shouldn't be . . . "

"He worked for the state," Pelayo said. "Didn't he, On-the-Ball?"

"Sure did," Paul answered. "I remember now, Doctor Fontaine. He was a chiropractor. But he gave medical exams to state employees for insurance . . . what a nutcase."

Tom rolled his eyes . . . then chuckled at On-the Ball's dilemma. "You guys weren't kidding," he snorted. "Disco clothes! Incredible. Wait till I tell Elaine. Boy she used to love disco."

"It's the perfect body suit," Paul quipped while starting to boogie . . . I *gotta be, a MACHO MAN! bumpa—bumba-bumba-bumpa!* The bass line was infectious. My butt started jerking instinctively as I jerked on my booties. Pelayo was doing the bump with the console railing, his hands clasped together and arms held high, his head pointed downward, like a matador.

"Got tons of these clothes in backa the closet still." Paul snapped. "Hate to see it go to waste." His finger was pointing skyward now, *a la* Travolta, his lips pursed and chin bobbing to the beat.

Ah, the memories . . . the *memories!* Dressed like human peacocks, tottering around on heels while slurping whiskey sours. Strobe lights, foxes in clingy skirts and huge clunky platforms, our pockets crammed with matchbooks scribbled with bogus phone numbers . . . no mortgages . . . no soccer games.

"Hey Pelayo," I said. "Tell Tom how it started."

"Oh geezus," On-the-Ball sighed. "Not again."

"*Yes* again," I countered. It's become a ritual when we take new divers out and they start making faces and raising their eyebrows at our get-up.

"Well," Pelayo started as Paul shook his head sadly. "The wife gave a garage sale last year. Had all my old disco pants and shirts on a ping-pong table in the front yard. Man, I hated to see that stuff go, sentimental value, you unnerstan'. Well, we'd been diving the day before, so I was walking over to get the dive bag outta the backa the truck. My jeans were hanging out of it. They'd ripped pretty bad and the flannel shirt had lost some buttons. I knew I'd have to replace them for the next dive.

"So I'm walking back past the ping-pong table and some people had drove up and were actually looking at the disco clothes now, chuckling to themselves and I says '*whoa!*'—that stuff's no longer for sale. And I snatched it up. It looked perfect to replace the jeans.

"The next week I brought it on a dive and everybody laughed. The week after that we was *all* decked out like Travolta. It caught on *quick*. Shoot, it's the same fabric as those fancy smantzy body suits they try to sell ya at the dive shops for two or three hundred a pop. I mean look at it, polyester don't absorb no waw-da. The guys on the rig always get a big kick out of it. You see 'em leaning over, crackin' up. We just wave."

Pelayo suddenly looked up. "Nobody on this rig though . . . or they'd be up there leaning over the rail. Geezum! Think about those poor bastards. How much excitement can they get out here?"

"They got one helluva lot of excitement when we brought out them German broads—those friends of Cindy's, remember?" Paul smirked. "They wanted to do a little sunbathing like they do on their Mediterranean vacations. *That* brought the offshore workers out to the railings. And those kraut chicks didn't seem to give a damn. They're used to that type of stuff . . . man, maybe we're on the wrong side of the Atlantic."

Tom was doing his best to be a trooper, but his eyes gave him away. The disco antics had cranked down the voltage a little, but his nervous system was still buzzing. His eyes were too wide. His smile came out bent. Tom was still terrified, but I could tell his spear gun wound had nothing to do with it. He'd already stopped the bleeding. He was thinking of the dive.

This whole crazy business is what had him spooked. And who could blame him? His last dive had been Palancar reef off Cozumel. Sunny skies. Calm seas. Shallow azure waters. A palm-shrouded coastline within sight. He was aboard a spacious, stable craft. He was surrounded by lithe, smiling yuppies encased in their blinding kaleidoscope of elegant scuba-suits.

Now look at him. Poor guy. Stuck in a twenty-foot boat in heavy seas and a vicious current. Three dudes decked out in skin-tight angel flights with bell-bottoms that look like mini cast-nets and shiny shirts sprouting collars the size of kites, bumping and gyrating around him. They're putting scuba gear over this get-up. He turns away and watches filthy brown water foam around a maze of rusted steel beams that span the length of a football field.

What he can't see from here is that those beams descend 500 feet to the Gulf's mud floor. We'll see that in a minute—hopefully. A hundred feet above, they support a huge platform with engines, compressors, and living quarters for thirty men. The thing emits a hideous industrial racket—non-stop. It's like ten eighteen-wheelers passing you on the highway. Or the engine room of a tanker. This thing has been sucking crude oil from beneath the Gulf, non-stop, for twenty years.

Tom started diving ten years ago, at the age of thirty-three, when he lived in Florida. Like most contemporary divers his environmental views are fashionably green. His musical tastes turn to jazz. This whole scene must be a nightmare. The scenery, the racket, the rationale for the racket, the disco-suits—he actually looks pretty good considering.

He was born in California and moved out while young, thank God. If he'd grown up there this scene might cause him to collapse, jerking spastically, bleeding from the ears and foaming at the mouth. This whole *thing* is an outrage to fashionable California sensibilities . . . a scene to boil the blood and foam the brain of any Sierra Clubber.

If meat-eaters are "cannibals" guilty of "species-ism" and "mass murder" as proclaimed by Ingrid Newkirk of the Fund For Animals—then these people better stay away from south Louisiana. Or come crammed with sedatives.

In the Fund For Animal's annual "Body Count," which scores states in its "Cavalcade of Cruelty" by the number of animals "murdered" by hunters as reported by Fish and Game agencies, Louisiana was: NUMBER ONE! The last two years running!

I'll quote directly from "Body Count," on their website: "If Louisiana is a Sportsman's Paradise as its license plates boast, it is an animal's hell. "Louisiana *leads all the states* in the Outdoor Cavalcade Of Cruelty with 7,376,541 animals killed by hunters."

And that's just the half of it. Here *we* are. Here's this rig: a huge steel spider sucking greedily at Mother Earth's molten innards and converting them to lifeblood of the very system bent on shackling, defiling, and mutilating her. Industrial capitalism's very lifeblood courses through those pipes. The black gold will be pumped to shore via pipeline and start the evil process; refineries will belch their flatus towards the ozone layer; they'll poison streams and wetlands with their toxic excreta. Cars will clog the freeways and foul the air with noxious exhaust. Shell Oil will profit, stockholders will gloat, and workers will be exploited. Fossil fuels, pollution, "obscene" profits . . . and *ye Gods!* a boatload of southern drunkards capitalizing on it all, playing macho around the steel legs, killing defenseless fish for the sheer thrill of it between slugs of beer and belts of whiskey, their boat decks awash with beer foam, empty cans, and the slimy blood of huge fish with sad eyes and gaping holes in their flanks. That evening at a marina crammed with the yachts of the oilfield gentry (rich white trash), a forklift will unload the carcasses amidst a drunken din of whoops, high fives, rebel yells, and sexist jokes. Every rule broken, every ox gored, every sacred cow yanked up on a hook and slit open—then butchered, diced, marinated, skewered, grilled, chewed, gulped, and crapped out of rectums reddened and inflamed by cayenne pepper and whiskey.

Still in no hurry, Pelayo finished off his Bud with a thunderous belch and started peeling the wrapper off a Twinkie. Paul sat on the bow, disco-suited, Bud in hand, staring glumly at the swells. I stared blankly at the ugly dark horizon . . . some flashes in the distance. Tom kept looking around, from us to the water, to the rig, to the lightning flashes, then back, feigning calmness, his eyes asking: "Well . . . ? We're here, aren't we? We're suited up. Now what?" But his mouth was mum.

Pelayo noticed him. "Sit back and stare," He growled at him. "We got plenty time . . . rest up. Grab a bite . . . or a beer." Masticated Twinkie bits shot from his mouth. Finally he gulped. "I know you're a tofu and bean sprouts man, but grab some high energy stuff, some quick-burning fuel." He peeled back the wrapper and finished off the Twinkie with one massive bite, stuffing it in with his muscular electrician's fingers. White goo clung to his mustache. "You need energy for these dives," he mumbled while swallowing. "Quick energy, fast burning carbos, my man. None of that slow shit like carrots. You need *quick* bursts of energy down there . . . to dodge dem hammerheads."

Paul was chuckling silently from the bow, making eyes at me and pointing at Tom. Yep, time to give him The Routine. Every diver we introduce to the rigs gets it—with both barrels. And Tom was fresh meat served up on a silver platter. He'd been in New Orleans for two years now, seen Mardi Gras from a Bourbon

Street balcony. He'd read about three rig-diving fatalities in the
Times Picayune. He'd attended a dive club meeting and come
away stuttering. He was ripe for The Routine.

"Those bastards are fast, man." Pelayo continued. "You'd never
think an animal that big—a fifteen-foot, two-ton monster like
that—could be so fast. But you'll see. So you gotta get the angle
on 'em." He licked his mustache and fingers. "But just for a short
burst. Just to duck into the middle of the rig. See those pipes
there?" Pelayo turned his head and pointed with his chin towards
the middle of the platform where a cluster of pipes formed a rec-
tangle. A huge swell broke through them with a head of ugly
brown bubbles. Then came the wave's trough, sucking out the
water and exposing a hideous array of rust and barnacles. "See
them?"

"Yeah, Yeah," Tom was trying to smile, but his face looked like
a driver's license photo. "Sure, I see 'em."

"See how close together they sit? About two feet, right? Well,
they stay like that all the way to the bottom—that's five hundred
feet down." Pelayo's face was rigid. "You'll *barely* fit between 'em
with your tanks." Pelayo made the motion with his body, hunching his shoulders like squeezing through bars.

"The hammerheads we got out here," he said, "their heads are
about four feet across." Pelayo spread his arms wide, looking
from hand to hand and pursing his lips. "Those heads won't even
fit through dem pipes. But they'll try. The stupid suckers always
try. Banging that big ugly head into the pipes. Bong! Bong! Bong!"

Pelayo was demonstrating, holding up two arms and smashing
his head against them like a bull against a picador's horse. "Just
like on those shark shows, like those stupid great whites. They
keep banging that cage. The camera guy shitting on himself,
ducking into the corner and all. Well, here, that hammerhead—
he'll be tearing off barnacles, opening his mouth, banging away.
The pipes'll probably be shaking. All kinda shit—but don't
worry." Pelayo looked straight at Tom, not smiling. Now his eyes
light up a little. "He *can't* get through." Pelayo shrugged and
licked his mustache. "Only little ones can make it through. The
little eight and ten footers. And there's very few of those out here.
You gotta remember: Sharks are cannibals. They'd just as soon

eat another shark as a dolphin, sea turtle, or a manta ray. So, those little ones stay away from this area, or they get eaten. So, don't worry."

Paul was losing it, sitting on the bow doubled over but silent, his torso quivering. Pelayo still kept a straight face. And Tom looked like he'd been plugged into a light socket.

"If you're too far from the middle of the rig, Tom?" Paul blurted, recovering his composure. Tom jerked his head around. "If you think you can't make it? If you're sure he'll grab you before you can reach those pipes? Here's what I like to do." Tom's lips were quivering. "Sometimes the real big ones charge up from below, out of the bottom murk. Sometimes from above. Always from your blind side. If you're stalking a fish or pulling one off the shaft, you don't always notice that huge shadow lumbering through the murk above you—until he's right over. Then you notice that it's dark."

"But it's hard to tell," Pelayo blurted. "Cause it's pretty damn dark down there anyway. Ain't much sun penetrating through sixty feet of murk. Ever seen those videos of the Titanic on the ocean floor?"

Tom flinched. "Yeah! Um . . . sure, I *think* so."

"It ain't *that* dark, but close. Then you'll notice it gets suddenly darker, where you can't even see your air gauge."

"But hell," Paul said. "That could also be a hundred-foot supply boat rumbling up to the rig with his six foot propellers churning away, blocking out the sun . . . " Paul looked around. "There! See it?" He pointed towards a supply boat about a half-mile away, chugging towards a nearby rig. Tom jerked his head around and nodded jerkily." That's what I'm talking about." Paul said.

"Sure," Pelayo added. "But, Tom, after a while you'll learn to distinguish the rumble of a supply boat from the rumble of the rig's compressors or from the roar when a pipe blows and starts spewing hydrogen sulfide . . . 'cause you don't wanna surface when a supply boat's up there."

"Or even come close to the surface," Paul whistled. "Those things," and he pointed at the boat again, "have five foot propellers. Two thousand horsepower. They'll suck you right in from fifty feet down . . . "

"And mince you like celery in a Popil's Veg-o-Matic." Pelayo blurted, his arms outstretched and going up and down, mimicking the process. Then he looked over at Paul and me. Tom followed his gaze, jerkily, wide-eyed.

Finally he broke. "Look guys," Tom smirked. "Wait a minute now. I mean . . . what about dive flags? I mean, that's pretty standard. I mean, don't . . . ?"

"A joke," Pelayo blurted. "Those boats ignore them. Or can't see them." Tom kept looking around, trying to smile. Searching desperately for a smile back, or even a hint of one.

"Half of those captains are drunk," Paul said. "See all those dents on those pilings?" Paul pointed to the docking area on the platform. It wasn't just dented, but cratered, a rusty gaping hole in the middle beam. "It's a wonder any of these platforms are still standing." he said. "The way those big boats ram them. Those captains are seeing double half the time."

"Or hallucinating," Pelayo added. "On-the-Ball and I worked on supply boats plenty summers." They looked at each other nodding seriously. "Damn good money."

"But damn dangerous work." Pelayo added. "You're surrounded by drunks and dope fiends and criminals, twenty-four hours. These are the guys that used to join the French Foreign Legion. They're crazy, man. They'll go sideways on ya in a heartbeat, especially the captain. He stays up for two and three day stretches at a time, popping pills. When he grabs the bottle of black jack—watch out."

"Remember," Paul snapped. "There's no law out here. *He's* the law. Or he thinks he is. We had to call the Coast Guard once. The captain and first mate were waving .357 magnums around, raving drunk on the bow, shooting porpoises."

"That's *terrible!*" Tom shrieked. "I can't *believe that!* What kind of . . . ?"

"They were feeding them hot dogs," Paul continued. "Throwing 'em off the bow, then when the porpoises came up—you know how friendly they are."

"Sure," Tom said. "I dove with them in the Bahamas. They're wonderful, real playful."

"Right," Paul snapped. "They'd come rolling on the surface

with that smile of theirs, then—BLAM! BLAM! BLAM! They'd empty that cannon on them, every cylinder, whooping and hollering and rebel-yelling, as the water turned red and the big gray corpses just sank, quivering, pouring blood from three or four holes."

Tom looked on the verge of a crack-up, "I can't believe ANY-ONE would . . . !"

"We got pissed at them," Pelayo snarled. "The bastards!"

"Well I *guess SO!*" Tom gasped. " Anybody'd do *that*, hell, they deserve . . ."

"The bastards wouldn't give us a turn!" Pelayo snorted and rolled his eyes. "They were hogging the guns—just like a captain to do that."

"Oh, *come on!*" Tom wailed. Don't tell me you'd . . . "

"Maybe not," Paul said. "Maybe not at the dolphins, but when the water turned red, the sharks showed up. Don't take long out here."

"That's when the fun *really* started," Pelayo nodded. "The mate went inside and got his M-1 Carbine with the banana clip. Put it on *full-auto*, my man: BLA-A-A-A-A-M!! Emptied it into that school of sharks in five seconds flat. Water was boiling, churning white and red. Shoulda seen *that* commotion! "

"We saw our chance," Paul said, while they were reloading. We ducked inside and called the Coast Guard on the radio. We told them we had an emergency on board. They were alongside in half an hour in ninety-foot cutter."

"With the water cannon aimed and loaded," Pelayo added. "Gave a few blasts of water over the bow to make themselves clear, then boarded. The mate was raving, drooling drunk by then, cursing at em, waving the gun around . . . they maced him."

"I mean *hosed* him down good." Paul laughed. "His eyes swelled up like ping-pong balls. He was red, choking and puking as they swarmed over him with the nightsticks. Wound up with a concussion. The captain tried to hide but they pulled him from a closet by his beard, whacked him on the head, neck and shoulders with billies, and hauled him off in a chokehold. We heard he was hoarse for a week afterwards."

Tom just nodded disgustedly. "I can't believe . . . I just can't."

"Anyway, Tom," Paul continued. "When you see a big shark and he's acting hungry, look around for some big cut-off pipes. See those big ones?" He pointed towards the corner of the platform, where discharge of some type was flowing from a pipe into the filthy waves.

"See 'em?" Tom nodded wearily. "This very rig, in fact, has a couple beams cut off at about a hundred feet." Paul said. "Me— when the big hammerheads burst upon the scene—I like to duck into those pipes feet first. The pipes are about three feet across so you'll *just* fit into them with your tank." Paul poked his arms down straight against his torso and made the motions. "But you *don't* wanna go in head first, might not be able to back out." Paul rolled his eyes and let out a low whistle. "Especially if . . . "

"Big wolf eels, Tom." Pelayo blurted from the bow. "Ever seen one?"

Tom looked over, his eyes still tense, but curious now, still trying to smile. Not sure what to make of all this. "No. No don't think so," he said smiling. "Seen some morays down in Belize though. Even petted them. Got some pictures. They're . . . "

"You *don't* wanna pet a wolf eel." Pelayo quipped. "No way . . . you don't wanna go *near* one. Don't even spear them."

"They're kinda like a moray." Paul continued. "In fact, I think they're a giant subspecies of moray. Dr. Thompson, a marine biologist at LSU, told me they were."

"But they're bigger." I blurted.

"And meaner!" Paul gasped while arching his eyebrows and nodding.

"Much bigger and much meaner!" Pelayo continued. "They're a *deep*-water fish. You find them here 'cause we're so close to the continental shelf. Chris, that crazy bastard, speared one a coupla years back out here—got him right through the head, fortunately. Stoned him. Shoulda seen the fish clear a path as he carried it up. I mean even the black-tip sharks were streaking off. They know. That thing stretched out to almost ten feet. Body looked like a flattened truck inner tube. Teeth like the monsters from *Aliens*. Ugly thing man, creepiest thing I ever saw."

Tom looked worried, and confused. "I've never heard . . . "

"They're usually near the bottom." Paul said. "They eat lobsters and spiny oysters. They just crush them to mush with those teeth and jaws."

"They also live in those pipes," Pelayo quipped. They like the darkness, the murk, which is why I said don't go in head-first. They grab you in the face or neck and you're in big trouble. Their teeth are like a moray's but bigger, more like a barracuda's"

"But a barracuda's don't curve back," I said. "These curve back like a moray's or a snake's fangs. Once they grab—CHOMP!" I made the motions with my hand on my arm. "There ain't no getting away." I tugged on my bicep to mimic the effect. "You're better off in the jaws of a pit bull."

"Or a Nile crocodile." Pelayo huffed. "Good thing you saw Bob's bubbles coming outta the pipe that day, huhn, On-the-Ball? He'd still be down there."

"Good thing indeed." Paul said with a mock shudder. "Geezus, how could I forget? That big tiger shark showed up and I headed up."

"Me too," Pelayo said, whistling slowly and nodding. "Bob was right by the pipe. He'd seen a big grouper duck into it when the shark lumbered up outta the bottom murk, almost right under him. Scared the hell outta him. Guess so. When Bob saw it, that monster was ten feet away from him. Christ, *we* panicked and we saw it from across the rig. Looked like a submarine. Anyway, Bob ducked into the pipe, feet first."

"Yeah," I said. "He'd come down well after us so he had plenty air left. But a half hour later he hadn't surfaced so Paul suited up and went back down—with the bang-stick, just in case. I had some bottom time left. Left Chris and these bozos," Paul pointed towards Pelayo and me, "on board with their bottle of Jack Daniels. So I get down there and see his line of bubbles coming from the pipe, and his spear gun poking out. I swim over, look in, and almost fainted.

"Bob was looking straight up at me. His eyes looked like cue balls—wild, crazy, he starts thrashing around, banging the spear gun around. He's screaming through his regulator. 'BRRRRULL!—BRUUUUL!!' Bubbles going every way. He was trying to say something, but I couldn't for the life of me figure out what.

"But it was obvious he was stuck. So I grab his arm and start pulling—and *pulling*—and PULLING! Something's got him good! He's still screaming, bubbles flying. He's carrying on like crazy. I finally get him to where his hands are at the lip of the pipe and he grabs hold—dropping his spear gun in the act. Then I drop the bang stick . . . couldn't grab either in time. Guess they're still down there, at four hundred and eighty feet. Anyway, now with him pulling for all he's worth and me helping by grabbing his arms we're making progress. He's coming up—slowly. We're fighting against something strong, man. He's inching up slowly, a little more, just a *little*—and I see *he's naked below the waist!*"

Tom laughed nervously, looking around at each of us. Looking for a cue. But we're poker-faced.

"Well, he comes up further and I see his disco pants all balled up around his fins! His white ass is all red and scratched from barnacles and urchins. Then I see the freaking eel! His head anyway—looked like something straight outta *Aliens*, man. That mouth locked on the bell-bottoms trying to pull Bob back down and drown him!"

"Wolf eel you say?" Tom rasped. "Don't think I've . . . "

"And a *big* one! I'll never forget THAT, man. Turns out Bob had ducked into the pipe when the shark approached. He said the shark circled a few times then lumbered off. So Bob starts coming out—but can't. Something's got him—got him by the leg, by his pants leg. And that polyester's strong man, wasn't tearing or giving. He could feel some creature tugging against him like a monster pit bull. So he knew it was a fish of some type.

"So naturally he's starting to panic. But being in that pipe—in that tight fit— he couldn't reach down to stab it or to cut his pants or even to see it or anything. So he's really panicking. His air's going fast, remember. He's down at eighty-five feet. So he finally unbuttons his pants and unbuckles his weight belt. The belt drops but the pants can't get past his fins. And he can't bend down to take them off. So he's stuck! And his air's going fast."

"Oh man!" Tom nods. "That sounds . . . "

"Then I show up. And help pull him out. But I'll be damned if I'm putting my hands down there to take his fins off with that *thing's* head down there. And the eel still had his tail wrapped around something inside the pipe. Only a foot of him was outta the pipe. He wasn't budging any more. We're in a hell of a fix. I look at Bob's air and he's below five-hundred lbs. We gotta do something here—and fast."

Tom was rapt by now. Like a little kid listening to a ghost story around the campfire. No sign of incredulity.

"So I take out my knife," Paul continues "and Bob goes nuts again, screaming again and bubbles everywhere. He's panicking—I don't blame him. I motion that all's cool, nodding my head, giving the OK signal. But I didn't wanna stab the freakin' thing. I was afraid it might let go of Bob, then grab *me*. Finally I had no choice but to put my hands down there. I reached down and started cutting the strap on his fin. The wolf eel's jaws were about a foot away as I cut. So I was nervous. But Bob's air was down to two-hundred-and-fifty and his regulator was howling with every breath. We had to get with it. Finally the strap gives. Bob kicks it off and the pants and the eel goes with it.

"He reached down for the other fin, jerked it off, and, man!" Paul motioned with two fingers upraised over his head. "We headed up... we hit the surface, first thing we hear is these bozos," he points at Pelayo and I, "singing . . . *'But I would not feel so ALL ALONE . . . EVERYBODY must get STONED!'*" along with Dylan on the boom-box. Then the empty black jack bottle shatters on a beam right above us.

"Christ, I thought. They finished it off. So we swim to the back of the boat with these guys singing away—joined by some rig workers now. We clamber aboard . . . and they go crazy howling. You guys"—Paul nodded towards us again—"were *shit-faced*"

"Last dive of the day." Pelayo shrugged. "Man, we like to die laughing when we see Bob, his naked ass, all scratched and stuff."

"But Bob's in no mood for that shit." Paul chuckles. "He was rattled. Badly shaken up. And he starts screaming 'SHUT UP! JUST SHUT THE HELL UP!' Remember, guys?" Paul's laughing now, and Tom too.

"Do we!" Pelayo roars. "Man, he was shaking one fist at us and scratching the urchin wounds and hydroid burns on his ass with his other hand. 'SHUT UP YOU BUNCHA ASSHOLES!' he kept screeching. Finally he started crying. I mean bawling like a hysterical old woman, shaking—shivering like crazy—let's face it, poor guy'd been through some spooky shit—enough to spook anybody. Anyway, he's wild-eyed, red faced, veins poking outta his forehead. Looked like his head was gonna explode."

"Naturally that just made it worse." Paul said "We were doubled over. I mean *dying*, looking up at the rig-workers lined up at the railing laughing along with us. Bob was raving. Looking up at them. Then down at us. Then he's trying to punch us, still naked. Going nuts. We thought we were gonna have to tie him up with the anchor rope. Finally he slipped on a tank and went down, bashing the hell out of his knee."

"By now we could hardly breathe," Pelayo laughed. "I can still see him, blubbering and moaning, on top of the tanks, his white ass poking out, all red and scratched up. Then I snuck up behind him and started pissing on his ass. . . . He came up swinging the gaff."

"Till I grabbed him in a hammerlock from behind," Paul laughed. "'It's the *treatment!*' we kept yelling. He was kinda new to diving at the time. 'Chill out! You're *supposed* to piss on urchin wounds, man! The uric acid helps cure it, helps cut the stinging.' Anyway, he didn't dive with us for the rest of the season."

"Didn't dive with *anyone*," Pelayo corrected. "That was two years ago. But he started again last year. You'll meet him tonight at the camp-out on the island, Tom. I get the feeling the topic may come up, hunh guys?" Pelayo and Paul chuckled.

"He stays away from those pipes, though." Paul nodded. "Y'all about ready?"

"Just about," I said while reaching for a tank.

We'd exaggerated just a *little*. Shrink the sharks, scratch the Coast Guard and captain stuff, change the name "Bob" to "Lance." Change "wolf eel" to "big ball of monofilament fishing line," and the story pretty much corresponds with events.

"I'm about set," Pelayo said while fiddling with his spear gun bands. "On-the-Ball? Hand me my fin over there, will ya?"

Three

SHARKBAIT

Terry "Poppa Smurf" Migaud, at fifty-one, the grand old man and historian of the Helldivers Dive Club, was diving with club mates Stan Smith and Louis Rossignol, both over twenty years his junior. I won't get into a detailed physical description of Terry. His nickname is quite apt. His philosophy of diving is equally succinct. "We're always looking for a little excitement," he shrugs. A typical rig-diver here. No pretense, no artifice; a stand-up guy. He's a lifelong New Orleanian and a Helldivers Club member for going on thirty years. For years he held the Louisiana shark record with a 407-pounder speared in 1984—then Stan "The Man" Smith burst upon the scene.

On this dive these three avowed shark slayers were together, prowling the shallower rigs (70-foot depths) just east of Breton Island. While we sought peace of mind in deeper, cleaner water, they sought huge sharks in shallower and murkier water. Their six-foot spear guns were customized for maximum range and penetration, the shafts strained for release against six bands of extra-thick surgical tubing apiece. Their riding rigs were ready, either to ride with a speared shark or to finally "tie him off" to the rig itself if air ran low—if they weren't too tangled or narked.

Big predators—apex predators—need a place to hide. Just the sight of them sends their prey scurrying. They also need a place to seek revenge against those who presume to muscle them off their "apex" perch—Helldivers, for instance, or big game hunters, their terrestrial counterparts.

Peter Hathaway Capstick titled his best-selling book on African big game hunting *Death In The Long Grass*. That's where the lions and the leopards stalk their prey. They also leap into it when wounded—then double back on their trail and lie in ambush for whatever caused their pain. Blasted by a high caliber bullet that hits vitals but misses heavy bone, a lion makes for it every time. He's enraged, bleeding, staggering, spouting blood from mouth and nose, drifting in and out of consciousness—no matter; he hangs on. He hunkers down flat against the grass, panting, leg muscles coiled for a savage rush—his last. Blood from his burning lungs foams on his lips and nostrils with every breath. He clutches at his flickering life with a death grip, fighting to clear the haze in the head. Revenge is a marvelous stimulus. *"Please!"* he implores his deity. *"Just five more minutes. Give me enough time and strength to catch this little punk with his little safari outfit who ambushed me at my meal, popped off that noise and sent this searing, throbbing pain into my flank. Let the spark linger in my stiffening joints till the little bastard bumbles down this trail. Give me one last charge, then the vigor for a final frenzy of slashing claw and chomping fang. I wanna hear him scream, wanna see his eyes pop when I rip into his face and mangle it . . . I wanna feel his chest shredding under my claws, ripping into human hamburger as he screams. Please, Earth Goddess Gaia . . . just . . . five (I'm getting weaker) more . . . minutes—YES! Here he COMES!"*

Under a rig, the murk performs much the same function for sharks: The Long Grass.

"All I saw was teeth coming at me," remembers Bobby Geanelloni when he speared his 350-pounder. And he was luckier than Helldiver Carl Loe.

A few years back, three Helldivers were diving 30 miles off Cocodrie at a fairly shallow rig—120 feet deep. Carl Loe, usually among the more venturesome of Helldivers, was chillin' out this dive. He was sitting on a beam at about 100 feet, shooting sheepshead, of all things. These are small, slow, and clumsy fish. A ten-pounder is considered huge—great eating, though. So they're typically targeted by novices or by meat divers not interested in a huge trophy.

Each species has it's own division at every rodeo and the biggest brought in merits a trophy. So Carl was shooting for the winning sheepshead today, and he had some nice ones strung up already. He was just sitting on a beam near the bottom—his legs actually dangling in the murk. He didn't know that Art Bukafske was in the murk below him, finning slowly through the "Long Grass," finger on the trigger. Terry Migaud had just emerged from the murk and was passing near the stationary Carl when "Poppa Smurf" suddenly saw Carl's body jerk violently.

"That shark grabbed *both* Carl's legs in one bite!" says Terry. "Then he was trying to twist them off! Jerking back and forth." Fortunately for Carl it was a sand tiger. They have a mouthful of mean teeth, all right, but they're long and sharp, and there are several rows of them. They're made for catching and eating fish—unlike a tiger shark, bull shark, or hammerhead. Those sharks have serrated teeth, made for sawing, tearing and ripping. A sand tiger's teeth are like a trap. They're made for piercing and gripping. Bad enough. But if it had been a bull that grabbed Carl, he might have lost his legs.

The International Shark File and the book *Shark Attack* list the attack on Carl as "unprovoked," because that's how it was reported in the *New Orleans Times Picayune.*

"Yeah, those newspapers," Terry and his Helldiver buddies snicker when they read it. "They believe anything. No, no," Terry says. "Believe me, that shark was *plenty* provoked. That shark had a spear in him." And it wasn't Carl's.

Contemporary dive lore regards the sand tiger or "gray nurse shark" as languid and generally harmless. At worst he's the Jekyll and Hyde of the shark clan: schizophrenic, unpredictable. So let's go back a bit: in the 1960s the U.S. Navy compiled a Shark Danger Rating list. It describes the gray nurse as "swift and savage," and somehow rates it *atop* the tiger shark for danger. So there.

A 1953 book titled *Fishes of South Africa* by marine biologist J. L. B. Smith says that in that country, "probably most shallow-water attacks are due to this shark . . . the jaw of a ten-foot specimen could easily sever a human head or thigh." Dr. Smith watched a sand tiger feeding while underwater. "The upper jaw shoots out, the inner teeth become erect in both jaws, and the snout forms a grotesque pointed hood over this projecting, fang-lined cavity of horror which can snap shut with bone- shearing force."

Carl's bones weren't sheared, but Terry vouches for the rest of the description. "Those suckers have row upon row of teeth, man." Carl, however, got no preview of the jaws closing on his leg. He didn't see it, just felt it.

"Man, Carl started whacking that shark on the head with his gun—WHACK! WHACK! WHACK!" says Terry. "Looked like he was digging a posthole. That shark was twisting back and forth, shaking Carl around. Finally after a hard whack to the eyes it let go and Carl starts swimming up, blood pouring out of his lower legs, a green cloud spreading through the water. Then I see Art, coming outta the murk below, gripping his gun for dear life, as if something's trying to jerk his arm outta the socket. Then I see the six-foot sand tiger twisting and jerking and thrashing and biting on the end of his shaft.

"*Now* it made sense. Turns out, Art, that crazy sucker, was down in the murk and had shot the shark. It was twisting around on the end of the cable, mouth open, biting like crazy. Carl's legs happened to be around, and—*wham!*—they got grabbed."

Picture that smoky stuff always hovering over the ground in the old Wolfman and Dracula movies . . . I mean the *old* ones, 1930s stuff. Better yet, think of the stuff released on the disco floor around midnight, in the midst of the pounding, deafening beat, at the height of the twirling frenzy, when we were all hopelessly crocked, red-faced, idiot smiles; prancing, gyrating, bumping, leaping, groping madly throughout the floor, fondling all the chicks who had blown us off earlier in the evening, and who were now getting that glassy-eyed giggle and a fondle right back. Picture the smoke that, though it covered the flashing floor to a depth of two feet, barely reached the top of our heels, and thus left the magnificent flares on our angel-flights unobscured as we leaped and pranced, flapping gloriously in full view, fanning the smoke in great billows . . .

Well, *that's* what the bottom murk looks like at a rig, same consistency, same visibility—a layer of thick fog stretching anywhere from 10 to 50 feet from the bottom, sometimes 100 feet, but usually more like 20. The bigger and more sedentary fish—snapper, grouper, jewfish—generally seek it for protection. They're either in it, or hovering right above it. And since sharks are ambushers, this murk makes an ideal place for them to ambush prey, as befits the apex predator of this realm.

That is, until the Helldivers' show up. Today, Terry, Louis, and Stan—clutching their six-foot spear guns, were hoping to inculcate a few lessons about "apex predation" to these big, toothy, swaggering bastards. And they weren't looking for small ones either—none of those little four- or-five-foot blacktips and spinners that follow you up to the boat, snatching bites from the snapper or AJ on your spear. None of that. They needed at least a 400-pounder just to *tie* Terry's record of a few years before.

A bit to the west of us some divers from Baton Rouge, the Bayou Bandits, were getting in their last licks.

"Man, I was feeling no pain down there," Clay Coleman says. That "down there" was about 220 feet. Clay shot a 150-pound Warsaw Grouper at about 160 feet. He was diving the Mississippi Canyon Rigs that day, so he had another 400 feet of Gulf below him.

"Water was cobalt blue that day." he says. "You know how *that* is—how easy it is to just drift down, and down—and down."

If ever there was a "tempting, all-embracing vastness" that Hans Hass warned about, it's the 600 feet of purple-blue water surrounding the massive coral-encrusted beams that stretch to seeming oblivion under the set of oil platforms known as the Mississippi Canyon Rigs . . . those big legs stretching down into the blue void . . . schools of massive fish finning below.

It's more than a temptation; it's almost a suction. Like the jagged peaks that beckon mountain climbers to ascend, these blue depths beckon our descent. To look from afar is simply not enough. Add prey and the lure becomes irresistible. Cayman's Wall comes to mind but, but in sorry second place. It can't compare. Yes, "The Wall" stimulates the instinct to explore. Mississippi Canyon does likewise, but titillates with prey. So the hunting instinct kicks in, too. The effects of these glittering depths, the surreal structure, and the big fish on a healthy male in scuba gear with a six-foot spear gun are downright aphrodisiacal. Clay succumbed.

You can never actually *see* the bottom on a Louisiana rig-dive. The bottom at Mississippi Canyon was 600 feet down. "You just see those beams and crossbeams stretching down and down into the blue void. And in that cobalt water they look so close. Next thing I know I'm at 180 feet, then I see a huge Warsaw grouper on the other side of the rig. He looked like a Volkswagen. So I start finning over, slowly—but he wouldn't let me get too close. After a few minutes of stalking and with him heading down, I said I better take him—the shot's a little long, but it's now or never. So—*schluunk!* But I hit a little low, under his eye.

"Then, *whoom!* Down he goes, and me with him. I know those big Warsaws. There ain't no stopping them at first. Just ride him out, I'm thinking. And sure enough, there was no stopping this one. I was rushing down with him, but somewhere in the back of my mind I knew I had to stop him. This rig was over 500 feet deep. My head'll crumble like a thin-shelled egg, I remember thinking. My freakin' eyes'll pop out my head like ping-pong balls—all kinda crazy shit started going through my head. So I'm looking around for a beam to wrap my cable around, get some leverage on this big bastard. But he's heading down and down. I guess I wasn't too narked out cause I knew I had to stop him—knew I was probably getting too deep.

"And I sure as hell didn't wanna let go of the gun. I'd already lost a couple and the ole-lady was hassling me about the expense. So like I said, I couldn't been *too* narked out to remember this. Well, finally a crossbeam got between me and him and I looped the cable around it, but right at the gun.

"Aha, I'm thinking. Now I got him! So now I'm relaxed. I was just sitting there, right under the beam, looking straight up. Content with the world, holding my spear gun, my cable going up around ten feet then making a half loop around a crossbeam. So, I look over and see this *huge* grouper right next to me, finning around plain as day. That's kinda funny, I remember thinking. And he's not even fleeing like all the other ones. What's wrong with this stupid fish?"

Clay was about three martinis into that "soft and cozy butterfly net" Hass warned about. "Then I look over and there's another one! Another gigantic Warsaw. And this one's got a spear sticking out from below his eye. Hummm. Weird fish down here today, I'm thinking. So I'm just sitting there digging it." Clay plays guitar for a rock band—he actually talks like that. "I just remember being very calm, very serene. Then *shlunk!* I see a shaft hit the first one. And he goes crazy. And in the commotion mine goes crazy again. Then I feel something tugging on my vest, I mean yanking me up hard, and I look up to see my dive-buddy Evans Byrd nodding and pointing up like 'Let's *go!*' With the other hand he's holding his spear gun and fighting the other grouper. So I look over at my computer and see we're at 220 feet. *Hmm.*"

"But what's the rush? I remember thinking. Until I look over and the computer's flashing. Hey look at that pretty red light, I'm thinking. But Evans is still tugging away at me and so we worked our way up. Warsaws give a big rush when you first hit them. I guess mine was played out. And Evans got a good crippling shot. We just worked our way up. But you know, to this day I still wonder: if Evans hadn't grabbed me down there? I was just feeling so calm, so content, I mighta stayed down there—and drowned."

Divers and fishermen have encountered huge sharks in great numbers in this area for decades. Recently Marine Biologists have come up with a possible reason. This area of the Louisiana coast, bordered on the north by Mississippi Sound and on the south by the Mississippi river delta, is looking more and more to them like a shark "mating and pupping ground," an area not to be confused with the "shark nursery" that lies on the other side of the river, around the rigs a few miles west of here. This comforting theory was made available by Dr. Bruce Thompson of LSU's Coastal Wetlands Institute.

Mark Grace of the National Marine Fisheries Service confirms from the air what we see in the water. "Yes, when we fly over that Chandeleur-Breton Sound region," he says, "we look down and they're all over the place. We see literally *hundreds* down there. And I mean some *monsters.*"

Wonderful news. "And remember," he continues. "Sharks mature fairly slowly. So it takes a *big* shark to mate and spawn. So that's what we usually see out there, *huge* schools of HUGE sharks."

Now to what geological quirk, to what oceanographic feature do we, who dive in this area, owe this blessing? Mark and his ilk suspect that it's because of the sandier bottom on the east side of the Mississippi river. There's abundant food, in the form of finfish and rays, because of the adjoining estuaries. Currents have a lot to do with this. Gulf currents run east-west. So the mud from the river's discharge gets washed west. The areas east of the river stay a little sandier. And so the water's a little clearer. Also, the egg-layers among the sharks—the tiger sharks for instance (the shark described by University of Miami's shark guru, Dr. Samuel Gruber as "the most dangerous shark in the world") like to lay on sand, not on mud, where the egg capsules would be buried. That's why more show up in the Breton Sound area.

If a shark's around, we like to *see* him. Make sure he's keeping his distance. Make sure he's not acting jerky, erratic, hungry, menacing . . . or worse: horny. This explains a lot of their behavior out here.

They call Breton Sound and Main Pass "Sharktown," and quite appropriately in our view. Us, we try to steer clear of sharks. But that's really more up to them than to us. We've seen them often enough, on practically every dive east of the river. You generally spot them early in the dive. They lumber around, scowling, swaggering around like Richard Pryor and Gene Wilder in *Stir Crazy*: "Yeah!—We Bad!"

Sharks don't flee for the depths like red snapper and grouper. They're not skittish like the jacks. They don't panic and scatter like the schools of bluefish. No sir. They wait for everything to clear a path for *them*. "Nothing in the water would *dare* mess with *me*."

Then they meet a Helldiver. "Not only will this clumsy, bubble-spewing peckerhead not move away, he's actually *approaching!* The nerve! And what's he holding? And pointing at me? Probably one a dem sticks to jab me away if I get too close . . . or one a dem cameras . . . yeah, dat's it . . . like that Eugenie Clark broad . . . but dis guy's dressed a little different from divers who use dem things . . . ain't never seen bell-bottom on a diver before . . . and a flowery shirt? He's getting closer . . . he's—OUCH, *hey! What the?* That's your ASS, pal! You done stuck THE KID! You're in a world-a-trouble now, PUNK!"

Time for evasive action. "All I saw was teeth," says Baton Rouge's Bobby Geanelloni about events right after he sent a six-foot stainless steel shaft into a 350-pound shark from twenty feet. "I ducked behind a beam. And just in time . . . I was down about one hundred and fifty feet and saw him below me, swimming away. He was about a three-hundred-pounder I estimated, about twelve feet long. I hit him in the back from above, missed the spine, no kill shot. He flinched a little when the shaft hit him but no big deal. He kept swimming. And I said, man this is a breeze! What's all this stuff I been hearing about badass sharks? I was ready for a ride, to swim with him. Thought he'd take off and start towing me around like a big grouper or amberjack. Man, I was *set*, had a good grip on the gun, plenty of air, wasn't too deep—I was set.

"Well, a second later he hits the end of the cable—and stops. Whoops, I thought. AJ's and cobia don't do *this!* What now? Do I just haul him up?

"Then he *turned around*. Whoops, again. Ain't never seen a fish do *this* before. Then he saw me. And he musta sensed, right away, that I was the cause of his troubles . . . 'cause man, then *all I saw was teeth!* Comin' straight at me. I said 'shit!' and ducked behind a beam. CRUUNCH! he ripped into it right below me. Man, I wrapped the cable around the beam a couple of times and went up—got the hell outta there. Got another gun, came back down and finished him off."

And that's a sand tiger, or ragged-tooth shark, normally harmless. Try it on a bona-fide tiger shark and things get even dicier. Just ask another Baton Rougeite, Terry Brousseau: "Anything got in his way, and WHOOMMP! He crunched down on it and mangled it—or tried to."

Terry had a 14-foot tiger shark on the end of his shaft. "I saw him under me when I was down around one hundred and thirty feet. He was inside the rig. I was younger then, crazier. I wanted him. Well, I ease down to good range, aim—*schlunk!* And he's off. Man, I'm tied up with a submarine, I says to myself. But I went with him. Then he went crazy. He was chomping the very rig, man, grabbing the beams and trying to twist them . . . putting up a cloud of barnacles, coral and teeth . . . I'm trying to stay outta his way. Trying to stay above him. So I look over and there's *another* one! He was all excited too, all jerky, following the speared one around. Man I said this is it—but I didn't wanna let go of the gun. Then I look over and there's my dive buddy—aiming at the other one! SCHLUNK! And he sticks *him!*

"But no kill shot. Nothing like a kill shot. So now we got *two* of the suckers going crazy, pulling us around, twisting our cables up—And every time one came near a beam—CHOMMMPP!!—teeth and barnacles flying every which way. You better believe I kept a tight cable and stayed above that sucker, and hugging a beam, ready to duck behind it. Well, I finally had to grab a beam to get some leverage on him. So I've got my bare arm—had a short sleeve shirt on—wrapped around the beam, with the other gripping my spear gun, hanging on as he's trying to bite a steel beam in half. . . .

"I'm scared, man. All this commotion going on right under us with two tiger sharks going nuts—but I'm excited too. You know the feeling. I didn't want to let go of the thing and lose my gun. I *wanted* that shark. So, I'm sitting there kinda catching my breath and I feel something, biting my arm. 'OUWW!' I look over and there's nothing there. No shark or barracuda or anything. Then it starts stinging. And stinging like HELL! Terrible pain like a hundred hornets stinging at once. Man, I'm freakin' out now.

"I let go of the rig and look at my arm. There's this thing wrapped around my arm like a big bracelet. It's an ugly thing, red and white, like some kinda huge caterpillar or centipede. And I mean huge, over a foot long. Christ! I'm thinking What now? Like I ain't got enough problems with two tiger sharks in a chomping frenzy twenty feet below me! And man, I'm hurtin' by now. The sharks are still going crazy, now I got something outta some horror movie injecting some kinda poison in my arm. Feels like somebody's holding a welding torch on it!"

Terry had tangled with a bristleworm, or fireworm. Just to look at a picture of one is to shudder. To find one wrapped around your *arm*—I can't imagine. A hideous and terrifying creature. When she designed this thing, Mother Nature was on the rag. I mean she was seriously pissed. Stephen King on acid couldn't come up with this thing. The white that Terry mentioned consists of thousands upon thousands of bristles that cover the length of this disgusting marine slug. Each is a hollow spine tipped with a barb like a fishhook. And each injects venom like the fang of a cobra, then breaks off, leaving the poison, the barb and half the spine inside the flesh of the poor sucker who touches one.

I've read that some divers have had fingers amputated as a result of touching small ones. I guess to some people a small one looks harmless, almost complementing the other colorful creatures on the coral reef; "here nice little coral creature, let me— OOOUUWWW!"

But back to Terry. "So man, I grab that thing to rip it off and OOOOW! Now my hand's burning like I stuck it in a wasp nest! And my arm—shoot, my whole side, half my body's throbbing. So I grab the gun back with my good hand. I'm getting numb all over by now. I guess the adrenaline was keeping me going . . . I still wanted that damn shark. To make a long story short, the sharks finally quiet down a little, actually started swimming towards the surface, so we just kinda went with them. We winched them aboard and, man, my arm was swollen up like an inner tube. Then the whole side of my body started swelling up. I was in the hospital the next day, getting antivenin shots like if I'd been bit by a rattlesnake. Swelling finally went down after a couple days. But I'll tell you, I was hurtin' there for a while. One shark was fourteen feet the other was twelve. We had our thrill, and we got some dynamite steaks."

Like I was saying, Florida lists more shark attacks—by far—than anyplace else. But that makes sense. Florida, obviously, has more people in the water for more time than any other area in the United States. And this being the U.S., more attacks are reported. But you'll never convince me that a place like, say, the Philippines, with its thousands of miles of tropical coastline and millions of people, doesn't have hundreds of shark attacks a year.

And we could probably quintuple the ones from Florida if we include the Florida Straits. It's estimated that for every Elian Gonzalez that makes it safely to shore, four of his desperate compatriots perish at sea like his mother. Roughly forty thousand have made the crossing in the past thirty years. (I'm talking *rafters* here. Not the Mariel boat-lift.) It's an ugly thing to contemplate—especially for me, a harrowing thing to put my calculator to. I've known some of these people, and believe me, the last thing on their mind when they hit the shore is calling some newspaper to report a shark attack. In fact, I know of a very special two who never made it at all. Almost every account of *"balseros"* (rafters) I've read mentions sharks harassing them along the way.

Frank "The Knife" Olah lives on Grand Isle and makes his living running a charter fishing service and cleaning fish, hence the name. "More like choice sirloin than fish," he tells me about shark. "Me, I cut 'em into steaks, but *across* the grain of the meat. Then I marinade them in fajita marinate and Italian salad dressing for a couple hours. Then I throw them on a hot grill—and I mean *hot*—to sear them just like a steak. I tell ya, I've had people from all over the country eat my grilled shark and rave."

I met Frank as the mate on an offshore fishing trip. He was a pleasant surprise. In Louisiana a mate does more blabbing than any "mating." That's his job, of course: entertaining the clients. And Frank had us in stitches the whole trip long. Too many off-shore fishing trips nowadays come off like a commando operation, with hair-raising penalties for any breach of schedule or orders— a vicious, hard-bitten captain (usually a retired combat-Marine if male, housewife if female) barking orders from the bridge. Everyone else scrambling around in stark terror. Remember the movie *Patton*? Remember the poor soldier with battle fatigue in the hospital in Sicily? He got off easy compared to a first mate I met on a trip some years back. "I just can't take it anymore!" he blubbered after some lines fouled.

"Why you lily-livered, yellow skunk!" The captain snarled on his way down from the bridge "I oughta use you for chum! In fact I oughta!" And he reached for the fish billy.

"No! No! Please . . . *Please*, it was an accident! AHHHHHH!"

Pelayo and I cowered behind the fish box, convinced we were next. I held a bait bucket for a shield and had a good grip on the gaff. Pelayo grasped a fire extinguisher. He'd spray the captain in the face with a blast and I'd trip him as we made our dash to the bridge and radio. We'd capture the high ground, then I'd sum-mon the Coast Guard on the radio, while Pelayo poured down a withering fusillade from the extinguisher and flare guns, pinning down the crazed captain until the Coast Guard arrived with the water cannon, net, and straight-jacket . . . or so we imagined.

None of that with Frank-the-Knife and Captain Rice though. This crew persisted in the crazy notion that we were out for a day of fun and relaxation. Should have guessed Frank was a serious rig-diver. He was typical of the breed. Nothing bland or stan-dardized about him. No cubicle worker here. Frank's been diving for almost thirty years himself. For a while he was more of a meat diver than a competition diver. He even did it commercial-ly, selling the fish. As such he needed to be efficient. A machinist by trade, he's always tinkering, and this ingenuity led to him to design power heads.

"Man, I got tired of losing guns," he says. "I'd done let go of at least three already. . . . Some huge grouper starts dragging me off—I'm looking at my air, my depth, finally—bye-bye! There goes fish, gun, every damn thing—another two hundred bucks. *Had* to be a better way, especially if I'm looking to turn a profit at this thing. I had to come up with something better for stoppin' these big suckers."

And Frank's skills were perfectly suited for this type of innovation. He went into his workshop and applied himself diligently, like the Nutty Professor. But a few adjustments proved necessary.

"Almost blasted a rig down," he says, shaking his head. "Man, I thought that thing was gonna topple over."

As Frank says, "Hey, you're always looking for maximum power, right? I mean, if a thirty two-caliber is better than a twenty two-caliber, then how about a twelve-gauge, in three-inch magnum? Ain't that better than a twenty-gauge? Sounded sensible to me.

"Turns out I missed the fish and hit the beam—Ba-LOOOOM-MM!!!" Man, that shaft ricocheted back— peewwwrrnn! All I saw was a little line of bubbles come whizzing past my head—didn't know what the hell it was at first. 'Man that's some fast fish,' I said.

"No fish—it was the shaft, man, ricocheting back like some kinda missile. Five inches lower and it woulda taken my head off. A foot to the left and it woulda run my dive buddy through the belly—spread his intestines all over the water for a real nice triggerfish feeding frenzy. A foot higher, it woulda castrated another guy. Over a bit and it woulda wacked another one's leg off.

"I'm just sitting there in a daze—still in shock, can't hear or nothing after that blast—terrible concussion underwater, you can imagine. It was like a bomb going off in your bedroom. I mean, that was some BLAST! Finally my head cleared a little and I remembered my dive buddies, and I looked around.

"Well, they didn't look much like 'buddies' right then. Good thing you can't hear down there—can't hear *good* that is, 'cause even with being one hundred feet underwater, even with my ears ringing like crazy from that blast—even with all that, I could still hear these suckers. BRUULL! BRROOOLL! BRAAALL! You never seen such a scene. Bubbles billowing from their regulators in huge clouds, heads jerking up and down, all shaking their guns at me, shaking their fists in fronta my face, heads bobbing and jerking, pointing at their heads and ears—it was a sight.

"Then I looked over and there's a big silver circle, about the size of a hub-cap, on the rig's leg. That magnum blasted off the barnacles, paint, rust, every damn thing. We decided to go back to the thirty two-caliber after that. That was fun enough. With power heads you don't have to worry about aiming all that much. I mean, you hit 'em in the freakin tail or the nose—*blam!* and they keel over. But after a while that got old and we went back to competitive diving with regular points."

A power head is what's on the end of a bang stick: a little cylinder with a firing pin holding a bullet or shotgun shell. Bash it into a fish and it goes off. You see this a lot on those sanctimonious shark TV shows. You know the ones. They revel in slow-motion close-ups: the cruel hooded eyes, below them, rows of four-inch teeth that chomp, twist, and rip child-sized chunks off some ox carcass. Then they dump fifty gallons of ox blood in the water, jump in, and start waving dead fish around:

Yes, Jacques, as we can see, sharks are not in the least bit aggressive. They've been miscast as ravenous man-eaters when in fact they're harmless scavengers. Primarily they—oops, this one's getting a little close—there, just shove them away. See how docile and harmless? Yes as we were saying, they're more afraid of man than— oops, this ones getting a little frisky here, yes, a little close, a little, Hey watchit!—WATCHIT!

BLAAAM! and they whack him. The mangled shark twists around crazily, then sinks.

Yes, as we were saying, sharks are perfectly harmless. In fact, they're a vital link in the ocean food-chain. It's sad and tragic how so many unenlightened and sensationalized accounts depict them as brutal or—

Anyway, put one of these power heads on the end of your spear gun shaft and you're talking one hell of a weapon. Your chest puffs up involuntarily. A power head makes you feel like you're strutting around with a .44 magnum on your hip *a la* Dirty Harry. A hammerhead swaggers by, eyeing your stringer of fish . . . he swings close and your eyes meet in a steely stand-off... "I know what you're thinking, *punk.*" You growl. "Does this guy have a power head on the end of the shaft? Or just a regular point? Well ya know, in all the excitement I kinda forgot myself. But being as this might be a twelve-gauge magnum and it can blow that flat ugly head *right off* . . . *y*ou might ask yourself: *Do I feel lucky today?* Well, do ya, PUNK?"

There's no denying the rush of strutting around with serious firepower at your fingertips. Anybody offended by this banality can't possibly be reading this book by now. With a power head, you can blast a hundred-pound fish into a huge fish-stick from twenty feet. As such, these weapons are anathema to competition divers. And rightly so. Hell, they don't give the fish a chance. There's nothing to it. Gone is the brawl *mano a mano*. Gone is the "harsh confrontation with the animal's fierceness, the struggle with it's energetic defense," as Ortega y Gasset calls it. The bastard keels over dead the instant you hit him. No drama. No gallantry. No sport.

But you talk about a kick in the ass. You see a huge cobia or amberjack lumbering by—*schlink—Ba-LOOOOM!!* and the big sucker stops in his tracks. Must be the same rush as shooting an elephant between the eyes from close range—POW!—and watching him collapse like a dynamited building. I used to love to watch that on the old *American Sportsman* shows, that splendid program from the late sixties. I believe it was Rick Jason, of the TV series *Combat*, who was the featured hunter that whacked an elephant. Then there was William Shatner, arrowing a grizzly, Bing Crosby and Kurt Gowdy massacring doves by the dump truck–full. Ah, those were the days. Incredible that Hollywood used to allow such things.

Coast Guard records show no shark attacks on divers off Louisiana. But what do they know? Unprovoked attacks, sure. None of those. But the key word here is "unprovoked." Stick a six-foot steel spear in their flank and they feel plenty provoked, believe me. And some rig-divers just love provoking the hell out of sharks. Ted Nugent could tell you why: "You can't grill 'em til ya kill 'em," is a favorite quip of his. Crunching the trigger and sending that stainless steel shaft into their flank starts the process that ends up with this flesh, cubed, drenched in lemon butter, and skewered on a shish-k-bob between chunks of green pepper and pineapple, or on Frank-the-Knife's grill.

In fact, according to the official records, the shark responsible for the most attacks globally is the innocuous nurse shark.

Yes, that placid reef-dweller that looks like a big goofy catfish. It makes sense, actually. The voyeurs on their chaperoned reef dives are always pestering nurse sharks. They're always grabbing them by the tail and stuff for a cutesy picture. Then, CHOMP! and they go crying and whining to the dive master. "That mean ole shark *bit* me!"

"Don't grab him then, you twit! Leave him alone! He's trying to sleep. Been a long night!"

Point is, *all* sharks have teeth and they're easily provoked.

"Sharks are ambushers," according to Peter Benchley in *National Geographic*. "Once he knows he can't surprise you he won't expend a lot of energy to get you." That's a hungry shark now. One looking for food. A pissed-off shark is quite a different matter. And sharks definitely get pissed when you poke a spear into them. That's the first step involved in converting them into shark kebobs. No way around it.

A few miles west of us some Helldivers had that very thing in mind. While we were fleeing from the bastards, they were *seeking* sharks, prowling through the bottom murk for the very purpose of finding them, and at close quarters. "Close" as in a few feet. "Close" as in when you bump the wall on the way to the bathroom at 3 A.M. Not much room for maneuvering down there, not when you extend the spear gun and can't see past your wrist.

JBL, the nation's biggest spear gun manufacturer, sells more guns in Louisiana than in any other state in the union, though we have fewer certified divers than Illinois, Pennsylvania, or Colorado (PADI statistic). We're not even in the top ten. But the (relatively) few divers in the state are possessed of a raging and unquenchable blood lust, as befits the winning state in the Fund for Animals' "Cavalcade of Cruelty." You don't get cuisine like ours without it.

But our marine assassinations require certain modification of factory spear guns. Takes power to pierce a shark's tough hide. Takes even more to penetrate the cartilaginous flesh and cold-cock him with a brain shot, which is how Terry got his 407-pounder in 150-foot depths years before.

"Good thing, too," Terry says. "I was almost outta air on my way up. Then he shows up right under me—offered an ideal shot, man. It was irresistible. If I'd a missed the head or hit a little off, I'd a probably let go of the gun . . . *bye-bye!* Didn't have much air left. Not enough for a big drawn out fight—especially if he came after me, which they'll do when wounded. None of us had been bit up till that time, but we'd just been lucky, and quick."

The memory of that kill was still fresh for Terry on this dive with Louis and Stan. But he was out to beat his own record. And he knew where such a creature was likely to lurk: in the "Long Grass," below, exactly where Art had found his at the Timbalier rigs the previous year. No getting around it.

"Water was murky from the top down at this rig," Terry recounts. "This was a fairly shallow rig, 70 feet or so."

They plunged in and headed down through the gloom. "But the murk never really broke. We never got more than ten or twelve feet of visibility down there." Terry says. "But fish were everywhere. I looked over and saw Louis shoot a nice sow snapper and string it up. He just sat on a beam and was surrounded by them, shooting away."

But Terry kept descending, the tip of his gun barely visible on the way down. Past schools of snapper, past some chunky grouper. The hell with them. He was thinking *shark*. A long shadow looms ahead . . . it takes shape—*ah*, a beam! He sat on it for a second and looked around, checked his bands, his cable, his riding rig. Some more snapper materialize from the haze around him. "And I mean some beauties." The stripes of sheepshead and spadefish were everywhere. A wall of bluefish roared by. A triggerfish was starting to nip at a loose nylon strand from the riding rig. But nothing huge, no sharks around.

So back to the stalk. He pushed off and kept descending . . . the murk getting thicker . . . thicker. Finally the gloom closed in around him even tighter, almost suffocatingly so. "I knew I was near the bottom now," he chuckles. "Man, I couldn't see six feet in fronta me."

Here's when most of us want company. You're fumbling around in that gloom with your heart hammering near your glottis. You're almost hyperventilating, your mind (mine, at least) flashing pictures of assorted versions of deep-sea doom and dismemberment at music video rates—then finally . . . there he is! Your dive-buddy! The bubbling apparition gives you the OK signal and you return it heartily. *Whoooo!* Comforting indeed, for a few seconds anyway.

It's instinctive I guess. Phil Caputo captured that feeling in *A Rumor Of War.* "In the jungle, men tended to draw together, seeking the reassurance that comes from being physically close to one another, because even the illusion of being alone in that haunted, dangerous wilderness was unbearable."

So Terry slowed down; his fins barely moved but his eyes were sharp and vigilant. His head swerved from side to side, scanning all around. Whatever happens down here happens at close range and fast. His finger was tense and on the trigger. He picked up the fin tempo a bit and started making a slow sweep around the perimeter of the rig, finger tightening on the trigger. Ready for instant action. Like Tom in the boonies of 'Nam decades before, or Hemingway trailing a gut-shot cape buffalo before that, Terry down in the murk, stalking sharks.

In fact he was just checking his depth gauge, barely visible in front of his face in the murk. It read 65 feet. This told him he was in the bottom murk. Yes, he was definitely in the "Long Grass." Big snapper and grouper loomed through it at close range. But none were big enough for Terry that day.

He'd just looked away from his gauge when everything scattered. "Those fish just shot off," he says. So he braced for action. Something massive and dangerous was close by. Most divers say they can somehow *feel* when a shark's around. Under a rig, with its ever-present schools of fish, it's easy, and requires no extrasensory powers. You simply notice you're suddenly alone. *Uh-oh* . . . you see fish shagging ass all around you, over you, through your legs. Look close and you'll see the fear in their very eyes. Spadefish and sheepshead aren't particularly swift. Much like Uncle Joe they're always "moving kinda slow." To see *them* shagging means a serious predator's around. And in a feeding mode, or a jerky pissed-off mode, barracuda don't generate that type of panic under a rig. Nor do divers. Only sharks.

Terry tensed and gripped the safety and trigger. "Those rig compressors pound pretty loud under water." Terry says. "But right then, my heart-rate was louder." His temples throbbed and he finned forward, slowly . . . just as a huge gray tail lashed the water inches in front of his mask, almost bashing it off and propelling him backward.

"The thing was about three feet high, man," Terry says. "I knew it was a shark's tail right away . . . and I knew it was a huge one. But he was already bookin'. I figured he was hit."

So Terry, remembering Carl, booked out of there too. "I knew that sucker was gonna start biting."

Stan had been no more than twenty feet from him at the time, and had seen the monstrosity looming under him: "looked like a submarine. I could see a fin here, then another *way* over there. Put it this way—I knew he was *big*." He shot, without much aiming, or even much thinking. "Then I just held on," Stan says. "I knew it wasn't a kill shot, so I knew what was coming."

Fortunately they were on the very edge of the rig, almost outside of it. So at least one peril—that of getting tenderized against the barnacled beams like a round steak as the beast rocketed around the structure—at least *this* threat was missing.

And off they went, on a wild ride all right, but mostly outside the rig. "Not that I really knew it at the time" Stan says. "I mean, it was dark and murky. I just held on and went with him. Barreling through the murk. Kinda knew I had a record if I could hang on, if I could somehow boat him."

Remember, the U.S. Navy rates this shark "swift and savage." J. L. B. Smith described the mouth of a 100-pounder as a "fanglined cavity of horror which can snap shut with bone-shearing force." Christopher Coates, Director of New York City's aquarium says, "Sand tigers bite like hell. We don't trust them." And Wiley Beevers of New Orleans gives a hearty "freakin'-aay" to that.

In the mid '80s Wiley's part-time job was donning scuba gear and feeding the fish in a 135,000-gallon aquarium featured at a disco in suburban New Orleans named Sharkey's Reef. The tank contained assorted Gulf fish and a six-foot sand tiger shark. Every time Wiley entered the tank, the resident DJ made it a point to play Hall & Oates's "Maneater." And we'd all turn in midboogie, point at the tank and sing-along, *Whoa-a here she comes . . . watch out boy, she'll chew you up!* as the sand tiger swaggered by, yards away, with that menacing, tooth-bristling grin and those cruel, hooded cat-eyes. Wiley always raised his arms and shook his head in mock fright as he passed. Great fun, this Sharkey's Reef.

And you guessed it. One night Wiley got chewed up in full view of the boogie-ers. But Wiley wasn't "watching out" like Hall, Oates, and we all advised. The toothy brute blind-sided him as he fed the sheepshead. Then dragged him around the tank in a billowing red cloud, shaking his head, jerking Wiley around like a dummy. The girls stopped in mid-spin, tottered on their heels and shrieked in horror. The guys whooped and cackled (tequila shot night) our collars flapping like kites. Yep, we finally got what we came for. They should have charged a cover charge *that* night. Wiley required a hundred stitches.

So what happens when you're attached to a sand tiger *five times* that size, in a much fouler mood and in the visibility equivalent of nighttime in the boonies?

"You hang on," according to five-foot-seven-inch Stan Smith.

When speared, amberjack and cobia immediately aim for a beam to wrap the cable, and you in it, if not careful. Stan had shot his share of big fish. But he'd never gone for a ride like *this*. He was plowing through that murk like on an undersea boogie board pulled by a 500-horsepower outboard, holding on for dear life.

The possibilities were endless. Let the monster double back towards the rig, and Stan might be smashed into a barnacled piling—a piling he wouldn't see till it smacked him like a three-hundred pound linebacker. Let the shark continue on course and there's all that jagged pipe on the bottom around a platform. The shark could weave through it. Stan could not. He'd be in a human chipping mill. But the triggerfish would love it. Shredded Stan, julienned Stan—a feeding frenzy for sure.

He could also get tangled in discarded cable or fishing trawls. The pipe and cable on the bottom often snag the deep shrimp trawls that ply this area. The shrimpers feel the boat lurch to a stop. They curse and rant. They try backing up—nothing doing. Finally they cut the lines, leaving the net. Stan could find himself enmeshed in one, struggling helplessly, like a tuna in a gill net, gasping, sucking frantically at his regulator, sucking harder and *harder*, hearing it groan— till it stops giving. I had my guts flash-frozen in just such an incident at 90 feet once (with spent air, not nets. I'd strapped on a tank that was only half full). I jerked around, wild-eyed on the verge of a freak-out—and there was On-the-Ball, living up to his nickname, extending his octopus. He'd noticed the dearth of bubbles above my frantic movements and me.

No such succor for Stan down here. He was alone. Nobody would find him in that murk. And of course, the Dr. Jekyll he'd speared could turn into Mr. Hyde, or Mr. Sharkey. The shark could turn and open his manhole of a mouth, and Stan could get a close-up of that fang-lined cavity of horror right before it closed around his head and shoulders, or made off with an arm or leg. Wiley got a nice little adrenalin jolt, a free ride around the tank, and a hundred stitches. Carl paid with hundreds of stitches for his dive-buddy's shot.

Stan would pay for his own. But 150-pounders hit Carl and Wiley. Minnows compared to the thing barreling through the gloomy depths with Stan in tow; a *third* its size, to be precise. Stan wouldn't get off so easy. He probably wouldn't get off at *all*. Carl was surrounded by dive-mates, rescued by a helicopter and stitched up. Stan was alone, literally blind in the murk, and attached to a shark that could *swallow* the one that hit Carl. Here was potential for much more serious damage.

But hey, this is Stan's recreation. Let's not get melodramatic here. In *Death In The Long Grass* Capstick wrote: "You will only have half-lived your life if you never feel the *icy clutch of danger* for its own sake."

No danger of that for Stan. The key is to feel that "icy clutch" in your gut but keep your head clear. In talk after talk with kick-ass, deep-diving, monstrosity-spearing rig divers like Stan and Terry, the refrain's the same. "Don't panic. Stay calm. Keep your head." That's how they explain their weekly defiance of the laws of physics, the laws of medicine, and—to many—the laws of sanity.

African big-game hunters say the same. And it sounds easy enough, when you're in their living room on a couch with a brewskie. Attorney John Jackson III of New Orleans has a trophy room crammed with African game: lions, buffalo, and elephant tusks. Some of these creatures charged him through the Long Grass. John knows something about that icy clutch. And as befits anyone with those instincts who lives in New Orleans, John was himself a rig-diver. Twenty years ago on a dive near these very rigs he looked below him and saw a huge shark, probably smaller than Stan's. "I got the hell outta the water," he says smugly.

I mention this to put Stan's exploit in perspective.

Finally Stan knew he'd have to surface—wherever he was. Fortunately this was a fairly shallow rig. At 200 feet a big wounded shark is a different matter (ask Stan). This one gave a final lunge, then seemed to slow down. So Stan aimed for the surface. But which way was *that?*

After bumbling through the murk like a gyroscope, it's easy to get disoriented in that stuff, especially after a twisting, turning roller-coaster ride through it courtesy of a five-hundred pound, fourteen-foot shark, and no rig structure around for orientation.

But remember Stan's admonition, "keep your head." It's not idle chatter to him. He had the presence of mind to observe his bubbles. This told him which way was up. He followed them, tugging the shark along.

Imagine tugging a five-hundred-pound grizzly on a leash. Imagine it at night, in the bushes. Now you get a feel for Stan's predicament. He started swimming up, trying to tow him along, finally budging the brute. The tension against his spear gun was a good sign—a sign that the shark was pulling *against* him. Wonderful. Nice to feel. A slack cable might mean the beast had turned—might mean that mouth was closing on him unseen, *a la* Sharkey's Reef. And it wouldn't be a measly one-hundred stitches if it did.

Yes, that tension felt comforting. He had fifteen feet of cable and another six for the gun. So he could reach the surface by only horsing him two-thirds of the way there.

"Man, we were starting to get worried," Terry recounts." I'd gotten outta that murk fast—remembering what happened to Carl. I didn't want to be down there with a wounded shark."

Terry swam out of the murk and into the still murky mid-depths. His other dive buddy, Louis, was sitting on a beam shooting big sow snapper. They signaled to each other. And Louis seemed unaware of any shark. "That's how murky the water was." Terry says. "I saw Louis almost immediately when I came out of the heavy bottom murk, maybe twenty feet away. But he hadn't seen a thing. I swam around for a while but couldn't find Stan—no bubbles, no nothing. I figured the shark had taken him off. Louis and I surfaced and got in the boat."

This was a shallow rig, so at least Stan was in no danger of being tangled in the cable and dragged towards the black abyss till his air ran out or the pressure crushed his chest like a thin-shelled egg. The shark couldn't take Stan down. But it could sure take him away.

Terry and Louis waited anxiously on the boat. Minutes passed and no bubbles rose. Their own tanks were nearly depleted, so Terry and Louis knew Stan didn't have much more. Still no bubbles rose. They started worrying.

Three years before, dive-mate and beloved friend Warren "Whip" Mermilliod failed to surface from a dive. Terry was on board waiting, then down under looking. They found Whip's spear gun with a sixty-pound barracuda attached. Three days later they found Whip's body, showing massive head injuries. The Coast Guard had given up the search two days before, but—typical of these guys—Whip's dive buddies *had not*. Tom tells me Marines have a similar philosophy about never leaving dead buddies behind the lines.

"Not again." Terry was thinking. "I can't go through another one of these things." It was Whip's wife that Terry was thinking about. It was for her sake that they refused to give up the search. It was for her that Terry, Val, Gerry, and a few others tied themselves together with rope, gripped lights, and plunged into the murk at 150 feet, groped through that nightmarish gloom, that lair of sharks, that jagged steel, that tangle of cable, looking for their buddy.

Amazingly, they found him. "Small consolation." says Terry. Now the possibility of another such scene with Stan—a newly-wed, no less.

"Then we hear this shout." Terry chuckles. "And there's Stan-the-Man! About two hundred yards away from the rig, yelling and waving, I mean he was waving up a storm. *Whooo!* We were happy to see *that!* Man, that shark had dragged him a-*ways!*"

They unhooked the boat and sped over. They were even more relieved to see that Stan was all right and still battling something huge. "Stan knew he probably had a record." Terry related. No way he was letting go. And no way he was gonna let any of us help him. We handed him another gun and he went down and finished it off.

"Stan comes up, huffing, shaking, panting, we're whooping—you can imagine. And now we had another problem. We had Stan aboard, everybody's alright. He's got a huge fish, probably a record. All that's great. And now we can't get the damn thing in the boat! We only had a twenty-three foot boat that day. There was no way the three of us could pull that monster on board."

So they looped a rope around the shark's tail and towed him back to the rig. Once there, Terry got out on the rig and threw the rope over a beam. Now they had the shark on one end, the boat on the other and rope angling over a beam. "Then we gunned it." Terry continues. *Wrunnn! Wruuunnnn!* And slowly—ever so slowly—we started raising the shark out of the water. Finally his whole body was out. "And we were freakin' out, man, when we saw the size of that thing."

Then they looped the rope around the beam a couple times to secure it and keep the shark elevated. They carefully untied it from the back of the boat so the shark was just hanging in the air. "Now we moved the boat under it, and slowly lowered it into the boat. Man, I thought we'd sink. Good thing it was a calm day. That thing just draped over both sides of the boat. We took water the whole way in. Thank God the bilge pump was working. Took us almost three hours to make it back to the marina. But we made it."

Four

THE DOG AND PONY SHOW

No putting it off any longer. Time for the Dog and Pony club to take the plunge and enter the Helldivers' Rodeo. Paul jumped in first, stopped briefly to adjust his mask and found himself behind the boat, struggling against the current. "Lookit that crazy sucker!" Pelayo barked. "Here! Hold out your gun!" And Paul stuck it out while pumping his legs maniacally.

Pelayo grabbed the tip of his brother's gun. "I'm surprised you didn't cock it already!" he said shaking his fist down at Paul . . . then he turned to Tom. "Last time I did this I found myself looking down the shaft of a *cocked* gun!" Paul was about even with Tom now. He took out his snorkel, spat out some water. "Bad current!" he gasped up at Tom. "Hell of a current!" Then he got in the lee of a beam and finned like crazy for the rig. Once there he looked back at us, emptied his mask, waved, and disappeared through the murk in a cloud of bubbles.

"Geezus," Pelayo nodded. "I knew it'd be a bitch today with the current. Two-foot tidal change, the tide tables said. But I didn't think it would be *this* bad." He plunged in from the bow, closer to the lee provided by the big corner beam, and finned rapidly to the beam itself. He waved and vanished through the ugly foam.

My turn now. I was sitting on the edge of the boat, nervous as always at this stage, making last-minute adjustments to the weight belt. Spitting another loogie—half Budweiser—into the mask and spreading it around with my tongue. Checking the bands on the gun, the detachable point. *Pfffffft—pfffftt*, a little more air in the BC—the inflateable vest officially known as a "buoyancy compensator." Last year I plunged in forgetting that detail and with only the snorkel in my mouth. I hit the water and thought nothing of it, then I started sinking like a stone. "No sweat," I thought. "I'll take a breath . . . *ummmmmph!*" A mouthful of water! I still had the goddamn snorkel in my mouth! I started clawing for the surface like a maniac . . . I'll never forget that.

The first dive of the year is always like this. Basically, I'm spooked, looking for excuses to delay the plunge. Hemingway defined bravery as the ability to stifle the imagination, Mencken as a "disinclination to think." Well sorry, I'm not brave right now. My brain's going a mile a minute. Always happens this way. Then I look over at Tom and feel better, because he looks about to faint.

It's amazing, I say to myself. I've been doing this crazy shit for over ten years now and *I'm* spooked. Imagine poor Tom. His first time out here. A world beyond his ken. Nothing we told him could have prepared him for this. But damnit, we *warned* him, and he insisted, pleaded—begged us—to bring his ass out here.

Well, here we are. "Buy the ticket, take the ride" as Raoul Duke says. "Ready? I looked over at him and it was the weirdest smile I've ever seen—bent, contorted. Worse than the one when he was listening to our bullshit shark and wolf eel story. The bottom part of his face was trying it's damnedest to form itself into a smile but his eyes gave the game away. They were turgid with fear. He was breathing rapidly. His hands trembled. I almost felt sorry for the bastard—almost.

"Shit, Tom!" I blurted. "We *told* you this stuff wasn't like Belize. What the hell did you expect?"

"I'm fine!" he croaked. Sounded like he had a wad of phlegm in his throat, like his mouth was dry, parched. "There's nothing wrong with me. Let's *go* man. I can't wait to shoot some fish!"

"Ready to go, hunh, old sport?"

"You're damn right!" he gasped. His mouth was still parched, I could tell. He kept licking his lips, gasping for breath. "Man, I'm pumped! Let's do it. Shoot, we don't want Pelayo and Paul to get all the good fish . . . *ha-ha!*"

"Tom." I said. "Let me tell ya something, pal. You'd make a piss poor actor. Good thing you got into sales."

"Hey?" he said, and shrugged. "What else? Shit, man, I'm a liberal arts major. What better training for a life as a bullshit artist than a curriculum which features nothing but essay questions?"

Man had a point. But I was lying about his acting prowess. I've been on many calls with Tom. Brando and Olivier would sink to their knees in front of the performances. Tom himself calls us salespeople, "the highest paid actors with the best job security on earth."

"And it's only fair," I second, "considering our level of performance." But Tom wasn't on a call here. So he was slipping. He reminded me of Alec Baldwin, that's how unconvincing was his little gig.

"But you're right." I quipped. "Pelayo and Paul are getting the pick of the big fish and scaring the rest down into the murk. Let's go."

Tom still looked like a zombie—not that I didn't.

Finally I plunged in and pumped my legs against the raging current towards the beam. It was actually easier than I expected. But only because I'd seen what happened to On-the-Ball and prepared myself. I got to the lee of the current behind the beam and started catching my breath, preparing to descend blindly through this filthy slop—but close to the beam, with the beam in sight at all times.

Drifting blindly through the murk gets you in trouble every time. Next thing you know you're in limbo. What's up? What's down? I replaced the snorkel with the regulator and checked the bands on the spear gun as a sudden, huge swell pulled me away from the beam. I scurried back and grabbed a length of nylon rope that hung from one of the huge truck tires they use for bumpers on the rigs, for when the supply boats pull up. Despite Hemingway's advice, my brain was still raging. So, Freddie's story naturally came to mind.

Growing up in Miami, our friend Freddie Tablada had cut his teeth on Caribbean and Keys dives. How different could this Louisiana rig-diving stuff be?

He discovered shortly after a job transfer here. He went on a rig-dive with some new "buddies" off Cocodrie. "Man, you'll love this shit," they assured him. Twenty miles off Cocodrie, he was sitting on the side of a friend's boat, suited up and watching the dirty water foaming around the rig's legs, not smiling, worried. His dive-mates had assured him the slop was "only a few feet deep" right before they disappeared into it.

So Freddie jumped in, adjusted his mask, and started swimming through it, following his dive-mates. "They said to jump in and just swim to the pilings," he told me. "Sounded easy enough. So I jumped in—couldn't see my freakin' hand in front of my face—and started swimming, and swimming, and swimming, and paddling. At first I figured I was actually moving forward. But I had no reference points. I swam and swam and kept swimming. More murk, more murk. Nothing clear. I couldn't see shit. Finally I said, the hell with this, and started ascending—at least I *thought* I was ascending. I couldn't really tell. And it turned out I *wasn't*, because fifteen minutes later I was still at forty feet and my air was down to eight hundred pounds! So I inflated the BC knowing this would send me up—and boy did it. I was nervous, man, on the verge of a freak-out and just slapped that button—*PPPPFFFFFTTTT!*—the BC inflated and I started *shooting* up."

"Christ! My lungs'll explode! I'm thinking. So I start breathing like crazy trying to compensate. I'm damn near hyperventilating, then I start flapping my arms like some drunk buzzard—but backwards, trying to slow down! Man, I'm panicking, flapping around like a lunatic. Finally, I pop to the surface . . . I made it! *Wonder if my lungs are okay*, I'm thinking, when—whack! A wave slaps me in the face. I swallow about a gallon of water and almost drown. I'm choking. I'm coughing like a maniac, trying to suck in air between the convulsions of my diaphragm and the waves . . . after a few minutes I finally calm down. I finally look around . . . and there's the rig, about a half-mile away!

"I almost crapped in my pants! With all the swells I couldn't even see the goddamn boat! So I started blowing on the little whistle on my BC—I mean I was blowing, podnuh! Tooting away like a crazed owl. Like they could hear it against the wind from a mile away, you know? *Yeah, right.* But I was scared man—I was panicking! Who wouldn't? I figured this might be my last chance to have *anybody* hear me! Meanwhile the current keeps hauling ass, with me in it.

Then my imagination starts going crazy. As luck would have it, the kids had gotten *Jaws* at the video store recently. Nice touch. So of course it started figuring heavily in my thinking about then . . . but I'm trying to forget about it when a gray fin slices out from the top of a swell about ten feet away. Damn! I thought. This is *it!* My insides froze. It was like somebody plugged me into a light socket. Then another fin slices through closer. Then I see the huge gray shape and by now I'm almost passed out. My stomach feels like a deep freeze. I'd been trembling from hypothermia for about an hour, my teeth were rattling like castanets—I mean I been in the water a *while!* Now *sharks!*

"Make it quick, I'm thinking. Chomp in half with one bite, please. I was almost too numb to think by then, too numb to care. So they come closer and closer—and I see it's dolphins!

"Well I'm so freaked out it doesn't really help much! I'm thinking these things may start ramming me with their snouts, like they do to sharks and kill 'em. I'm waiting for the pummeling to start . . . I'd also seen that Time-Life video with the killer whales batting the seals around through the air with their tails . . . I mean all kinda crazy shit was going through my mind. I'm seeing myself like one of those seals, flying through the air like a badminton birdie, back and forth with the dolphins batting me back and forth with their tails, yakking and laughing like Flipper . . . I'm sure I was starting to hallucinate at this point.

"I mean, my last dive had been at Pennencamp reef in crystal water fifteen feet deep and twenty other divers. Now look at me! Well, the damn dolphins keep circling and rolling on the surface, closer and closer. They go away, then show up again . . . then they finally disappeared.

"Well, three hours later I see a helicopter flying over. But there's all kinda helicopters out here because of the rigs. They bring the crews out and stuff. Then I see him slowing down . . . make a long story short: the helicopter rescued me, plucked me outta the water in a basket. My dive buddies said they'd searched for me for about an hour in the boat, then, since they work for an oil company, they alerted the helicopter.

"See me? From now on I'll go back to the Keys for *my* diving. I'll fish the rigs all right. I like that. But I'll dive where I can see where the hell I'm going from the *moment* I jump in the goddamn water until the *moment* I get out. You can *have* that rig-diving, pal."

Tom had heard the same story, word for word, the week before around a keg at Chris's house. He'd been convulsed in hysterics with the rest of us. Now it didn't seem all that funny. It seemed too real. And where the hell was Tom anyway? He'd followed me in, I knew. I'd looked back and saw him plunging in . . . geezuz, should I wait? Pelayo and Paul were already on the way down. Their bubbles were flowing all around me, though most were surfacing well behind me, carried by the current. They must be quite a ways down by now, I was thinking . . . shit, what should I do?

I bet Tom hit the water and just started down, like Freddie had. Now he's swirling around in that murk somewhere out there, clawing aimlessly at the water, probably dropped his gun by now, his weight belt, everything . . . he's clawing for the surface and actually heading down or sideways. God knows.

My dive's ruined, I'm thinking. I should have had another beer to calm the "negative vibes," man. Should have guzzled *two* more, like Pelayo, and plunged on down. Every man for himself. Tom's a big boy, a 'Nam combat vet for God's sake.

I was bobbing in the swells, deliberating, on the verge of heading back to the boat, when I saw him surface about fifty yards behind the boat and start paddling frantically forward. He'd almost blown it but seemed to be making progress, pumping his fins like a paddleboat. He's probably had it by now, I thought. He'll probably get to the drift line, grab the life preserver and sit there gasping a while. Screw this, he'll probably think. Then he'll pull his way to the boat, climb aboard and fish till we surface. To hell with this rig-diving bullshit.

We've seen this often enough with first-time guests to this racket. But no, the plucky bastard made it to the boat, sat in the water catching his breath, and waving at me. Then he started swimming over. Macho-man indeed. He was pumping away, gaining on the current. Finally he was yards away. I took out my regulator for a big gulp of real air and to greet him with hearty salutation just as another swell lifted me and slammed me against the tire, and Tom against me. His spear jabbed my leg.

"Ahh-bruuooolll!" I howled, then—*bluup!* another wave crested and slapped my mouth in mid-howl. It turned the howl into a spasm of wet coughs.

"WHAT?" Tom belched . . . he took out his regulator and spat . . . *what? What happened?"*

"Shark!" I screeched. *"Shark must have got me!"* I grimaced and clutched my leg. "Or a 'cuda!"

His face was a mask of terror. His eyes looked like melons. "No! Oh man!" he screeched. "Where? Where'd he getcha?"

I shut my eyes tightly and grimaced, just groaning, blowing bubbles in the water.

"You alright? You alright?" He was grabbing me by the shoulders, shaking me, sputtering mouthfuls of water, forgetting about his gun, which was pointed down and jabbing me again.

"Aaahhh!" I screamed as the point sunk in again—then another swell lifted us and covered his face.

He came up coughing, hacking and spitting—*"Wha?"* he gasped. "He hit you again?" Tom's mouth was contorted and his eyes blazed. It was shock, horror, sympathy, guilt. His eyes were plastered to the front of his mask. "Where? What? Aaahhh!" Then *he* screamed, let go of me and started fumbling downward with *his* arms. "I think he just bumped ME!" he shouted. "Ahh! Again! He hit me again!" Now he started jabbing my fin with his gun, jabbing the hell out of it.

"That's me, you idiot! That's my freaking FIN!"

"No!" He coughed and gasped. "No way! I felt it BITE me!" Then I realized *my* gun was pointing at him; it wasn't cocked but the detachable point was sticking him.

I started roaring with hysterics. I was almost drowning, laughing crazily, coughing, howling, hacking, drooling. Tom's face changed. He saw I was laughing and was puzzled. Finally, he started laughing himself.

"No sharks, no 'cuda, man." I sputtered. "We're jabbing each other with our *own guns*, man! What the hell are we doing out here anyway? Christ, we oughtta be petting the goddamn manatees! Feeding the parrotfish!" Wild laughter now.

"Let's go buy some body suits and glow sticks, why don't we!"

"Or those little pads to write cutesy little notes to each other underwater! Geezuz, we're a buncha old ladies. Let's take up golf!"

Thing is, I *knew* it was his gun jabbing me the first time. I was trying to mess with him, shake him up. Then when *he* started screeching, I flipped. "Geezuz, what's going on!" I thought. Serves me right I guess.

I was still slobbering and sputtering, "You jabbed the hell outta me with your godamn gun!" My angel flights were ripped but the sturdy polyester had performed brilliantly, cushioning the worst of the jab.

"Where the hell were you?" I gasped.

"Man, I thought I was right behind you!" he snorted, then started coughing. His eyes were wild. "I couldn't see anything after I jumped in!"

"I *told* ya." I huffed. "Geezum, how many freakin' times did we warn you about this murk? Ready to go down?" I gasped. He nodded and jammed the regulator back in his mouth.

I started deflating the BC and sinking behind the beam. I was hugging the beam and still almost blind. Barnacles, barely ten inches in front of my mask, seem a mottled blur through this silty river slop. I stuck my hand out past the beam and the current jerked it back, like the wind outside the window of a speeding car. Tom's fins were tapping me on the head. Good, he's still coming. I could see the faint stripes of sheepshead and spadefish, which were also seeking refuge from the current. Soon they started bumping my legs and torso. *Damn*, I thought, *I don't care how often you do this—you never relax.*

My brain was still going a mile a minute. The crazy episode above had left a mark. Predators hold in the murk, I'm thinking. It hides them, like the tall grass of the African veldt. From here they make the deadly rush at prey. Nothing like watching a school of thirty-pound jacks bolt and scatter as a huge shadow looms through the murk you just passed through, like last week. They start a chain reaction and soon the spadefish, sheepshead, and blues join the frenzy of flight and panic. I love the looks on their eyes as they flash past. You never think of fish eyes as being particularly expressive. The poor suckers just sit there in your cooler or in the case at the fish store with the same blank stare. Even the ones finning around at the aquarium seem listless and bored. Then you see a school of panicked Jack Crevalle blazing past six feet in front of your mask and their eyes are *almost* as wide as yours. Those gazelles and wildebeest on the Discovery Channel know how they feel.

Bubbles kept rising all around me, but I knew those were Pelayo's or Paul's. Where the hell was Tom? Was he lost *again?* Did I descend too fast? I stopped descending. I thought he was above me. But if he was, his fins would be tapping me on the head right now. *Don't tell me . . .* I was preparing to head back up, feeling responsible for his welfare.

Then I turned around. The water had gotten a little clearer down here and I saw a weird shape with a baby blue sweatshirt, spewing bubbles outside the rig. He got closer, closer.

Laughing is not wise with a regulator in your mouth, but I couldn't help it. Tom's legs were pointing straight up. He was grabbing my shirt trying to stay down. He'd apparently lost his weight belt. I looked into his mask from up close and guffawed into the regulator, releasing huge gouts of bubbles. His eyes made Marty Feldman's look normal. The poor guy was mortified. He'd also lost his spear gun, apparently, because his other hand was free. And he kept pointing *up, up, up.* I nodded and made the circle-finger OK signal, then started up with him. He was still clutching my shirt.

We were only down 30 feet, but in that murk it seemed like 300. When we hit the surface Tom tried to smile. His mouth was trying to twist into a smile, anyway. His eyes, like before, were wide and tremulous, about twice as wide as they'd been in the boat.

"Where's your gun?" I gasped after taking out the regulator.

He nodded, shrugged, and pointed down all at the same time. "I was trying to grab my weight belt" he gasped and spat some water just as another swell slammed us against the tire. "The buckle came loose somehow. I think I had it on backwards and hit it with my gun. Well, I'm grabbing for it and the current's taking me off again. I look up and don't see the beam, don't see you . . . I guess I dropped the gun sometime in there. You go down. I'm going back to the boat to fish."

"Alright." I stuck the regulator back in my mouth, deflated the BC, and started the descending routine again, much calmer this time, for some reason. Until I got 40 feet down and the murk still hadn't cleared.

I was descending through this swirling gloom and felt the water chilling rapidly . . . then a sudden suffocating blackness all around. *"That's it!"* your brain screams at this point. *"I don't need this shit! I'm heading up!"* But fight that, because you've made it. This cold dark water means the clear stuff is coming up.

Sure enough, suddenly that muddy broth from the river vanished and the genuine Gulf water kicked in. Visibility shot from ten inches to ninety feet. Another ten feet down and it spread to one hundred and twenty feet.

This might happen when your depth gauge hits 30 feet. It might happen at 10 feet. It might happen at 60, like today. If so, you're shrouded in darkness. Little sunlight penetrates sixty feet of murk. The deep gloom that normally cloaks the ocean depths at 600 surrounds you here at 60. Your eyes adjust slowly and the massive steel labyrinth starts taking shape around you; it spans three acres across down here. Huge schools of silver fish (everything's silver or gray down here) dart through the dark structure and your legs.

The special effects people from *Aliens* or *Star Wars* might chill your innards with the surface of a sunless planet or underground city on Pluto. But they'd throw up their hands at replicating this. An inky world pulsating with fish with a monstrous man-made structure as surreal backdrop. And the deep rumbling of the compressors two hundred feet above traveling down the pipes add a soundtrack to shame anything in *Dune, Star Wars*, or even *Jaws*. "In space no one can hear you scream," says the ad for *Aliens*. For some reason I always think of that down here. They call this "inner space."

My air lasts about ten minutes down here. I'd hate to check my pulse rate. In brief, for a diver fresh from petting the manatees or feeding the parrotfish, it takes a little getting used too. What am I saying? I'm out here practically every weekend from May to September. And *I'm* sure as hell not used to it.

Fish are everywhere. I look up and Jack Crevalle blaze around near the border of the murk above. It's a weird sight, looks like the clouds that accompany a wet cold front, the kind you like to see from a duck blind—thick, gray and ominous. There's three 'cuda right behind me. The hell with them . . . and down there?

From far below, a little line of silver bubbles. That's On-the-Ball, I'm thinking. Man, he's deep. Let's see . . . I'm already—*geezus!* One hundred thirty-five feet! Remember, I didn't get out of the murk till sixty feet. It always happens this way. You finally hit that blue water and feel like the descent just started. You look down and it seems like you could touch the bottom down there. It's so easy to keep drifting down further, further . . . or *is* it Pelayo?

Yeah, that's him. He had the angel flights, I can see the bell bottoms billowing from here, even his collars flapping around like kites. What a scene. It looks like he's after an amberjack. Looks like a school out in front of him. I see the gun out in front. He's pointing it, and now the biggest one turns broadside—*schlinnk!*

There he goes. From up here it looks like a minnow wriggling on a hook. I know better. I can compare his size to Pelayo . . . and *ah* . . . there's Paul to my right. Good. So much nicer when you've spotted everybody down here. You suddenly relax a little. Paul's got a nice grouper through the gills. His gun is up around his shoulders through the bands and he's pointing down, towards his brother, the amberjack, and the action.

Yes, I nod vigorously, giving the OK signal. Too bad we can't high-five down here. The rest of the school is still finning around as Pelayo plays his fish, so I head down.

That's prey down there, and I'm finally getting into the hunting mode. In the murk I felt like prey. Now, in the clear stuff, I'm predator. Yes, sir, finally relaxing, finally getting in tune with my surroundings . . . *feeling good, feeling right it's Saturday night, the hotel detective he was outta sight.* Feeling a little giddy too. Probably narked out by now. Rapture of the deep. Those "jiggle party jags" Cousteau wrote about in *The Silent World*. No escaping nitrogen narcosis at these depths. It usually hits me at 90 feet, and now I'm at—Christ!—145! Deep, for me.

Yes sir, I'm in my favorite role—the hunter, the predator in the genuine sense of the word. I feel like killing something, but first I've got to stalk it. That's the most fun—*stalking.* I'm a stalker now.

The AJs are getting closer, they're starting to circle me—that black stripe on the head clearly visible from here. But they're not nearly close enough. Better slow down, stop blowing such a volume of bubbles, that always spooks them. But holding my breath could cause my lungs to explode—or so they say. That's only on the ascent anyway. I'll stay level . . . get behind this beam on the edge of the rig and blow out a few teensy-weensy bubbles, just to be safe. Yeah, that's it . . . a big one is angling this way . . . three more behind him. Now another one swims up from the black void below me. What a sight . . . getting closer . . . closer. Ten more feet, pal, and you get a spring-steel shaft slammed through the gill plates.

No other form of hunting nowadays—not even bow hunting—demands such intimacy with the prey as spear fishing. A rig-diver also makes his hit from intimate quarters. We close on the hapless, lumbering fish—*wham!*—from ten feet. Hopefully he'll turn over quivering.

But he's still thirty feet away, and now he's heading down, and the rest of the school after him—dammit! Guess I blew too many bubbles. Swam too fast. Forgot to use the beams for cover and camouflage. I lost my cool. Jose Ortega y Gasset writes: "hunting is not a human fact, it is a *zoological fact,* it is an imitation of the animal, in that mystical union with the beast a contagion is immediately generated and the hunter begins to behave like the game. He will instinctively shrink from being seen, he will avoid all noise, he will perceive all his surroundings from the point of view of the animal." You're right Jose. But it's easier to do when I'm hunting deer. Up there I can at least breathe through my nose.

Ah . . . and there's Pelayo on my right, wrestling with his AJ. Is he waving? Is he beckoning me over? Or is he just trying to hang on? It's hard to tell down here.

No, he's all right. Just grabbed the big silver sucker through the gills. Now he's reaching in with his gloved hand and ripping them out. Blood clouds the water. The fish thrashes crazily, bucking Pelayo around like a rag-doll. Maybe I should help. Nope, that's the AJ's last thrash. The green blood-cloud gets bigger, envelops the fish's head, and he starts calming down. The blood now shrouds half of Pelayo.

"Blood," the liquid that carries and symbolizes life" wrote Ortega, "is meant to flow occultly, secretly, through the interior of the body. When it is spilled . . . a reaction of terror is produced in all nature—yet after this bitter first impression, if it flows abundantly, it ends by producing the opposite effect: it intoxicates, excites, maddens both man and beast . . . the Romans went to the Coliseum as they did to a tavern, and the bullfight public does the same . . . blood operates as a stupefying drug."

Anyway, the AJ's blood isn't red down here; it's green. But I can imagine it red. So it "excites," "intoxicates," and "maddens" just the same. Or maybe I'm narked.

The big amberjack calms. His wild bucking and thrashing turn to mild quivers. His life oozes out with the green cloud. Pelayo's got him under control. Didn't even have to employ the ice pick. Nice going.

As for me, I must be slipping. I lost track of my prey . . . ah, they're coming back! Back up from the darkness below. But Pelayo's heading up with his. On-the-Ball's nowhere around, probably on his way up, and the air's getting hard to suck through this regulator . . . geezum! Barely 900 pounds left! Musta sucked it all up during the episodes with Tom through the murk.

But, man, I hate to go up with nothing . . . and this AJ's coming head on at me, with three behind him . . . Look at that brute, huge, gorgeous. Bet he's sixty, seventy pounds. I move toward the corner of the rig but keep a beam between us, *almost* holding my breath. I shift my head and spot them. Still coming. Now I'm focused. Ortega again: "The tourist sees broadly the great spaces, but his gaze glides, it seizes nothing. Only the *hunter,* imitating the perpetual alertness of the wild animal, *sees everything.*"

Except his depth gauge, and air gauge, and watch. That's why so many of us get into trouble. That's why dive accidents befall spear fishermen at quintuple the rate of sightseers. Ortega's actually wrong in this case. We see everything, all right, but only until we spot prey. Then we see nothing *but* prey. We're focused, riveted, locked-in like a missile from a Phantom jet—on the prey, like your cat on that sparrow by the birdfeeder.

I raise the gun and he turns broadside at fifteen feet. An easy shot—a perfect shot, the kind of shot you *dream* about—but I wimp out.

Guess I'm not as narked out as I thought, or as focused. It's only the second dive of the year. Shoulda had another beer. I don't feel like wrestling the brute by myself down here with eight hundred pounds of air left. At one 150 feet, I'm too deep. I'm heading up. What a wussy.

My ears start popping on the ascent; that "reverse squeeze." And the air starts getting easier to suck through the regulator. Looking up I see Pelayo, clutching his quivering prey through the gills with both hands, the shaft pushed through and the gun dangling below. He shoots me the OK sign, readjusts his grip, and melts into the overhead cloud like some Jack in the Beanstalk. I'm about ten feet from entering it, the water getting warmer and visibility getting hazy when a huge form jerks my gaze to the side—*damn!* A shark!

No, wait. A cobia! Three cobia, actually. A monster with three little ones tailing behind. These suckers always pop up out of nowhere—usually from behind—and scare the hell outta me. Not much air left, but hell, I'm only at 65 feet—that's his ass. I point as he angles off, jerk the trigger—and nothing happens. The safety, dammit! Again—*schlink!* And the shaft jabs him right behind the gill plate, but a little low, not much penetration.

And there he goes, with me in tow. But not *straight* down, fortunately. He's shooting for the middle of the rig at a slight angle. Damn, but these suckers are strong. I let him take me about thirty yards, then I grab a beam just as he angles around one above me and starts thrashing around like a maniac, knocking a cloud of barnacles from the beam, the shaft battering the beam below it and adding to the cloud of pulverized barnacles and coral. In his frenzy, he's wrapping himself in the cable. Better you than me, pal. I've been wrapped up enough times by you suckers. Cobia always head for a beam to wrap around—*always*. The trick is to stay out of the way. Keep tension on the cable and the fish in front of you.

He makes the loop and angles back around where I see he's about to jerk off the spear. His skin stretches out where the blades on my spear gun point opened. Yikes . . . I hit him right above the belly, right where he shifts from dark brown to white. A lousy shot. I was too rattled. The shaft didn't go through him, didn't hit bone. Fortunately cobia have a tough hide, almost like sharks. Better grab him while there's time.

I stick my arm through the bands and jam the gun up around my shoulder, grab the cable, and start pulling. I make headway and now I'm lunging for the shaft. There! Got it! Now I start grappling with the brute, reaching for his gills. *Whack, whack!* He lunges, gyrates, and the shaft batters my legs. Forget it. He's too lively. Too strong. Oops, now he's swimming around me and the cable has me under the arm and snagged around the valve on my tank. He's jerking me upwards now and wrapping around another beam.

"Damn, this sucker's too BIG! Shouldn't have shot him this late in the dive with nobody else down here . . . *keep cool man.*"

I unlock my legs from the beam and pivot around to unloop myself. Ah, managed it. Now he's coming back around and I finally get a good look. Geezuz, must be a seventy-pounder . . . I lunge for the shaft again . . . and grab it! Whack! His tail slaps my head and knocks my mask askew, but at least the regulator stays in. *Christ*, that's all I need. That was close. But I'm still holding on. He's jerking around like crazy, whacking me around, bashing my legs, my head, trying to get the cable around me *again* . . . and *damn it,* now the air's getting hard to suck out again! I must be down to nothing!

I oughta let go of the fish, the shaft, every damn thing and shoot

up for godsakes—assuming I could get free of this cable . . . *whack!*
Now his gills bash into my cheek and his tail rips off another cloud
of barnacles. Pieces are floating around everywhere.

In the melee I finally jerk my gloved hand through his gills and
grab hold—grab HARD! Now the other hand . . . *aha!* Finally got
the bastard in a chokehold! Got him by the—well, if fish *had* balls
hanging from their crotch, I'd have the equivalent hold.

But maybe not. He's still thrashing, but I've got my polyester-
encased legs wrapped around the beam again and can control
him . . . oooops! . . . ooooops! Maybe not . . . I'm upside down
now, but still holding on to his lunging, thrashing bulk with my
hands and to the rig with my legs. I point his head up, and his
next lunge actually rights me again. Perfect. . . . No more tension
on the cable that seemed about to saw through my disco shirt
and into my armpit. He's still jerking me back and forth, but with
both hands through his gills I feel in charge. He's a powerful
sucker—dammit—oops! . . . almost lost my grip again—There!
Got him *good* now.

I've got him in a vise grip, white knuckles, bulging biceps, my
teeth chomping down on the regulator mouthpiece about to bite
it off. The fish's face inches from mine—I've got him just like the
big Kraut had the Jewish kid in *Saving Private Ryan*, as they
wrestled on the floor, grimacing and snarling at each other, right
before he stabbed him . . . point is—his ass is *mine!*

Like nature commands, I'm trying to kill this goddamned fish!
Problem is, nature commands the fish to try to kill me, or at least
escape me . . . oops! Suddenly the cobia jerks savagely and
smacks my head against the beam. *Aou!* but it comes out "bruu-
ull!" through the regulator. I'll have blood on my scalp when I
surface. I can tell. The blow or cut always seems minor down
here. You never see or feel the real damage until you surface,
usually on the ride in, when the adrenaline subsides. No wonder
the early guys used to wear football helmets while diving.

I tighten my grip with both hands, which means I can't reach for
the icepick, or start ripping out his gills. And he's still full of fight.

WHACK! His tail smacks my kidneys. Feels just like that cop's
billy during Mardi Gras back when we were in college. The guy
had no sense of humor. Pelayo had dived over him to catch one

of those long beads for Maria and the little uniformed hippo collapsed on the curb. His hat had flown off and was immediately trampled by the drunken crowd, which erupted in mirth as he thrashed around like a turtle on his back. He was short, fat, bald—looked like Clemenza in *The Godfather*. He finally righted himself and came up snarling and swinging his club. I was closest and got a savage whack to the kidneys and another across the upper back that almost floored me. I was knocked, breathless, into a huge black woman with a purple hat who stated howling "Aw lawd! Aw lawd!" Her sons, or nephews or neighbors or whatever—they all looked like Coolio—were moving in for the kill when they saw the cop, who was still swinging, trying to hit Pelayo, who'd deflected his attention by calling him a *"fat asshole!"* before fleeing through the crowd. His lithe form and athletic prowess allowed Pelayo to weave through crevices and duck through holes in the crowd.

The cop didn't have a chance. Imagine Ralph Kramden trying to catch Emmit Smith. He gave up after a short but energetic burst that knocked down two old ladies, trampled a comatose drunk who came alive kicking and shrieking about "Horses! Help! I'm being trampled by horses!," and started toppling a ladder with three infants strapped atop until the quick-acting father grabbed it. He was obviously a proper uptowner and reprimanded this errant member of the constabulary in the tones of an Eton schoolmaster, which earned him a billy club across the cheekbone that sent his glasses flying like something hurled from a float . . . ah, these crazy memories.

The cobia's still struggling for his life. Bashing me around and sawing through my gloves with his gills. His chocolate-colored flanks are gouged with white streaks from all the scraping against the beam. My hardy disco pants protect me. He's still thrashing around and I'm actually trying to straddle him now—get one leg around him to pin him to the beam. Seems like a good idea—but no go.

He twists free from my leg, knocks me off balance again and it's all I can do to retain my grip on his gills. This ain't like hunting deer. You never know when these brutes *actually* surrender. And right now, that would be a good thing to know.

Five

TO THE BOTTOM

"Don't worry, Pops" Gerry Bourgeois was suiting up. His younger divemates were trying to reassure him. "We'll look out for ya, Pops. We'll be right behind ya the whole time."

"Great," Gerry chuckled. "You guys watch out for me now." He was sixty-one, started rig diving in the late 1950s as a charter member of the Sea Tigers, a club actually older than the Helldivers. Oddly, he's still at it, plunging deep for massive fish. The only one among his contemporaries still so obsessed. The others—Mitch Cancienne, Val Rudolfich, Johnny Bonck—kick-ass divers for almost forty years, pioneers of the sport, have turned to free diving. Most others reserve it for Caribbean vacations. Gerry has learned a lot in those years.

"Don't stick your hand too far in a four-hundred-and fifty-pound jewfish's gills." Was a lesson he learned early, back in 1961, and at 170 foot depths. Monstrous jewfish—sometimes in schools—prowled under many rigs back then. "Even the shallow ones," Gerry reminds me. "Hell, the sixty- to seventy-foot ones. You'd get down there, and right above the bottom murk, it looked like a herd of cows down there. Sometimes if the murk was only a few feet deep you'd see their backs poking over it. Seemed you could almost walk over them."

But it was on a deep dive that Jerry tangled with his 450-pounder. "Back then we didn't usually go deeper than a hundred feet or so—no need to. But I was down at a hundred seventy, near the bottom, when I saw this thing. Now I'd seen a lot of big jewfish—hell, I'd *shot* a bunch of big ones, and been with Val and Mitch when they'd shot big ones. So I knew this thing was a record—or damn close to one. But I was deep and didn't have too much air left. 'What the hell,' I thought—and I let him have it, aiming for that kill zone between the eyes that Cousteau had shown us a few years before."

Gerry missed it. No brain shot. "That thing took off and I went with him. That huge thing was lunging around with me in tow, just missing the beams. I was ducking them just in time, or just glancing off them, ripping my jumpsuit, but not much of my skin."

Finally the fish slowed down a bit and Gerry saw he might have a chance to grab it by the gills—not the gills actually. When a diver grabs a fish "by the gills" he means the ridge that runs just under the actual gills, joining the mouth to the chest. Makes a handy place to get a chokehold, and to try and muscle the fish along. But not necessarily a 450 pounder, and especially not if you grab wrong.

"Down in that murk, with all the commotion, I stuck my hand in too far." Gerry blurts. "I actually stuck it *inside* the gills, way inside, past the feathery red stuff, into the hard bony stuff. Then—*clump!*—he snapped them shut. I pulled and—nothing. Couldn't budge it. Whoa-boy, I thought."

And well he should. He was alone. His dive buddies were all on board.

Val himself had just finished boarding a huge jewfish of his own. He'd gotten a kill shot but at a price. He'd approached the huge fish unseen near the bottom murk and marveled at its size. With a monster like this he definitely wanted a kill shot. His scars from the previous week were barely healing. No kill shot that week, and the jewfish had taken him on a merry, bumpy ride around the rig. His dive buddies were still calling him "Pinball."

No more of that, Val thought when he saw this one—which looked even bigger. So he approached and aimed *carefully*, by poking his gun straight out in front of him, pointing at that three-square-inch zone right above the eyes that Jacques Cousteau had shown him as the kill zone. Piercing to the brain was the only way to disable these buffalo-sized fish.

In the process of aiming, the butt of the spear gun was positioned inches in front of Val's mouth. And Val, a welder and machinist, was expert at customizing his guns for maximum power. These are souped-up guns—low riders, magnums. The six-foot shaft on Val's gun was straining at *six* extra-thick bands of surgical tubing. We're talking some serious penetrating power here—thus, some serious recoil.

The lumbering fish finally turned to face him, offering the perfect head shot, and Val crunched the trigger. *Whack!*—the gun smacked into his mouth, smashing his lips and teeth against his regulator mouthpiece like a trip-hammer. He was blinded for a second, stunned, dizzy. Recovering his wits he was happy to see the jewfish turning on it's side, "stoned," as they say. "Cold-cocked." Thank goodness for *that*.

But a strange sensation enveloped his mouth, a steely taste, and he felt things floating around in there. Now something green was staining the water in front of his mask. He sat there in his semi-daze, thrilled with his kill but stunned. Finally he felt around with his tongue and realized he'd knocked out four teeth with the gun recoil. Oh well. At least the jewfish was done for. Time to get the 250-pounder up.

Gerry saw none of it. And Val couldn't see Jerry pounding on his jewfish with the spear gun while trying to pull his other arm out of the thing's gills as it barreled around the Gulf bottom. "And there was *no* pulling my arm out." Gerry says. " I had gloves on and everything, and a long-sleeve shirt. But he had me *good*. I couldn't move my arm in or out. And now he decides to take off again! So there I go right with him. Like I'm hopping a freight train, ya know, hanging on the little ladder as it chugs off. That's what I felt like. But hell, with a train I could just let go. Not here."

So Gerry's bumbling around through the murk going wherever the beast wanted to go. "And remember," he says, "I was low on air to begin with. Well, at least he couldn't take me any lower than a hundred and seventy feet, I'm thinking."

Some consolation. "If all I'd done was shoot him, hell, I'd a let go of the gun by now. My air was going. But I kept yanking, ripping my damn hand and arm up but what the hell else could I do?"

What indeed, Gerry. "The jewfish was bucking around every which way, just jerking me around. I felt like a bull rider. Ever see how they get thrown off the bull but their hand's still caught in the rope? And the bull's bucking and running around dragging and bucking and stompin' the poor sap?

"Well, that was me. I'm gettin' jerked around just like that. Except I'm almost two hundred feet under the Gulf in the bottom murk and can barely breathe. The air was gettin' hard to suck out. Something was gonna have to give soon. I had trapper friends who told me of coons and mink actually gnawing their legs off to get out of a trap. I was wondering about that. But I couldn't even grab my knife."

Gerry finally hit upon a solution. If he couldn't *pull* his arm out. Perhaps he could *push* it out, using his other arm. This meant, of course, inserting his free arm through the fish's mouth—a mouth that, half open, could have swallowed him.

"Hell, I had to do *something*." He says. "Well, no sooner I stick my arm in his mouth than—*chomp!*—he snaps it shut, right around my elbow. Yeah boy. Great idea, I'm thinking.

"Now I got one hand in his gills up past my elbow, and the other in this mouth to the elbow! Now what? And off he goes again on another little romp with me flapping around like the bull rider while hugging his head!"

You hear from old timers that jewfish play out fairly easy. They give *bursts* of energy, spurts, lunges, then relax, unlike the sustained rocketing frenzy of an amberjack or tuna. "He finally seemed to be playing out." Gerry says. "So I said this is it, I've gotta try to take this sucker up with me. So I just kinda pointed his head up—I had the strength and leverage of *both* arms to do it with, remember—then I just started swimming up. And damn if he didn't come right along. He was spent. No more struggle.

"Up I go with him barely moving, my ears popping from the

decreasing pressure, the air getting a little easier to suck out as I ascend. I felt a helluva lot better—but I ain't outta the woods yet. I hit the surface near the boat and start yelling. The guys see me. Their eyes are poppin', man. The size of the fish for one thing, but also their faces are saying like . . . *what the hell?*

"A couple of the guys jumped in immediately and helped pry my arms outta the fish with their knives. The fish had lost strength, bloated, and relaxed it's grip. Finally I'm out. My arms are free—all scratched up—but free. Hell, when Val came over and smiled, I saw he had it worse. I like to die laughing when I heard how he got his jewfish—not that my story was *too* bad."

Point is, Gerry had earned his spurs in the sport of rig-diving many times over. This rodeo, over thirty years later, found him and a boatload of Sea Tigers aboard a ninety-foot shrimp trawler at deep rigs in the Timbalier blocks, out from Morgan city where the first rigs went up in 1947. But those were in 50 to 60-foot depths. These had gone up much later and stood in 300-foot depths. The deeper the water, the deeper the danger.

This past summer, dive instructor Chuck Buckley nailed a big grouper near the 200 ft. mark. He had been at depths far greater than what most would consider safe, though only fair-to-middling by Helldivers' standards.

His dive mate Randy Evans saw him spear the fish about fifty feet below him. "It looked like he had the fish under control," Randy told me. "So I stayed at one hundred and fifty feet, watching him ascend. He came past and we exchanged the OK signal. He looked fine. The fish was calm. I stayed down looking around for a few minutes, saw nothing real big, so I started up. I'm about halfway up when I hear the outboard crank up. Hum? Now *that's* kinda weird, I thought. We'd left a buddy on the boat fishing. Why would he be leaving us? So I hurry through my decomp stop and get to the surface. The boat's going off and there's no sign of Chuck . . . now this is really strange, I'm thinking.

"But I'm not really worried. The fish seemed to be under control and Chuck had looked fine. He'd shot much bigger fish. He was a dive *instructor* for heaven's sake. Well, finally the boat turns around and heads back to the rig. That's nice, I thought. Must have dropped something over the side and the current took it. No sweat. But I only see one person in the boat. When he's about thirty feet away he sees me bobbing around, hauls back on the throttle and screams: CHUCK'S DEAD!

"What a stupid joke, I'm thinking. What a *tasteless* joke. It didn't sink in. It *couldn't* sink in. This *couldn't be real*. That stuff only happens to those lunatics who go down to two hundred and fifty feet ten times a day during the Rodeos. We came out here to have fun and relax. I picked up Chuck at his house this morning. We were excited. The day's beautiful—calm, no murk, not much current. He's my friend. I know his family . . . It can't be! . . . what kinda bullshit is Dave trying to lay on me? And why?! Then he got closer and I saw his face and I knew it was true.

"His look said everything that needed to be said, without another word. He said he saw Chuck surface outside the rig screaming 'Come help me! Oh God, come help me!' So he unhooked the boat, cranked up the motor . . . when he got over there Chuck was face down. He pulled him in the boat and he wasn't breathing. He gave frantic CPR, everything. But he was dead."

The Coast Guard ruled an AGE (arterial gas embolism) as cause of death. Chuck also had barnacles embedded in his skull. "We figure the fish must have got his second wind closer to the surface—where the danger of an embolism is greatest", says his friend Randy. "Maybe he banged him around the beams, using up his air or knocking his regulator out of his mouth. But his tank still showed air. He never ran out. Like I said, Chuck was a good, careful diver . . . what happened? We'll never know for sure."

Dr. Charles Burchrell of the University of Southern Mississippi—himself a rig diver—has looked into several rig-diving accidents. He explained to me that an embolism is much more likely when you're struggling with something. "Think about it," he said while pretending to lift something off the floor. "When you're *lifting* something, or *pulling* on something, you have a tendency to hold . . . your . . . breath—right? Well we all know from Diving 101 that's a no-no—a BIG no-no. But when you're in a fight with a two-hundred-pound fish instinct takes over, right?"

I got the picture. Oddly, Chuck still had the riding rig around his wrist, and the fish was still on, and lively. Sometimes they win. A riding rig is a rope off the spear gun cable that attaches to your wrist, rather than to the spear gun. This way you can shoot and let go of the gun, which is attached by a cord to your belt. Then you grab the rope with both hands and go for a ride. Or you can simply loop the rope around a beam and tie the fish off. Let him fight the rig rather than you. With a riding rig, if things get hairy—say he's dragging you down past 250 feet, your air's low, whatever—you can simply let go, losing fish, shaft, and cable—but not the gun. Some rig-divers swear by riding rigs. Others prefer the shaft and cable attached to the spear gun the conventional way. They say it's easier to just let go of everything that way.

"We'll never know for sure"—the epitaph for Chuck Buckley's diving death, as for half of rig-diving fatalities. Jack Schiro was twenty-seven years old and had been diving for five years when he went down about six miles from here this past June. "He looked fine when I last saw him," says his divemate and uncle, Bob Larche. "He was cocking his gun and gave me the OK signal. I was on my way up. He was down around eighty feet, heading down. The water was beautiful, blue, without any murk, calm, not much current. We'd dove under *much* worse conditions, believe me.

"Well, I climb aboard and we wait half an hour for Jack to surface. That's about how long a tank's gonna last on our dives. Then we knew something was wrong. We suited up, went back down to one hundred and fifty feet, but found nothing. So we came up, got on the radio, called the Coast Guard."

Helldiver Stan Smith was diving nearby and heard the distress call. "We heard 'em on the radio. They were panicking, you can imagine. So we get coordinates and head over. Turned out we were only a couple miles away. I went down and at around one hundred and eighty feet saw a school of *huge* black grouper. I mean big ones. Right then I knew what had happened to Jack. Black grouper bore straight down when you hit 'em. If you don't get a kill shot, they give a burst of power and there's no stopping 'em at first. You just have to ride 'em out. Problem is if you're too close to the bottom, or too deep with too little air, or maybe wrapped in the cable, or narked, or whatever. When I got down there I saw that the murk started about fifty feet from the bottom. I started into it, but it was hopeless. I knew this rig. I'd dove it before. The bottom's full of discarded cable, scrap, pipes and other stuff from the platform. It would be real easy to get banged up and tangled up down there, especially attached to a black grouper—a big one. They head right into that stuff."

The Coast Guard gave up the search two days later. Jack had a wife and three kids. You hear a lot of sanctimonious types bad-mouthing those "crazy macho-type divers" like Stan, who risk their lives to "get their name on the board" or "pose with some fish." Stan's an insurance agent in his early thirties, been rig-diving since his late teens. The record books show Stan's name behind the top three sharks, each nudging five-hundred pounds. Each took him on "a helluva ride," in his own words, often through the murk. Somehow he evaded their teeth. But they were shot at shallower rigs and the ride was usually outside the rig. Stan went down into the murk at 200 feet that day, not "to kill a fish," not "to get his name on the board," but to try and rescue a diver *he didn't even know.* Crazy indeed. They were calling the Coast Guard, not him. He didn't *have* to show up.

Gerry's son, thirty-two, another Sea Tiger, was suiting up alongside his Dad and chuckled when he heard the "Pops" line. Darren "Gumby" Bourgeois owns Aquatic Technologies, a dive shop in suburban New Orleans. On his office wall hangs a gold plaque from JBL, the nation's biggest spear gun manufacturer. The award heralds the most spear guns sold in one year. A little dive shop right here in New Orleans sells more spear guns than any other dive shop in the U.S.

The Sea Tigers, like other dive clubs, often charter big (sixty to ninety feet) shrimp or crew boats and spend several days rig hopping. "Shoot, we might dive ten, fifteen rigs in one day," says Gerry.

Gerry, son Darren, and those guest divers who graciously assured "Pops" they'd watch out for him walked to the side of the big trawler and hopped in. This was a Rodeo, so they were going for big fish or nothing. And that meant going deep. "The water was beautiful," says Darren. "You could see across the whole rig and down forever." It's easy to descend in those conditions; also easy to lose track of your depth.

But "Gumby" was distracted midway down. "That sucker came straight at me!" he chuckles. "He was about an eight-foot sand tiger, nothing huge. But he caught me off guard. I'd seen my share of them, knew they got ornery at times. But we had great visibility that day—probably one hundred feet. So he wasn't mistaking me for a fish."

But *something* about Darren interested him. "I don't think that he'd completely made up his mind that I *wasn't* lunch, either." He says. "I mean, he was coming straight at me . . . okay, he'll turn away any second now, I'm thinking—Okay . . . Okay . . . Any time now! Okay . . . come on now! I'm a diver! A human! LOOK!

"WHACK! I raised my gun and smacked his nose. He swerved off. That's better, I thought . . . but I'm still watching him—then he turns around. And comes *back!*—Oh shit! I thought. Never seen them do *this* before. Usually one whack on the nose does the trick out here. So now he's coming straight at me again.

"POP! And I poked him with the tip—he swerves off again. Great, I thought. So I start swimming off, a nice snapper was under me. I was going after him. I look behind me—and here he comes *again!* So I turn around to face him. Now he's coming a little faster . . . closer . . . closer—JAB! I really poke him in the nose with the gun—I mean *hard*, felt the point sinking in—Now he jerked away and darted off—for *good*. That's better, I thought."

Darren looked around to make sure the shark had no buddies around and continued the descent. "Dad was always down below me. He knew where he had to go to find the big fish in this area. He was after amberjack. And they were descending steadily in front of us, down into the dark depths. He was following."

Indeed he was. "At one hundred and eighty feet I look around," says Gerry. "And there's my chaperones, the guys who were gonna watch out for "Pops," twenty feet above me, waving. They're heading back up, waving at me, like, *come on!* Ya crazy or something? So I waved back."

"Pops" was going after the big ones, his specialty. "I could see some big amberjack below me. Looked plenty big enough to put me on the board. So I cocked another band and just drifted on down."

Darren had also drifted past the erstwhile chaperones but not as far as his dad. Actually he was starting to worry, while looking at his depth gauge that read 200 feet. And still his father was descending.

"I knew good and well what he was going after," says Darren. "This was a Rodeo. You always push it a little during a Rodeo. And I knew that even after thirty years of this stuff, Dad had lost none of his passion for the sport, or for shooting the biggest of anything around. And I could tell those amberjack were big. I just wished Dad had looked at his depth gauge."

But "Pops" was focused on the fish. Remember your cat at the bird feeder. Remember that leopard closing on the gazelle on Animal Planet. Same instinct here.

Darren finned towards the middle of the rig, where some barracuda hovered near the center beams. But, nah. None were trophy size. So he continued down, towards the edge of the rig now, where the big AJs circled. What a contrast to the lazy 'cuda who weave slowly around the structure. None of that for amberjack. They're hyper, always on the move. Piscine candidates for Ritalin.

Darren looked again and now his depth gauge said 230 feet. And his sixty-one-year-old father is was below him, still descending. "He's pushing it." I thought. "The old man's gettin too old for this daredevil stuff. He's bound to be narked out of his head by now . . . is he acting crazy?"

Darren himself was succumbing to Martini's Law at that depth. "I was getting giddy, all right. But I knew if I was worried about Dad, I couldn't be too narked. That nitrogen narcosis is like drinking. You can't say: at such and such a depth you'll get narked. Any more than you can say, two drinks or so many ounces of alcohol get a person drunk. It depends on the person. Depends on a lot of other factors. Same with nitrogen narcosis. If not, we'd all been drowned a long time ago, me and every rig diver I know. Believe me."

Yet Darren decided to keep descending. But not because he

was reeling from "rapture of the deep," or even yearning to spear a big AJ.

"Hell, man," he says. "I was gonna swim down, grab Dad by the damn belt, and drag his ass up. He was *pushing it!*" Then he saw a grouper staring at him from slightly below. He swam over . . . maybe a forty-pounder. Nah. Not worth it right now. He descended past him.

Darren glanced back at his gauge—263 feet now. It was flashing red. "Okay, that's it. Dad's gotta be narked silly by now. This is it. He finally bought the farm. Hope I have enough time. I'm gonna grab him. Might already be too late."

"Then I saw the amberjack," he says. "Three of them. And monsters. I knew they'd push a hundred pounds each. They were below me near the very corner of the structure, just outside the rig. And that's when I knew it was all over. Those fish were almost at three hundred feet and Dad was drawing a bead on 'em, aiming the gun out in front of him while grabbing a beam with the other arm.

"It was hazy down there. Even with the crystal water, even with midday sun shining, it was hazy down there. It was just so *damn deep* [those Russian submariners on the Kursk were considered doomed at 342 feet] sunlight doesn't make it down there very bright.

"Swim away!" I'm screaming to myself down there. "Come on AJs! For my ole-man's sake—PLEASE SWIM AWAY! Don't give him a shot! Please! If he hits you—that's it!

A tank of air doesn't last very long down there, a few minutes. And supposedly, at those depths, what both were breathing was toxic. "So Dad had nowhere near the air for a wrestling match, for the dodging the cable, for the unwrapping himself—for all that stuff—not with a hundred-pound amberjack down here. Nowhere near it. Hell, a forty-pound amberjack almost drowns *me* at ninety feet. What's a hundred-pounder gonna do to a sixty-one-year-old man at three hundred FEET!

"We'd been on a lot of dives together, Dad and I. Hell, he started me at the New Orleans lakefront at age ten with a scuba-tank. So it's not like I wasn't used to his type diving. But this was getting spooky."

And the AJs stayed on course. A course that would take them ten feet in front of Gerry Bourgeois, who was hiding behind a beam already taking aim.

"I started finning frantically down. I was pissed by now. I was determined. I was gonna grab Dad by the damn BC collar and drag him up. I didn't want him to shoot. Hell, even if he stayed free of the cable, even if the AJ didn't go completely nuts and wrap him up—even without all the usual hysteria—he'd be in trouble . . . but if he did shoot, and if he hit one, I was gonna jerk the gun from his hand and let the damn thing go. We HAD to get UP! No two ways about it. No more fooling around down here! Enough is enough!"

And that's just about the time the biggest AJ angled in and Gerry crunched the trigger.

"The crazy geezer!" Darren thought to himself. "He shot! He shot the most powerful fish for its weight in the Gulf, at three hundred feet with almost no AIR! I was already trying to figure out how to break it to Mom . . . *Mom, come on now, Mom. It's the way Dad would have wanted to go. He was doing the thing he loved. He'd a wanted to be buried at sea anyway. You know that, Mom. Come now, mom . . . let me see you smile now . . . that's it. That's better . . .*"

But the fish was dead, not Gerry. Dead in its tracks. The shaft hit the amberjack and it turned on its side, quivering. A spine shot. "You talk about the sweetest sight this old boy ever saw!" laughs Darren. "I was floating there shaking from fright, from narcosis, from hysteria, from relief—whatever. Then Dad passed me towing the huge, trembling, silver fish. He looks over, his eyes calm, with an expression like: 'Let's go son . . . what's the matter? You look a little nervous. Don't worry. I got it all under control, no sweat.'

"You talk about *relief!*" Darren gasps. "You talk about ELATION! But actually I turned out to be wrong. He never made it down to three hundred feet. His depth gauge only read two hundred and eighty nine. And the AJs weren't hundred-pounders, like I thought. Dad's came in at ninety eight point seven."

Above: Author was mocked mercilessly for spearing this "tiny" snapper. The fillets, drenched in lemon butter and seared over a driftwood fire that night, silenced the mockers. (Photo from author's collection.) **Below:** No shark cages off Louisiana. We don't want photos. We want steaks.

Top: *"In space no one can hear you scream." said the ad for* Aliens. *Same underwater.* ~~e~~ *steel legs reach 800 feet to the Gulf's murky bottom.* **Left, Center:** *Nature, that bumbler,* ~~et~~ *to design a reef even half as prolific as an oil platform. Schools of Spadefish (here) bare-* ~~rt~~ *as you swim through.* **Left, Bottom:** *These barracuda could swallow the Caribbean* ~~without straining. (Photos courtesy of Nancy Cohagan. Seven Seas Dive Shop Baton~~ ~~e~~*, La.)* **Above:** *Johnny Bonck and Roland Reviere wearing some of the first scuba tanks* ~~nerica~~*, holding a big Warsaw grouper, circa 1952. (Photo courtesy of John Bonck.)*

Sea Tiger with monster Amberjack he wrestled up from 200 foot depths. (Photo courtesy of Aquatic Technologies, Harvey, La.)

Six

HAULIN' 'EM UP

I finally clear my head and get my bearings after another cobia-pummelling—his tail to my head this time, back and forth, like Mike Tyson on the speed-bag. The gauge hose ended up tangled over my shoulder during the melee, so I can see—Christ! Five hundred pounds, I oughtta grab my ice pick and jab this cobia through the skull a few times, quiet him down—but I'm afraid to let go with one hand to grab it. I don't think I can control this brute with one hand—*oops! There he goes again, another brutal lunge that almost jerks my arm out of its socket*—much less kill him.

Whack! WHACK! Now he's back to flailing the beam, my fins, and my legs with his tail. My grip slips a little and I try to straddle him again—but no way, impossible. He's still charged with life. My head jerks back and forth as he pummels me around.

Cobia never seem to give up, even on the end of a line. You hook one and they go crazy, running and lunging like mad, stripping line like a missile. They never seem to tire. But *you* do. You ride him out, back and forth. Finally he gets close, he's lumbering at boat-side and you gaff him—WHOOAA!—bash—clang—clang—clang!—and he goes nuts again.

These suckers never seem to give up. And I'm on the point of having to. My regulator's wheezing with every breath. And I'm only at 65 feet, can't have much of a reserve. Sure, if forced to, I could probably make it up with one breath, letting it out slowly. But why push it? Like I'm not pushing it already. I'll have to point his head up and just go with him. Hopefully he'll go in the right direction. But in that murk, who knows what direction *that* is. How will I know he's going up?

Hemingway's "Old Man" always puzzled me in the past. "Let go of the goddamn thing!" I'd always say as a kid. "Just let go! . . . Don't let him kill ya! . . . *Let GO* old man!

But it doesn't work that way. Now I saw his point. Sometimes you *can't* let go. I've invested too much time and effort in boating this fish. I'll have to kill him or he'll have to kill me. So I tightened my grip on his gills again and eased off with one hand, reaching below my bellbottoms for my ice-pick. There— got it! Got a *good* grip. I still have to subdue and boat this bucking, thrashing cobia before he drowns me. My air must be down to the double digits. I'll jab him and kill him—simple. Good grip on the ice pick. I'll kill him with one jab. Here goes— WHACK!

But no penetration! Felt like I hit concrete. Like a fool I hit too high. Cobia have a head like a cape buffalo, no getting through it except with a magnum . . . and there goes the ice pick. It jumped from my hand when I struck the solid bone. My hand is too numb from gripping his gills for what seems like hours now, but can't be more than ten minutes. Now the icepick's fluttering to the bottom—400 feet below.

Gotta start up, with or without this fish and my gun. No more farting around. So I get a two-handed grip on his gills again, unwrap my polyestered legs from the beam, and start finning up, through the murk and—*whooaa!*—the current.

It usually breaks along with the murk. Then cranks up again when you enter it. I'd forgotten about it. But it grips me the second I ascend into the murky maelstrom. I fin like crazy to the lee of the big corner beam, the cobia still bucking me around, my gun banging the beams somewhere below me, and continue up, blind, still struggling with the fish. My regulator groans with every breath. Christ, I'm down to nothing now. Won't even be able to inflate my BC.

Up, up, up further through the hot swirling broth, my ears popping, the fish actually helping me along now. I've got his head pointed up so his movement takes us in the same direction. Finally I hit the surface and spit out the regulator—

"Come grab this sucker!" I screeched.

Tom was reaching down at the back of the boat, helping Pelayo boat his AJ. On-the-Ball was aboard, jerking off his tank and BC.

"Hurry goddammit!" I yelled. "I'm outta AIR! My BC's not inflated!"

Half of what I screeched was underwater but they got the point and I saw Tom putting on his BC, then jump in to the rescue. Good, I thought. He swam over. "Whaddaya want me to grab?" he spat.

"Nothing!" I gasped "Don't grab anything! I've got the fish. He's still alive; I don't wanna let go. Look, just get behind me and push me towards the boat. I can't swim against the damn current while holding the fish."

"Okay—okay! Here!" and he started pushing. But we weren't getting very far, and I was gasping, swallowing mouthfuls of water and on the verge of dropping everything again, when I heard the motor growl. On-The-Ball was lifting the rig hook as Pelayo worked the throttle.

"Ah . . . great!" I gasped.

"Good idea." Tom blurted.

Soon they were idling next to us, and good thing, too. We were probably 100 yards away from the boat by now. Paul threw a heavy nylon rope with a big metal clip on the end like a huge safety pin. Tom grabbed it and stuck it through the fish's mouth and out—OOOOWW! *watch it!*—and out through his gills, and I finally let go.

My freaking hands were numb. I could barely make it the ten feet to the boat. I got there and clung to the ladder, gasping. "Come on," Pelayo groaned as he grabbed the back of my BC and jerked me aboard. I tried clambering up the ladder with my fins but stumbled back in, bashing my chin on the last rung and letting out a howl that died as a burst of bubbles.

"WAIT!" I screeched when my mouth cleared the surface. "Goddammit! Wait! My fins! My freakin' fins are still on!" I jerked them off, hurled them in to the boat . . . "let's try *again!*"

Pelayo grabbed the top of the tank and I finally stumbled aboard—where I immediately tripped over a tank made slimy by Paul's grouper and landed cheek down on Pelayo's amberjack. Paul was still hauling my fish in with the rope.

"Geezum!" he howled. "This sucker's big—plenty of fight left in him!"

"Shoulda seen him down there." I gasped, as I ripped off my mask and collapsed on a boat seat. I could feel the snot trail over my moustache and over my lips, but I just didn't give a damn right then. The cobia was finally at boat-side and Pelayo and Tom, seeing my condition, went over and helped On-the-Ball heave the big fish aboard. It flopped over the side and started thrashing around between the tanks.

"Watch it!" Pelayo shouted. But its tail smacked Tom, who pirouetted—waving his arms crazily trying to regain his balance—and finally he went down atop the tanks with a *clang!*

"You . . . alright?" I was laughing too loud to ask properly. So were Pelayo and Paul. And so was Tom. He got up rubbing his elbow, the same arm with the spear wound from earlier.

"My gun!" I suddenly howled. I'd forgotten about the gun, still attached to the cable, which was attached to the shaft, which was attached to the detachable point, which was still in the fish—but barely. I grabbed the cable that was still hanging over the transom and pulled in the gun.

I looked up and everyone was looking at everyone else. "Brewskie time?" Pelayo asked.

Freakin'-aay! Paul dug them out of the ice chest and tossed them around. Mine foamed all over my face, but I guzzled deeply. I wasn't even thirsty. The motor idled as we bobbed in the waves, chugged, and gabbed.

Those women who complain that men never talk should see this. It was a gabfest to shame anything on Oprah. Happens every time. Lots of things happened under water, lots of drama and emotion. But we couldn't shout to each other down there. So it's all pent up. Now it's uncorked and comes spewing out like shaken champagne.

"Tom?" Pelayo laughed while wiping at his nose. "Where the hell were you? What happened?"

"Oh, man," he moaned. "All kinda stuff happened . . . don't ask."

"Yeah," I quipped. "We got attacked by sharks on the surface."

"Whaaaaaaaat?" Pelayo and On-the-Ball both asked while looking suspiciously at each other. "Sharks? Don't look like it."

We told them the story; they cackled, drooled, gasped, finally recovered their breath, and started on theirs. Paul had shot a nice grouper.

"Man, I saw him as soon as I broke through the murk . . . surprised the hell outta me. They're usually much deeper, but this guy was just sitting there, his tail curled against the corner of the rig, staring up at me." Paul imitated the fish, his hands up against his armpits fluttering like a grouper's fins when it's standing still. His eyes looking up over his glasses, just the way a motionless grouper looks up at a diver—right before he darts off.

"Man, I just pointed down, hit the trigger . . . nothing! My damn safety, I thought. So I thumbed down the safety, hit the trigger again . . . nothing! Then I noticed my freakin' gun wasn't cocked! I forgot to cock the bands! Man, descending through all that murk and current I just forgot about it. I was too busy just trying to stay outside the current and behind the beam. Then I break through and the fish is right there.

"Well, the stupid sucker *stayed* there while I cocked the bands. But when I started aiming he started finning off. Then I went at him and he sped off . . . oughta know better by now. So I forget about him and start heading down for the big amberjack I could see *way* below. On my way down I look over and see the grouper curled up in a corner again—can't swear it was the *same* grouper, but he looked identical. I aimed—*wham!*— right through the top of the head. He keeled right over . . . I actually thought he was bigger." He was about fifty pounds.

After dropping off the shark at the marina, Poppa Smurf hooked up with another bunch of divers who'd chartered a big crew boat and were shoving off that evening, heading west this time, and staying out three days. There were ten divers on board from three different clubs, Helldivers, Sea Tigers, and Aqua Aces. Each diver brought fifteen tanks. This was no leisurely affair.

Terry met them, loaded up his tanks, which he'd stored in the back of his truck parked in the marina, and they shoved off, towards the Ship Shoal blocks, not far from where the Bourgeois themselves were diving. The first rig was in about 200 feet. They got to it with about an hour of sunlight left. Beautiful water again. Terry went down on the first dive with two other divers.

"I'd had a little excitement already that day," he says. "But, hell, when you see a buddy take a huge fish, like Stan's, makes you wanna outdo him. But I knew that'd be a helluva job, considering that shark!"

Terry prowled the depths down to 150 feet near the bottom murk for fifteen minutes and saw nothing worth shooting. No amberjack at all. "Just a few ten- and twenty-pounders." His buddy speared a nice mangrove snapper—about a ten- pounder— and was swimming up with it. The fish was dead, so he left it on the shaft, just pulling it behind him as he ascended.

Terry followed him up, thinking he'd probably had enough diving for one day. Hell, he had three days to go. And the weather forecast looked perfect. Why burn himself out the first day? He was about 30 feet from the surface, watching his friend's dead snapper coming up with the shaft through him when he caught sight of a huge form to his right.

"It was a monster amberjack!" Terry says. "I couldn't believe it! Here I'd been looking for a big one down at one-hundred and fifty feet and seen nothing. Now here's one at thirty feet almost under the boat!"

This is rare. You don't see amberjack that shallow, not big ones, not ever. This one came up only because it was following the speared snapper, thinking to snatch it. "He kept circling it." Terry says. "Coming close but never actually taking it. I'd never seen one acting like that. He was acting like a triggerfish. They're the ones who snatch the fish from your spear—and sharks, of course. I said, well hell, ain't this my lucky day."

Terry had shot his share of amberjack and knew this one had

to push a hundred pounds. "Looked like a cinch, man. I mean, we were at barely thirty feet, almost under the boat. Usually you shoot one this big way down deep—then the battle starts, wrapping the cable around the beam, dodging it, all that mess. Here I had one handed to me on a silver platter, and a big one. I knew he'd at least put me on the board."

So Terry took aim. But the big AJ noticed his new focus, saw him turn, saw him aim and zoomed off. "I chased him a little but I know *that's* pointless."

Terry figured he'd missed his chance. It was too good to be true. An AJ this big, this shallow, this close to the boat. It was almost cheating. He started back up, thinking to board and get a new tank for another rig-hop. He looked behind him one last time. . . .

"And here comes that big amberjack again!" Terry laughs. "Always seems to happen when you turn your back on these fish."

But it wasn't Terry that interested the AJ. It was that wounded snapper still wiggling on his dive mate's spear. Johnny Bonck had lured a massive jewfish out of bottom murk the same way forty years before. But that was intentional. "My buddy looked down and saw what was going on. But he couldn't do anything. He'd already shot. But he was pointing man! Bobbing his head like: LOOK!—LOOK! Shoot the damn thing!" The big AJ came up for another swipe at the snapper and Terry nailed him.

"But I shot too fast, hit him too far back. Wasn't *too* worried, though. Hell, I'm already up here at twenty five feet. I'll have him in the boat in no time."

Terry planned to fight him over just a bit so he could grab the boat ladder, like he'd normally grab a beam under the rig, and just hold on, waiting for the AJ to tire. A cinch.

"Yeah right!" He says. "That thing shot *off!* Straight *down!* I mean like a rocket. My buddy said he saw my spear hit that fish then—WHOOOOOM! He said I looked like the Starship Enterprise when it stomps it—ya know. I went from full body size to a speck in a nanosecond. But straight down, man!"

And down is not exactly where Terry needed to go right then. He'd already been down there a while, all the way to 150 feet.

He'd used up most of his tank down there. He was planning on surfacing when the big silver brute showed up so enticingly.

"That thing was zooming, like only an AJ—or a tuna—can go. Then he turned into the middle of the rig, I'm missing the beams by inches, glancing off of them like a car in a demolition derby." And still—down.

Decision time was coming up for Terry—hell, for most divers it was well past. Do I let go of the gun? Drown? Maybe embolize on the way up? Terry was below a hundred feet (again) and the fish was *not* slowing down. The shaft hit no bone or vitals, just meat. Terry was in for it if he wanted to boat this fish. His only option now was to tie off the fish and surface. But he'd better do it quick.

"Tying off" means somehow wrapping the cable around a beam with a few loops and leaving the gun and cable and fish down there, the fish fighting the rig while you surface in a leisurely manner. You check the computer for time, wait if necessary, then strap on another tank, plunge in, and retrieve the (usually spent) fish.

But again, this means slowing the fish down first to get leverage around a beam. "I knew I had to stop him. But how? He was too big and going too damn fast. But I didn't wanna let go, either. Hell, this was a Rodeo."

Terry was going too fast to grab a beam. They whizzed past him like lamp posts by a speeding car, and again, the direction was mostly down. His air was vanishing, his lungs puffing frantically, his arms and hands cramping. The decision looked simple: Let go of the *damn gun* for God's sake! Darren and Gerry will be happy to sell you a new one! Probably with a discount as a loyal customer!

But that would be hasty and an act of desperation. And like these guys all say when people ask them how they're still alive: "keep your head, don't panic." And in the midst of this madness, Terry kept his. Hell, he probably had a good minute of air left. What's the rush? And if he couldn't grab a beam, he'd simply ram one, using his gun to absorb the blow.

"Finally I said, the hell with it. It's now or never. We were heading straight for a beam and I just grabbed the spear gun with both hands and held it out in front of me crossways, like a chin-up bar or a pugil stick, thinking to ram the beam with it and maybe stop the ride. Or at least slow it down.

"So I'm holding it out in front of me . . . we're coming up on the beam—*whack!* CRACK! The freaking gun hits the beam and starts bending around it as the fish keeps pulling, and finally snaps in two.

"I'm sitting with my arms wrapped around the beam, like I'm hugging it. A little stunned too. I'd smacked my head against it. The cable was attached to the front of the gun so that was the piece in my right hand."

Amazingly, Terry was halfway into his tie-off now. He had the leverage he needed and the fish had slowed just a tad.

"I grabbed what was left of my gun with both hands and started trying to wrap the cable around the beam. I'm tugging away with both hands now, scraping a cloud of barnacles off the beam, flapping my fins like crazy for leverage—then pushing against the beam with my legs to get leverage with my arms . . . and I'm making a little progress—"

That crucial first loop finally made it around. "Hallelujah!" Terry thought. He went around again. Around again. The fish came back to life but he was fighting the rig now. A tie-off! And shoot, will ya look at that! A good 800 pounds of air left.

"Had him tied off now. Whoo! The point had opened through him, so he was secure. He wasn't gonna rip off the spear. Now, I said, I gotta get the hell outta here, gotta go up. I'm almost outta air. I'll strap on another tank, grab another gun, come down, finish him off with a head shot. And I got me a place on the board for sure. Maybe first place."

Sounds easy enough. Terry looked behind him as he finned up. The fish was secure, lunging but not budging the cable. His depth gauge read over a hundred feet. He'd gone for a hell of a ride. He hit the surface next to a boat. "GUN!" He screeched. "Gimme another GUN!" His dive mates guessed the reason. His buddy with the mangrove had filled them in.

Terry grabbed the new gun and started down. He'd neglected to get another tank. That 700 pounds was plenty enough. He'd be pushing it, but didn't want to leave the AJ down there for too long. Tethered meals like that always attract sharks. They'd rip valuable pounds off his prize fish, maybe take him out of the running. He'd also have to fight them for it. He was in no mood for an undersea version of *The Old Man and The Sea*.

But he lucked out. No sharks were shredding the AJ, which was spent. The big fish was in its death throes, finning slowly, jerking a little, then turning on its side. No need for a kill shot.

"I grabbed the cable and the little piece that was left of my gun." Terry says, "Unwrapped it from the rig and just started hauling him up. He'd had it. He was coming right along with me. I didn't even have to straddle him and ride him up." Terry chuckles. He was referring to a method of surfacing with lively AJs, perfected by his late buddy Whip Mermilliod.

"I saw him shoot a huge AJ once—had to go ninety- to -one hundred pounds. Dragged Whip way outside the rig, I followed to watch. And I'm glad I did. I see Whip catch up to the fish and grab the spear that was right through its middle—missed bone, though. I figured he'd grab for below the gills, maybe whack him with the dive knife and head up. But no—he grabs the spear on one side of the fish, he puts one leg over it, straddling it like he's gettin' on a horse! Then he grabs the protruding spear on the other side of the fish with his other hand. So now he's got a handle. Like he's leaning over holding the handlebars on a motorbike.

"Gidde-yup AJ! And there goes Whip! He points the amberjack's head up and just rides him up like a pony! He even waved to me. I was cracking up down there, swallowed a gallon of water—almost drowned I was laughing so bad . . . I'd been meaning to try that myself."

But this one was already spent. He wouldn't provide much of a ride. So Terry was towing him up with one hand, holding the spear gun with the other. "Then I look over and a huge brown shape's heading right for me! Whoa—a cobia! A curious one. A huge one."

It was too much. Another monster fish popping up and enticing Terry when he least expected it—and was least prepared.

"I wanted him." Terry nods. "He got close and started turning just as I hit the trigger and stuck him—but again—too far back . . . WHOOM! He's off!"

You'll remember Ben Hur? Or was it Spartacus? He was in the Coliseum with a chariot on each arm trying to pull him apart. Remember? Anyway, you get the picture. That was Terry. The amberjack got a second wind in all the commotion. And the cobia—about a seventy pounder—was doing pretty good on its *first* wind.

"So now I'm sitting there, both arms being stretched outta socket in opposite directions. I'm trying to ride with one, then with the other. And my regulator starts groaning, I'm down at four hundred pounds!

"But the cobia won. He was stronger at this point. And he wanted to go back down. I didn't have the air or bottom time for it—nowhere near it. But there was no stopping him.

"I was finning like crazy trying to get him outside the rig. The AJ played out again—thank God. So I started muscling the cobia up. Just pulling like crazy. Regulator's starting to groan. But it gets easier as I ascend. I'm pulling the cobia along, somehow. He's finally starting to come with me. I look up and—*whew!*—there's the boat. I'm almost under it. I got up there, tied the AJ to the ladder. Then managed to get the cobia through the gills and we hoisted him on board . . . hey, I didn't do too bad on that dive."

BRETON ISLAND INTERLUDE

We bobbed in the waves, the motor idling. Nobody felt like moving. Finally we gunned it towards Breton Island, about fifteen
miles away. We'd be spending the night there in tents, or maybe
aboard Glen's houseboat, depending on how many people
showed up. We had quite a party planned.

About twenty boats, some with divers, some with fishermen,
were scheduled to converge in a cove on the west (sheltered) side
of Breton Island this weekend for a massive blow-out. The
"Breton Island Blast" we call it, an adjunct of sorts to the
Helldivers' Rodeo. We park in the cove; assemble tents and tarps
on the island; fish for wadefish at dusk, and flounder at night;
ignite massive driftwood fires; cook fish and beans; shuck and
slurp down raw oysters by the sackfull; swat gnats, mosquitoes
and sand flies; bitch about wives and girlfriends—all the while
drinking.

It's beer during the day, rum and whiskey after sunset. Some of
the guys smoke dope. A few doobies always get passed around,
but nothing major. That mellow "munchies" crap would ruin the
atmosphere. Like they say: What's the difference between dope
smokers and drunks? Dope-smokers get stoned and contemplate

their navels. Drunkards get drunk and contemplate *other* peoples' navels.

Yes, sir. We need heavy-duty liquid crank out here, some serious buzzing. Tradition demands it. Those famous nocturnal boat races and the ever-popular nude bonfire leaping wouldn't amount to much without the proper stimulus. Things get interesting out here.

The plan was to meet our compadres, get the tents and sleeping arrangements squared away, shoot the shit, socialize, eat, and maybe get in an afternoon dive at some shallower rigs—that or some surf fishing.

Breton Island itself is nothing more than a glorified sandbar, the remnants of an ancient delta created when the Mississippi entered the Gulf at a slightly different angle from today. The river's been fickle, falling into its present track only nine hundred years ago—an eye blink, geologically speaking. Breton Island stretches for barely half a mile, and it's a few hundred yards wide. Hurricanes Andrew and George pummeled it fearfully, shearing it in half and shredding off about a third of its landmass.

But it hangs on. Vegetation is sparse, growing mainly along the edges, like hair on Danny DeVito's head. Some sea oats, saltgrass, bachiris, and marsh alders sprout on the sand dunes and cove edges. No trees grow on it. But that cove on the backside makes a perfect anchorage for houseboats, yachts, party barges, and whatever else makes the ten-mile open water trip from Venice or the thirty-mile trip from Hopedale or Shell Beach. Our chums would be converging from both directions, laden with fishing gear, diving gear, camping gear, beer, rum, and God knows what else. Breton's a mini Bimini. A Cajun Catalina. And, yep, we were ready for a little partying ourselves.

Breton's no Grand Isle, though. For pure *partying*, Breton can't compare to the barrier islands on the opposite side of the river, Grand Isle, and the adjoining Grand Terre. Fort Livingston squats between them overlooking Barataria pass, a major thoroughfare for crewboats and shrimpboats. A few years back, a few lucky ones chugged through just in time for their crews to first blink, then shake their heads, and finally gape at the incident which resulted in the famous photo, "Moons Over Ft. Livingston," involving Baton Rouge's all-female dive club, the —— and its president M—— B——. Sorry, but I promised. I can't divulge the names. But, locally, everyone knows them. Sure, I was tempted to lie. But if hell indeed "hath no fury like a woman scorned," then scorning a woman who routinely wrestles fifty-pound cobia from one hundred-foot depths onto a boat—and who carries a spear gun—cannot be wise.

Anyway, these women (mostly middle-class wives and mothers) had chartered a boat out of Grand Isle for a morning of rig-diving, then an afternoon of picnicking on the beach near Ft. Livingston. The dive went well. Scores of fish were stalked, tortured, and assassinated by these suburban moms. The picnic was going well also, the daiquiri supply depleting rapidly.

"Time for a group picture, everyone!"

"Sure! *Let's go!*" and they scrambled atop the fort.

"A little closer now, gang . . . there that's good . . . over a little, C——, there!"

"Hey!" the president shouted. "How 'bout if we turn around, so they can't see our faces, and pull our suits down!

"Great idea, M—— B——! But *you* go first!" (Remember, these are one piece bathing suits.)

"Okay, here . . . how's this!"

"Okay, I'll go!"

"All right, all right, me too . . . gosh, I can't believe I'm *doing* this!"

Finally, a dozen Louisiana scubababes were grinning at the camera with their vertical smiles. *Click-click*—and "Moons over Ft. Livingston" entered immortality.

The photographer was sworn to secrecy, so naturally the picture was featured the very next week in the Louisiana Council of Dive Clubs' official newsletter, where only about 5,500 people saw it. Imagine the time and effort involved in passing it around by hand to 5,500 people!

Word has it that for months afterwards Dive Club meetings in the Baton Rouge area involved contests among the males involving magnifying glasses. Come on guys! Let's *name that BUTT!*

"Huuuummmm—That's my ole-lady's right there! I ga-ron-tee
. . . look at those dimples!"

"No way! That's *mine's!* Lookit the mole on the left cheek, I'd
know that anywhere!"

"Mole? That ain't no mole! That's a hickey! . . . so I know damn
well that's my . . ."

And so on and so on. That was ten years ago, and controversy
still rages at club meetings—usually around mid-keg—as to the
exact identification of certain derrieres.

The fort was actually built in the 1820s at the very site where
Jean Lafitte once made his headquarters. They say it was quite a
place in its day, before the U.S. Navy swooped in, blasted it to
rubble, and torched it.

It was home port to Lafitte's armada of fifty ships and his crew
of one thousand privateers. As such it was built to accommodate
their roistering appetites. It boasted a gambling casino, slave quarters and a bordello. Why pirates patronized a bordello has never
been explained. Maybe they've been mischaracterized as raping,
plundering beasts. Maybe the moniker of "Gentleman Pirate," as
Lafitte was known among New Orleans Creoles, fit better than the
"Terror Of The Gulf" of his wanted posters.

The name, Barataria, some say, comes from the French word
barraterie meaning "fraudulence" or "deception." Others say it
was inspired by the island in Cervantes' *Don Quixote* where the
arch-rogue and buffoon Sancho Panza set himself up as governor. Either way it fits. This channel sees a lot of boat traffic, it
being the gateway to Barataria Bay itself and the entire Barataria
estuarine complex, a 4.6 million-acre expanse of swamp and
marsh including the ports of Lafitte, Crown Point, and
Westwego.

This watery wilderness was the buccaneers' lair. When the heat
was on, they'd grab their loot, pile it on shallow craft, and scoot
from headquarters on Grand Terre Island into this maze of shallow, alligator-infested bayous. The Spanish—or later, U.S. authorities—in their bigger boats were left stranded and fuming.

Fittingly, during the early years of Prohibition—that "noble
experiment"—this area of Breton Sound was a smugglers' haven
known as "Rum Row." In the early Twenties, schooners crammed

with contraband rum from Cuba and the Bahamas would anchor near this very Breton Island, which lies just inside the twelve mile territorial waters of the U.S. So the foreign schooners would stay a few miles offshore, about where the Main Pass Rigs now stand. Smaller craft would swarm out of the maze of coastal bayous like hungry ants, load up, and scurry back through the marshlands and into the fishing villages. The precious cargo was then offloaded onto trucks, and their convoys would head New Orleans-ward, that the wicked appetites of "America's Wettest State," as it was known at the time, might be slaked, that our "moral depravity" and "love of luxurious dissipation" might be indulged.

Nowadays the Barataria Pass is always crammed with oil company crew boats and shrimp boats. Remember, these type of boats are generally crewed by men. In many cases—especially for those boats *entering* the pass from the Gulf—by young men who have been offshore for a good while, several weeks in some cases. Several weeks during which no real, live women were visible; several weeks during which the only females around smiled and winked from the insides of magazines which had been encased in cellophane.

Such sensory deprivation drove mariners of yore to turn manatees to mermaids, which might have made sense if all women looked like Rosie O'Donnell. But as we know, many also look like Bella Abzug and Janet Reno. So why just the lust for manatees? Why not fantasize about humping walruses and elephant seals and white belugas? These live in the ocean. Manatees live along the coasts. I'm sure those horny sailors saw more of the former.

Anyway, such men as those entering Barataria Pass would be *particularly* appreciative of the fleshy display atop Ft. Livingston that fateful afternoon. And it turns out that some were in a position to see it. Some claim two, some claim three; some claim shrimp boats, some claim crew boats. Point is, several boats ran aground that afternoon. It's a tricky channel under normal circumstances. It requires careful scrutiny of the radar and depth gauges to navigate properly. I met a captain who had to wait three hours for the tide to rise in order to churn his way out—and with a now-damaged prop. He has no regrets.

"It was damn well worth it!" he snorts. "We'd been up for thirty four hours, man! We thought we were hallucinating! Though it was a freakin' *mirage!* It was gorgeous, man!—*GORGEOUS*, I tell ya!"

And speaking of enjoying ourselves, Breton Island's tallest sand dunes were just creeping over the horizon and On-the-Ball had just started gulping a fresh beer when—bash!—CLANG!—*splash!* We came down off a swell Pelayo had been riding (too fast) and smacked into the trough. Without noticing, we'd climbed to the crest of one of those rogue waves that show up out of nowhere . . . then we'd come off the top like a sky jumper—*whoa!*—WIPE OUT! Happens often when you're going *with* the waves.

The Bud smacked Paul's teeth, ricocheted off my knee and started foaming over my feet as the wave crashed over the bow, knocked down everyone in the boat, then swept out of the stern.

For a second Tom's legs pointed skyward as he seemed to be smooching the gunwale. Then I landed on top of him, bashing his kidneys with my knee, as Paul grabbed my ankle to slow down his flume ride towards the stern.

"Woo-hoo!" Pelayo shook the water from his face with a mighty whoop. He spit some out and gunned it into the crest of another swell.

"*Slow down!*" I gurgled from the stern. "*Are you crazy?*"

"EEEYY-HAAA!" Pelayo sounded like Slim Pickens riding that nuclear bomb down in *Dr. Strangelove*. His eyes were wild. A lunatic smile creased his face as we pitched down. "Yeah, you right!" Pelayo howled as he shook the salt spray from his face and spit out another saltwater loogie.

Paul's neck and chest glistened with beer and foam. Tom was rubbing his knee and shoulder again. A spent beer and a few bruises . . . tanks clanging around again—big deal! We'd been chugging Bud for six miles now. The effects were beginning to manifest. We were still pumped, whooping, yelling . . . red faces, convulsed in a laughter that dulled our bumps and bruises.

We were *feeling good, feeling right it's ALMOST Saturday night.*

Yes sir. We were cocky, loose. And why not? It had been an interesting day thus far. Much like the mayor of the Emerald City in *The Wizard of Oz*, we'd "laughed in the face of death, sneered at doom, and chuckled at catastrophe."

Slight exaggeration, perhaps. At any rate, we'd stared down or beat back everything nature sent to battle us. We'd set our jaws, hunkered down, and crashed out into the Gulf for fifteen miles, in the face of waves, rain, and lightning. We'd jumped in and fought against a raging current. We'd stared down the chocolate murk, plunging defiantly through 60 feet of it to the gloomy depths, where we finally cocked our guns and went on the bloody prowl. We'd stalked down some big fish, shot them, grabbed them, subdued them and wrestled the bastards into the boat. Nobody'd been hurt, seriously. And the boat was in one piece. We'd done *okay*. Time to gloat, to brag and bluster.

Hemingway wrote about his "confrontations with nature that strip away sham and compromise . . . in the lazy ocean you will be purified." If he felt purified after reeling in a fish from a forty foot boat, we felt downright antiseptic after skirting the continental shelf in a twenty footer and wrestling the brutes in their own element. Or maybe it's that second Bud on an empty stomach.

"Ease back on the throttle a little, okay Pelayo?" Paul smirked at his brother while grabbing his arm and edging back the gas. Yes, sir, let's kick back, grab a fresh round of brewskies and chug our way to Breton Island.

"Hope those suckers brought all our stuff," Pelayo nodded.

I was thinking the same thing. Since we were loaded up with diving stuff, we'd assigned our overnight gear—tents, sleeping bags, cooking stuff, food, booze—to Don and our old friend Chris, who had a bigger boat and expected to arrive on Breton Island near noon with my brother Rick—a fisherman, not a diver—and the rest of the convoy.

The eighteen knot winds had tapered to a gentle breeze by now. That spine-jarring chop dwindled to a gentle swell that we cruised over comfortably. The island finally loomed into the view. As we rounded a corner to the lee side we noticed the thin white breakers foaming along the windward side. "Not too bad," Tom said. "It's really calmed down from this morning." Just then some sun poked through a crevice in the clouds and illuminated the blue, red, and yellow of the tent city already assembled on the westernmost corner of the island. Nice touch.

"Looks like they're here!" Paul shouted, and we high-fived around the boat.

"They've here all right," Pelayo laughed. "That's Don, hunh?" A twenty-three foot Pro-Line was cutting a huge arc to our left. "Looks like Don's new boat, hunh? Looks like he sees us . . . look-it that crazy sucker!"

He was blazing towards us over an area that we knew was only a foot deep. The last hurricane had silted it up. "I can't believe it!" I gasped. "That new boat of his must not draw much water, geezum!"

It was Don all right, with Chris, Rick, and Bob on board—all of us high school chums—shooting the bird and heading right for us like a crazed kamikaze while yelling "BABY-WE-WERE-BORN-TO-RUN!" which was booming out of their sound box actually louder than the 220-horsepower outboard.

Tom and Paul were cackling. "Can you believe those crazy. . . !"

At about thirty yards Don turned sharply, and Chris joined Bob and Rick who were already in the stern mooning us, slapping their hairy cheeks as Don roared with mirth . . . until something loud and wrenching was heard.

Yep. We knew those shallows were around here. They found 'em. The outboard let fly with a ghastly roar that barely muffled all the knocks and bangs from inside the boat as the merry pranksters bounced against the hull, the coolers, and each other, while Bruce continued with "Strap your hands cross my ENGINES!"

And speaking of engines, good thing they didn't have the tilt locked. They'd be dead right now, instead of just stunned and bruised. Their prop was high in the air, spinning away. The engine roaring, water and sand spewing every which way as we howled and shrieked.

"Ah-HAA!—ahh-HAA!" Now we were roaring. I was in freakin' tears, slapping Tom on the back, pointing with my free hand. Pelayo tilted up the motor and we eased towards them, yelling, whooping, blowing rasberries and yes—mooning. I yanked down my shorts and joined Tom and On-the-Ball on the bow, wiggling and slapping our red-pimpled buttocks till we were twenty yards away from them.

"HEY-HEY-HEY!" Pelayo yelled, just as Don lunged for the ignition and slapped off the racket. "WHATCHA-GOT-TO-SAY!"

The famous Kool and the Gang song was a notorious inside joke. It symbolized another famous boating debacle from our late teens. And we'd all known each other since our *early* teens. That kind of thing happens often in south Louisiana. We don't move much down here, don't like to relocate. Ask any headhunter. In our circle, we're mainly salespeople; we get calls from them all the time. "You *from* New Orleans?" They ask. "Uh-huh . . . your wife? Unh-hunh... well, we wont bother to ask if you're willing to relocate . . . thanks anyway . . . if anything changes give us a call."

We'd make more money in Houston or Atlanta—*tons* more, in fact. But quality of life would suffer. Attend a New Orleans area party and ask ten people around you where they're from, originally. Probably eight are natives. Try that in Houston or Dallas . . . or shoot, just about anywhere in this country.

Point is, we have inside jokes. "Whatcha-got-to-say" was the song blaring from Pelayo's radio as he pulled an *identical* kamikaze run on me and Chris while fishing in lake Pontchartrain summer of '74, when the song was a hit. We were casting our lures along the Causeway (world's longest bridge) pilings about five miles from shore in Chris's skiff when we see this lunatic in an identical fourteen foot skiff blazing right at us, steering with his elbow, Miller pony in one hand, feet propped on an ice chest next to a huge boom-box and singing along with Kool and the Gang. "Hey-Hey-Hey," he'd shout with head bobbing and a shit-eating grin as he roared in. "Whatcha Got to SAY!" then he'd turn away at the last second drenching us with his rooster tail.

He made three such runs, and I was contemplating grabbing the flare gun, when my line snagged. We motored a little closer to the pilings to un-snag it. Now Pelayo was on his fourth run, almost even with us, head turned, chin bobbing to the beat, singing along "Hey-Hey-Hey! . . . Whatcha"—and heading straight for a concrete piling.

"WATCH IT!" Chris howled. I looked up from untangling my line to see Pelayo about ten feet from a piling. He saw it, too, and jerked the outboard's handle for a 90-degree turn. The boat turned on a dime, all right, throwing him overboard, then blazing off by itself towards the middle of the lake.

For thirty seconds I couldn't see or breathe for laughing, thought I'd need a respirator and a hernia operation. Pelayo surfaced and we saw that he was alive—laughing as hard as we were, so we went after the boat. The damn thing was almost *airborne*. Nothing to weigh it down. Nothing to control it, either. We gave chase, boring it out and laughing violently. But there was no catching it. We were in an identical boat with an identical twenty five-horsepower outboard—but with more weight. It was getting further and further. We couldn't gain on it.

Finally it hit a small wave that jerked the outboard sideways, causing the boat to turn sharply, like a bull chasing the cape when the matador twists it . . . then it sank, groaning and gurgling until the engine drowned—but not completely. These skiffs have built in flotation under the seats. So we lashed the anchor rope to it and hauled back to shore, along with Pelayo.

Same as now.

"Need some help?" Tom sputtered just as Bruce was howling that "The highway's jammed with broken heroes in a last chance power drive. . . ."

I don't know about anything *broken* here, but certainly bruised.

"Ooh, man," Don was rubbing his stomach, where the steering wheel had dug in. With the other hand he rubbed his forehead, where the windshield made contact. He was beet red, either from sun or from shame, trying desperately to laugh— forcing, coaxing, and doing a fair job. But a counterfeit laugh all the same.

Bob, Rick, and Chris added to the drunken din of whoops and guffaws—also counterfeit. They were trying to deflect or preempt ours. They'd taken a hell of a banging, their bodies *and* egos.

"Cause tramps like us," Bruce was still wailing from CD player somewhere in the boat.

"Baby we were borrrrnnn to RUNNNNN!" Everyone chimed in for that last stanza, grimacing crazily and pumping our fists, as befits the theme song of spring break '76. All of us (except Tom) were there, single, slimmer, hairier (top of head-wise—less so, back, nostril, ear and butt-wise), and *much* less in debt . . . ah, the memories.

That was Panama City, Florida, before MTV started whooping it up as a national spring break mecca. Back then it was more of a regional spring break mecca. It drew from LSU, Ole Miss, Alabama, Auburn, U. of Texas, Tennessee—basically everything south of the Mason-Dixon line and east of the Pecos. But plenty of time to rekindle those delectable late '70s spring break memories around the fire tonight. We brought the music for it: Bruce; the Eagles; Fleetwood Mac; assorted disco including KC, the Ohio Players, Barry White, Earth Wind and Fire; and especially—the Stones.

Nothing like music for this sort of thing—to beam you back in time. Tonight's when the rum flows, tongues loosen, and the hardcore reminiscing cranks up. "The past is a voluptuous siren," writes Jose Ortega y Gasset. "It engenders the strong undertow of a low tide. We must grasp the present well or the past will drag us down and absorb us."

Well, all week long we grasp the present with a white-knuckle grip, five mind- and soul-numbing days of it. By Friday it starts slipping like greasy monofilament. We start peeking behind us at the voluptuous siren. Tonight we stop kicking and thrashing against that undertow. We let go of that safety line. That "voluptuous siren," gets us tonight. That undertow takes us right into her arms. And that wench better watch out. We're as ravenous for her charms as Magellan's crew.

Yes, sir. We'll hear tales to shame Warren Beatty with all his starlets and Mick Jagger with all his groupies. These celebrities were sex-starved geeks compared to this gang of irresistable beaus from the bayous. The beach bunnies were helpless against us. Arrayed seductively on their towels, sipping their wine coolers, they'd spot us from afar. A gaggle of sneering, prancing studs, walking the beach and hurling a Frisbee. Beneath those sun-oiled bosoms their hearts fluttered, inside those sand-flecked thighs their muscles quivered at our approach, these strutting honchos, their loins encased in cut-offs with the frilly edges, gold medallions dangling against bronzed chests, beers in hand, LSU caps cocked rakishly.

Finally within earshot we'd glance over, nod perhaps, tip our caps—then let fly, usually allowing Pelayo the opening shot. "Do y'all believe in love at first sight?" he'd croon, wink, snicker, pause. "Or do we walk by again?"

Steve Martin and Dan Akroyd had nothing on us. We slayed them without fail. We were simply irresistible. The chicks would swoon collectively, cooing and chirping and giggling. We'd move in, give them a close-up shot, charm them from shorter range for a while; "If I told you you have a beautiful body," Chris would croak, his eyebrows in serious Groucho mode, "would you hold it against me?"

They'd erupt in cackles, covering their mouths and spurting out mouthfuls of wine cooler, their ripe little bodies quivering with glee. Then we'd arrange for the evening, where we'd really (and literally) shine: lime-green angel flights buttoned at the sternum, platform shoes to totter over the smoke that poured onto the dance floor, medallions (different ones for nighttime— much bigger) that blinded a dance-mate while reflecting the strobe lights, and—of course—polypropelene shirts with collars like kites, the kind that flapped like wings during a particularly spirited Hustle and poked them in the ear while doing the Bump.

They'd melt at the spectacle again, surrendering shamelessly to our every whim, especially after the fourth amaretto sour or slow screw. Don would request "How Deep Is Your Love" from the DJ at Spinnaker. Then time for some serious groping and dry humping on the dance floor.

By the second gallon of Bacardi it's time for "Hot Rocks" and the slashing rhythm of "Jumpin' Jack Flash." We strap on the air guitars—driftwood works well also—and slash away, frowning, grimacing—Keith Richards eat your heart out, podnuh. "It's a gas—gas—gas!" Mick, you don't know the half of it buddy. The poor seagulls and pelicans trying to sleep on the other end of the island are plugging their ears against the racket. Yes, sir, the boom-box blares and imaginations jump into overdrive. Now it's down to the nitty gritty: recalling how we split up for the night. And where we went—beach? car? room? and whose room? ours or theirs? And yes, maybe *several* of them were in the room together, drunk, or stoned.

We'll hear tales to shame *Penthouse Forum*—not that we read it. Compared to our exploits in *amour,* Don Juan's were those of a hopeless bumbler and Casanova's those of a sorry chump. We'll hear of conquest after conquest, of wild passion in the sand, of bed sheets stained and clawed to shreds, of the scores of panting breasts and broken hearts left in our wake—and all mouth-watering babes. Every last one of them. Not a dog or walrus in the lot.

Thus do ten ounces of rum, half a doobie, and twenty years affect the memory of married middle-aged men with an exclusive audience of other middle-aged men, and a weekend pass from wives.

Camille Paglia says, "males have only a brief period of exhilarating liberty between control by their mothers and control by their wives." She writes in *Sex, Art and American Culture*: "The agony of male identity springs from men's humiliating sense of dependence upon women." Ouch. She's right. So we'll celebrate that "brief period of exhilarating liberty" at every opportunity, every bachelor party, every hunting trip, every fishing trip, every diving trip. Historically, when males got together it was to kill things, either animals or other men. So be it.

And if our celebrations seem a little more raucous than most, if we harp on the past to a point where relative newcomers (like Tom and Glen) feel excluded, if we provoke the wives to cold-eyed fury when we huddle together at parties howling and cackling over times past—well it's because we spent that time *together.* Practically everyone dates from that brief period of exhilarating liberty, Paglia mentions: late high school and college. Call it the Ya-Ya Brotherhood.

"The old things are nowhere except in our minds now," Hemingway wrote to a friend in 1923. "We have them as we remember them and we have to go on. We can't ever go back to the old things or try and get the old kick."

Tell you what, Ernie baby: we come *damn close.*

Happens a lot in south Louisiana. "Human relations in such a place tend to assume a solid permanence. A man's circle of friends becomes a sort of extension of his family circle." That was Mencken writing of life in his beloved Baltimore. He might have been writing of New Orleans. He goes on: "His contacts are with with men and women who are rooted as he is. They are not moving all the time and so they are not changing their friends all the time. Thus abiding relationships tend to be built up, and when fortune brings unexpected changes, they survive those changes. Then men I know and esteem in Baltimore are, on the whole, men I have known and esteemed a long while. It is our fellows who make life endurable to us and give it a purpose and meaning."

Twelve of us would sit around the campfire tonight. No friendship was younger than a decade. Most spanned two. Any one of us looking around would find all six who stood in his wedding. Again, not unusual for south Louisiana.

We still had to get this boat out. I threw Don our anchor rope as Chris and Bob, groaning and chuckling, stumbled out of their grounded boat. Don made the rope fast to the bow. Pelayo revved our engine, prop churning, sand and water spraying—and nothing moving. He tilted it up a little more. WREEN!—WREENNN! Still not much progress. Bob and Chris went behind Don's boat and heaved a little . . . WRREEEN!—there we go—that's it— *bingo!* We whooped as it started inching away, slowly.

We towed Don's spanking new craft into the deeper channel, which was only a hundred yards away. He and Tom clambered in, cranked it up and we headed for the tents.

Looking up as we chugged along, I noticed that the black clouds that stained the sky this morning had melted into an even gray haze. I was feeling the sting on my neck and shoulders by now . . . getting a little red.

I was smearing on sun block as we eased into the shallow cove and threw out the anchor amidst a dozen other boats. A huge three-story house-barge with about five smaller bay-boats docked to it was anchored in the northernmost corner of the cove. The thing looked like a floating condominium unit.

"Check it out," snorted Paul as we jumped over the side into the foot deep water. "Really roughing it, hunh? Hand me that duffel bag over there."

"Lookit the *size* of that thing!" Tom croaked while he threw Paul the bag. "Whose is it? Did PETA make it?!"

For weeks, rumors had raced that People for the Ethical Treatment of Animals had gotten wind of this Breton Island Blast. PETA shudders in horror at our brand of amusement. Some said they were planning a demonstration.

"Fine," we said. "Let 'em come." I mean, PETA people regard the catch-'n-release fly-fishing of their yuppie and Hollywood celebrity soulmates as barbarous and cruel. Indeed they label fishing as— I swear—"the cruelest form of hunting." Out here where fish are jabbed, poked, stabbed, wrestled, sliced, ripped, clubbed, then hung up for photos—well, they'd better bring sedatives.

"Nah, that ain't PETA." Pelayo huffed "No such luck. Think of the fun. No, that's some oil company's house barge."

"Service company's" I corrected. "It's McDermott's . . . or Haliburton . . . one of the big service companies. They use it to entertain oil company big-wigs"

"Medium-wigs too, hunh?" Paul asked. "Didn't your brother tell us about staying on that thing?"

Rick, my brother, was an engineer for Shell Offshore. The energy service and supply companies spend more on entertaining people like him than on salaries. It's incredible. Skiing trips, Cancun trips, tickets to Mardi Gras balls, you name it. And "fishing" trips with luxurious accommodations, day-long open bar, cooks, manservants, and . . .

"Check *her* out!" Paul whooped. "By the railing, second floor."

"Oooh-yeeah" Pelayo whistled. And check out the one . . . is that? Looks like three of them, lying out on the deck. What the . . . ?"

"Sure is." Chris gasped from behind. He was splashing in from the rear, carrying an ice chest. "Gents, it's babe-a-rama out here this year," he whooped. "Titty-city. We noticed 'em the minute we pulled in this morning. A few of them were wade fishing."

"Man, we thought we were hallucinating," Now Don huffed from behind. He was catching up, splashing through the sandbar, carrying a sleeping bag on each shoulder. "We couldn't believe it.

You know how it goes out here. You might see the odd chick out here now and then. You know . . . like last year. Maybe a coupla wives who come out to fish, splash around a little in the evening. Work on the tan while the ole-man fishes. But these don't look like no wives. No way. So we idled pretty close to 'em. They were actually catching fish and started waving us off, like they were pissed. Like we'd scare the school away, mess up the fishing. They were serious about it, man, waving and screaming. So we backed off. But let me tell ya man, all that waving with those *microscopic* bikinis? Some serious bouncin', some delicious bouncin'. It was heavenly."

"Ummmm-*UMMMM!*" It was On-the-Ball, the only single one left amongst us. He was peering through some binoculars he'd yanked out of the duffel bag he was carrying, splashing along and mumbling. "MAMA-*MAMA!* he sighed. " FOXY-*FOXY!!*" he whistled while waving back at the babe with the yellow tanga and long brown hair, smiling, waving and wiggling from the second floor of the floating condo.

We splashed ashore and about ten tents had been set up already. A driftwood fire was smoking and smoldering, a grill over it with sausage and redfish fillets, about ten aluminum chairs set up around it. But only one chair was occupied . . . and it looked like . . . a female? Impossible.

"Who's that?" I asked Bob who finally huffed ashore carrying some gear. "I mean, I thought it was no ole ladies out here? Shoot, I'd a brought Shirley if I'd known. She'd a come. The kids were all out this weekend."

"That's no ole lady." Bob smirked as he shuffled past, rum fumes pumping up from his lungs. "She's *mine*, podnuh. All mine . . . the perfect woman." He grinned and jogged up to his tent, opened the flap and threw in his stuff.

Bob's always talking in riddles. And I was in no mood for subtleties, so I let it slide. "What's with the chick?" I asked Chris and Don who'd just come up behind, lugging their gear.

"Come see," they chuckled. "She's Bob's date for the weekend. The perfect woman . . . here." Chris handed me a Bud. I popped it open and chugged.

As I got closer, the chick looked oddly stiff, even a weird color.

Good Lord, I thought, what kind of broad did Bob dig up this time? Then it hit me: she was an *inflatable doll.*

"Got her in the quarter last weekend after the bachelor party," Bob said as he patted her head. "Y'all left early, right after we left Pat O's. Remember? So Chris and I walked over to Bourbon Street. Sat in Papa Joe's for a while, for ole times sake. Then we walked in one of those sex shops. She was beckoning from the wall. Just look at this mouth!" He groaned while squeezing her cheeks. "She's a *goddess!* A *goddess*, I tell ya! I fell for her." He started smooching her.

Bob was already looped, as anyone could tell. His eyes where rheumy, face red. He whacked her on the side of the head and stumbled off through the sand to his tent.

I went over and sat her back down. She was a slutty-looking thing. Red round mouth, opened in an O. Arms outstretched. A dog collar. A pink haltertop with "The Perfect Woman" emblazoned in bold red across her tits.

Geezuz, I thought. These people are shameless. Still, it's impossible not to be horny right after a hunt. Sure, we come home tired, dirty, and bedraggled—but always with a carnal gleam in the eye. Ask the wives. And there's good reason for it. For 99 percent of our species's history *apres*-hunt was nookie time. The brutes came in from the hunt bragging and blustering about who killed the most or the biggest. The women sat around, smiling coyly, but sizing up the kill. The best hunter was naturally the best provider. So he got the best poon-tang. Nothing's changed. They do the same thing now, except the hunt takes place in an office or boardroom, and the kill is a paycheck. Who are we kidding?

"Over here!" Chris was calling me from the shore where he was struggling with an ice-chest. "Gimme a hand."

I walked over. "What the hell ya got in here? Man, it's heavy." And he opened the lid. "Oh-yeah! Man-o-*man!* Are they salty?"

He'd picked up a sack from an oyster boat at the marina this morning like we'd wanted. They'd been iced down for three hours by now. The oyster knife was in the box, so I grabbed one with my bare hands and pried it open. No sauce. No lemon. No nothing . . . sluuurp—"UMMMM!" Nothing but the fabulous taste of the raw salty gulf. "Man, these are *good!* I mean *good—*

salty, salty, salty—and cold! Let's get 'em up there."

"Told ya I wasn't gonna buy them unless they were salty," Chris smirked as we huffed it up to beach towards the chairs. "The guy let me taste them first. But I was pretty sure they'd be good. All that south wind lately."

Rule of thumb for Louisiana oysters: eat them after a few days of southerly winds, if possible. South (and east) winds push the salty Gulf waters into the estuaries where oysters grow. A few days of that and you're guaranteed salty oysters, at Acme and Felix's in the French Quarter, or, of course, straight from the boats themselves, like in our case.

I've met exactly *one* male in Louisiana who isn't fond of raw oysters. About half the women love them. Food snots talk about caviar as some "erotic" or "sensual" dining experience. And maybe it is. They say *good* caviar tastes like a "breath of fresh clean ocean air." I guess it's like wine. The best ones taste like nothing; flavor and price are inversely proportional with wine as well as caviar. But not with oysters, and we'll take raw oysters any day—the fatter, colder and saltier the better.

"Let's go," I huffed. Chris was adjusting his grip. "Got it? Let's go." I couldn't get them over to the tents fast enough. "There." And we dropped the ice chest next to the pile of driftwood. I dug a glove out of my dive bag, reached in for another oyster, and popped it open with a quick twist of the knife. It was actually steaming—in reverse, I mean. Vapor was issuing from it because the oyster was ice-cold and the air hot and humid.

"Tom! Come over. Check out the oysters."

Pelayo dug out another oyster knife and half the sack vanished in half an hour. A nice little pile of oyster shells grew next to the driftwood. Not an ounce of any kind of cocktail sauce was used to mask their marvelous salty flavor.

"Another beer?" Tom asked as he went for the cooler.

"Naw . . . not right now. Think I'm gonna . . . yyyAAWWWNN!— think I'm gonna zonk out." It was getting that time. Almost two in the afternoon. We'd been up since 4 A.M. lugging tanks and gear around, then fighting the waves, the current, the fish—a six-pack on an empty stomach. Now a half-gallon of raw oysters percolating in the gut. Yep, time for a nap.

But not in the tent, too hot. It wasn't set up anyway, a tarp was, and a nice breeze was blowing. I walked over, set up my cot in its shade, spread my sleeping bag on top and plopped down . . . that's nice. Better than a bed at home. The breeze was heavenly, the gentle lapping of the surf fifty yards away a soothing lullaby. I drifted off in seconds—then back again as somebody let fly with a bray of laughter from nearby . . . then another . . . and another . . . more of the gang meeting the Perfect Woman.

I didn't mind, actually. I was drifting off again in seconds. Their outbursts granted me more time to savor the delicious sensation—those thirty seconds of bliss before you conk out into sweet oblivion. And here I was succumbing with a Gulf breeze caressing my face and the soft serenade of the surf.

No beating a nap. Just ask us Cubans. Sadly, for many of us the traditional siesta was another of those things Fidel stole. This country's not right for it, but you'd still be amazed by how many people in Louisiana sneak away for an hour or so after lunch, especially in summer. Not that it necessarily means getting in a bed, or even a recliner chair. Office cubicles, so touted as increasing productivity in the workplace, if properly provisioned, make ideal sanctuaries for post-lunch siestas. Let the lunch include a margarita because of a co-worker's birthday, promotion, or retirement and it's a clincher.

A nap lets you actually *feel* the sleep, especially out here in the breeze, with the waves . . . it lets you *savor* the slumber. It's a lighter form of sleep, with more vivid dreams that you remember.

Suddenly, I felt something wet on my face—felt it again, then opened my eyes to see a hideous white, slimy orifice inches from my nose. So PETA made it out here after all.

"UH!" I jerked sideways and fell off the cot as the laughter erupted all around me. "What the?" Looking back, Don was cackling and holding a *stingray* by the tail.

"You crazy bastard!" I wheezed.

"We cut it off, man. We cut the spine off . . . see?" He wiggled the creature at me again. Yep, no spine on its tail. "Sounded like you were having an erotic dream man . . . wanted to help." At least ten guys were still stumbling around in the sand holding their sides. "Look at this sucker's mouth . . . looks good, hunh?" Don roared.

A stingray's mouth does have a certain labial or anal look to it. Though most dive guides say the mouth looks a lot like a human mouth, indeed like a smiling human mouth, a smiling female mouth. Leave it to this bunch of degenerates to find it erotic. But I wasn't in the mood for these idiots right now. I usually wake up from a nap in a foul mood, especially with a quasi-hangover. So I got up, ran past the cackling gauntlet to the surf and dove in, as much to get away from those assholes as to wake up.

The water felt delightful—not hot like it'll be by next month, not cold like during Easter. A black skimmer was working the shoreline. These crazy birds suffer from a hideous underbite, like Springsteen. Their bottom beak protrudes about an inch past the top one. They stick it in the water and just fly along, literally "skimming" the shallow backwash from the surf in search of a tidbit. If the beak touches a fish—*blip*—they flip it in the air and gulp it down.

Always seemed like a terribly inefficient method of eating to me, unlike that of the brown pelicans out behind me. They stop in mid-air over a pod of mullet rippling the surface. They cup up and dangle their feet almost like a decoying mallard. Then they point their heads down, sweep the wings back—*swoop, splash!* Right before they hit, they twist their heads and open their beaks, smacking the water atop a swell, and get upright in seconds, with a mullet jerking around in their elastic pouches. Then they tilt their heads back, bob it a couple times—*gulp-gulp,* and down goes the fish.

These terns are pretty good too. *Kreek-kreeek,* their constant, noisy cries sound like the proverbial fingernails on a blackboard. They wheel, flap, and hover over the waves, always peering down. *Whoops*, one stops and hovers for a second. *Aha!* You can almost see his face light up. *SMACK!* he hits the water, always with a belly-buster. But terns don't submerge like the pelican. They grab the shiner on the very surface, then flap back into the air in a split second, the little morsel wriggling in their beaks. Terns are after smaller fare than pelicans, little menhadden, glass minnows, or anchovies, or just bits of them, brought to the surface by feeding speckled trout or Spanish mackerel.

"Fishing the birds" is a summer staple along the Louisiana

coast. Find some terns smacking the water, head over, and start casting under them. It's one of the surest ways to catch trout down here. Which reminded me—*something* was causing all these little swirls and eruptions under these terns. I splashed ashore.

"Chris, Rick!" I yelled. "See those birds? Something's ripping up the baitfish out there—trout or Spanish!"

I grabbed a light-action spinning rod, and the three of us waded out, casting plastic coca hoes around the little swirls and splashes atop the swells. Every now and then a fish would leap completely out of the water. "Looks like Spanish mackerel!" Rick yelled, just as his reel started singing.

"Yeah, that ain't no trout." I said. "Lookit him go . . ." and *wham!* just then my lure stopped in mid crank. I lifted the rod high and rared back. "They're HERE!" And another Spanish went on a spool-sizzling run. I held the rod high, letting the little silver rocket run, savoring every sizzling second. And speaking of sizzling, wait till we get his fresh white fillets, drizzled in lime juice and sprinkled with garlic powder and creole seasoning into some sizzling butter atop the fire tonight.

I tightened the drag a bit to slow him down. These fish are unreal. With their savage strikes, frantic runs, and sheer line-stripping power, any two-pound mackerel shames any four-pound. speckled trout. It's no contest.

"Trout over here!" Rick was shouting as he lifted his rod with one arm and lunged with his landing net with the other.

Soon we had five people wading and casting. The action stayed hot for a half hour or so, about half trout and half Spanish, with a few ladyfish and jacks mixed in. Then the school moved on.

So I hobbled back under the tarp and dug in Don's cooler for a cold Bud.

Don walked over. "Man, right after you fell asleep I was wading to the boat to get the grill," he chuckled, "and so I look down and this freakin' stingray is right in fronta me! Another step and he mighta got me. I came back, got the gig and wacked him. Then we saw you squirming around over there on your cot and Pelayo got this great idea and I said, 'why not?'"

"Very funny . . . good move. How 'bout the afternoon dive?" I said, then guzzled again.

"I know Chris, Bob, and I are going . . . y'all up for another one?"

"Damn right we are . . . let's go. Y'all brought our extra tanks, hunh?

"Yeah, sure, they're still in the boat. One of 'em almost broke my ankle when we went aground on the 'Born to Run' run—but we got 'em. And oh . . . check this out."

Don was digging something out of his shorts pocket. "A few of those chicks were walking the beach while you were sleeping," he mumbled. "Shoulda seen *that* shit. They'd been fishing again, having trouble with the spool on one of the reels, huge tangle. We went over and helped them out." He held out a business card of some type. "Bananarama," it said. It showed a drawing of a lovely lass with dreamy eyes peeling a banana; in the corner was a phone number.

"Escort service?" I asked.

"Exactly," Bob snorted from behind. He was dripping, blowing his nose, just in from the water. "Shoulda seen these broads. They're *gorgeous* man. Like the ones in Rick's Cabaret, not the ones at the Shobar or Papa-Joe's. I mean, these ain't no bow-wows. High-caliber shit, my man. Those service companies know how to take care of their customers, all right. You know that 'customer-focus' bullshit we keep hearing about in sales meetings? Well, whoever owns or rents that houseboat takes it *seriously*."

"And guess *what?*" Don whispered. He moved in close, a weird look on his face. *"They invited us over tonight."*

"Good God," I snorted.

"Yeah!" His face was aglow. "Invited us aboard. They have a chef out there, open bar . . . everything. Just like your brother said, but for some reason he's not real hip on going."

"I'm game!" I quipped.

"Same here!" Bob laughed.

Pelayo and Paul had just walked up. "We'll be out there tonight, alright. They say most of their *clients* are leaving this evening. They've been out here three days. Say they're tired."

"Oh, they're tired all right." Don quipped. "Tired of kneeling in front of old, potbellied yokels with snakeskin cowboy boots and Rolexes."

"Yeah, sure." On-the-Ball said. "Now they're ready for more debonair types," he smirked. "Casanova types. I don't know, man," he shrugged, "but they sure seemed friendly. Maybe they think we're rich or something. Well, y'all ready for another dive? Let's go, it's almost four o'clock."

Eight

CHUNKS OF FLESH

The Gulf was much friendlier for the afternoon dive. We roared over the gentle swells at a good thirty-five miles per hour, heading towards shallower rigs about ten miles northeast of the island. Pelayo, Paul, Tom, and I led the way in Pelayo's boat. Chris, Don, and Bob were blazing alongside in Don's boat. Then they angled in close, like on another "hey-hey-hey" run. Don't tell me they're into the rum already, I thought.

Instead they pointed towards a set of rigs to our left, waved, and veered off. We waved back and nodded. "Pompano rigs," Paul said. "Don and Chris nailed a pile of them last year right there. Remember? Guess they're hoping for a repeat."

Amazing how often that happens to us. We've been at this for fifteen years now and keep a log. It's almost scary how it shows the same species of fish on the same dates at the same rigs year after year after year. We even started naming the rigs after fish. "Pompano rigs, cobia rigs, mangrove rigs, and the ever-popular hammerhead rigs."

We were definitely pumped. Conditions looked ideal. The

morning dive had taken the edge off for me. I couldn't wait to get down there, but Tom looked worried; *his* dive hadn't gone as smoothly. And now, for some reason, he kept bringing up sharks. I was almost sorry for subjecting him to the Routine. It seemed to have affected him, even after we laughed it off.

On the island while I'd been snoozing under the tarp he'd been wade fishing with Glen, hearing about the shark that grabbed his stringer of trout while he was wade fishing last year. Probably bullshit. Glen probably forgot to tie the damn stringer and it slipped off. But to hear him tell it, he was almost dragged to his doom, pumping and clawing frantically as the sixteen-foot hammerhead tried to drag him to a watery grave.

Lots of speculation about that story. Like most of us, Glen's in sales. But he's one of those that's *always* at the top. He's got more bullshit than Joe Isuzu. And he was fishing alone during the famous shark incident, so no one *saw* it. But we sure heard about it, and it was enough to scare a little curiosity into one of us in particular.

"*Forget* sharks!" Pelayo finally blurted at Tom, who kept asking about them. "They *won't* bother you! It's all bullshit! We were bull-shittin' ya this morning . . . geezum! How many times we gotta tell ya?" He glanced at me, nodding and rolling his eyes. "Just watch out for the triggerfish—vicious little bastards."

Tom turned away with a bent smile. "Triggerfish?" he muttered. He looked at me with a feeble smile, shrugged, and turned his gaze back to the dolphins frolicking off the bow. Dolphins do it every time—especially for beginners. You see those dark gray shapes, those fins poking out of the water . . .

"Cut him some slack." I barked at Pelayo. "Shit, remember when we started diving?" I turned to Tom smirking. "We were scared shitless. Remember?" I turned back to Pelayo. "We were asking Buzzy and Floyd the same questions—almost word for word. But they were more patient."

"Patient, huh?" Pelayo huffed. "Patient? That's not what I remember. They were trying to scare the hell out of us. Telling us all those bullshit stories about shark attacks, about Floyd getting nailed from behind and losing half his ass. Then who was the other one? Oh yeah, Terry beating one off with his spear gun and getting his shoulder ripped open, showing us the scar and every-thing . . . come to find out that night that the scar was a mortar wound from 'Nam."

It worked. Both Pelayo and Tom were smiling again. "No shit, Tom," I continued. "Pelayo's right. Forget sharks. We'll probably see a few, but they never get close. But again, watch them trig-gerfish."

Tom's face was creased with a wise-ass smile. "Triggerfish, hunh?" he chuckled. "Yeah boy, I'll sure watch out for *them!*"

He figured we were using triggerfish on him like Buzzie and Floyd had used sharks on us. He figured this was another bull-shit story like this mornings' Routine. And he wasn't about to fall for it again. "Do they take me for an idiot?" he was probably thinking. "What could be crazier? Trying to scare me with a god-damn aquarium fish?" Grey triggerfish rarely grow over fifteen inches long. Goofiest looking fish in the water. "Fudpucker," they call him in Florida. Even named a restaurant chain after him in Destin. Their logo shows a harmless, bucktoothed, cross-eyed lit-tle buffoon of a fish.

Actually, I couldn't blame Tom. Like all of us, he'd tuned to the Discovery Channel two nights ago. Happens every year. Their "Shark Week" coincides with our Breton Island Blast. What tim-ing. It's hell on beginners. All those great whites lumbering around, smashing into cages, ripping leg-sized hunks of flesh from some mangled goat carcass. Those cruel hooded eyes, all those teeth. Then that bimbo in a steel mesh wetsuit that looks like something out of *Monty Python and the Holy Grail*, waving dead fish around in a middle of a shark feeding frenzy. One final-ly obliges by grabbing her arm, then almost yanking it off at the socket. Then another one grabs her head and almost twists it off. Then everyone gasps back on board about her close call.

Good TV, all right. But all that contrived drama distracts new rig-divers from the *genuine* perils under a rig, from *genuinely* dangerous fish, from fish that don't require any tricking or goad-ing to chomp on a diver.

Tom was learning the hard way. I could tell because underwater, a howl appears as a huge cloud of bubbles. Judging from the size of the cloud, Tom must really have been screaming. I wasn't actually able to hear him because of the rumbling from the rig, but I bet I could have if he'd been thirty feet closer . . .

A few seconds ago he'd been swimming over to show off his first fish of the day, a nice snapper, nailed with his spanking new spear gun. Now, however, the snapper was in shreds, and Tom was swinging his gun around him like a crazed samurai while bubbles spewed from his regulator in enormous clouds. About a dozen blood-crazed triggerfish had him cornered against a beam. He'd be out of air in five minutes at this rate, I figure.

In truth, for sheer fish life, the scenery under an oil platform surpasses anything in the Caribbean. The panorama simply staggers. I've seen divers fresh from Cayman's Wall surface from under a rig too wired on adrenaline to do anything but stutter and wipe spastically at the snot that trails to their chin. I've seen an experienced scubababe fresh from Belize climb out from under a rig gasping and shrieking at the sights and sensations, oblivious to the sights and sensations she was providing with her bikini top near her navel.

I've seen the less venturesome surface and vow never to rig-dive again.

It's all in the eyes—the *eyes.*

With schools of spadefish, bluefish, mangroves, and red snapper finning around, we felt on top of the food chain—Tom certainly did. Even the little (six-foot) blacktip shark we saw on the outside of the rig kept his distance. He circled the rig politely, even after Pelayo enticed him with the thrashing amberjack on the end of his shaft.

Pelayo was still tussling with his AJ on the opposite end of the rig when I noticed Tom extending his spear gun downwards. Focusing, I saw a school of circling snapper right above the silt layer. *Schlink!* went Tom's gun, and the snapper went berserk at the end of the shaft. No kill shot there, I thought. Tom pulled the cable in and grabbed the snapper through the gills like an old pro. I pumped my fist in his direction in a mock high-five.

Tom was waving the snapper in my direction and doing the OK

signal with the other hand as he finned over to show me the prize. He seemed jaunty, pumped. The water was gorgeous, the scenery spectacular. Fish were everywhere. Rig diving was everything we'd promised.

He didn't see the school of triggerfish closing on him from behind. He slowed down to adjust his grip on the snapper's gills, and they surrounded him. They went for the snapper first, like always. But I knew it was just an appetizer. Tom didn't seem too concerned at first. He slid the snapper off the shaft with one hand while shooing them away with the other.

Nothing doing. They wouldn't shoo. Three of them ripped into the snapper right at the spear hole and chomped off chunks of meat in a burst of scales and tattered skin. Now came another. And another. In seconds I lost sight of the snapper as a pack of ravenous triggerfish ripped into the mangled carcass, covering it completely, like a pack of starving wolves on a hamstrung moose.

Fish blood stained the water. A cloud of scales, skin, shredded snapper flesh, and little gray triggerfish all but obscured Tom, who wouldn't let go of his snapper. More trigs converged on the feast from every corner of the rig. Their frenzy was starting, and I knew Tom was recalling our banter on the boat. "Geezum!" he was probably thinking. "It's true! I'm in a goddamned school of salt-water piranha!" That was my reaction almost twenty years ago. But nobody had warned me.

Tom had much more meat on him than a ten-pound red snapper. His turn would come. I finned over to join the fray and started swatting and poking with my spear gun as Tom flailed and punched around him, dropping his spear gun in the process—a spear gun he'd neglected to attach to his waist with the cord like we'd advised repeatedly. He didn't seem to notice, so I plunged after it and left him to fend for himself.

I snatched the gun five feet above the murk, in an ear-popping dive, saving Tom 150 bucks. But now I was wondering if I could save *him*. Custer had better odds at Little Big Horn. Still more triggerfish joined the melee from all sides. Must have been two dozen now. Their little pig-eyes twirled crazily, flashing with blood lust, as their buck-fangs nipped, slashed, and reduced the snapper to a tattered mass of skin, bones, and scales. Still Tom refused to part with it. It was the principle of the thing, dammit. His first fish out here.

An inexperienced diver looking at Tom right now might think he was waving. I knew better. That's the motion of a hand that's felt a hot stove, or a poorly placed hammer blow . . . or a triggerfish's teeth. Yep. That huge cloud of bubbles erupting from Tom's regulator confirmed it. He was trying to swat at them with his uninjured hand, but then another triggerfish grabbed *that* one. Now Tom was waving *that* hand around, with *the triggerfish still attached.*

The triggerfish's fangs were caught in the glove webbing. Tom was trying to pull him off with his previously-bit hand but one nipped that thumb and he started the waving routine again, with the other triggerfish still yanking away at his other hand. Oh, for a video camera.

My swatting and poking availed little. We're talking a full-fledged feeding frenzy here. Tom's lesson was coming, with a vengeance. He jerked his head sideways and his hand shot to his ear, rubbing and tugging frantically at his earlobe. The clouds of bubbles spewing around him almost looked like a blown regulator hose.

Again, I knew better. It was just his lung-emptying howls of terror and confusion spawning those bubbles. Nothing like a human earlobe to titillate a hungry triggerfish. That morsel of tender pink flesh jutting out from under the mask strap drives them to a tooth-popping frenzy. And nothing, but *nothing*, so terrifies a veteran rig-diver like the *thomp-thomp!* of triggerfish teeth popping at your ear.

The sound didn't scare Tom, though. At first he didn't know what it meant. That's normal. First time you hear it, you're never scared. You're confused. What the hell's that? you think. Did I pop a strap or a hose? Then you turn and look into that little bucktoothed fucker's face, his eyes twirling crazily, dinky little fins going a mile a minute.

Still you're confused. Your hoses and straps look fine. You don't associate the sound with the fish. And the fish looks harmless and stupid. It makes no sense. So you turn back. Then, *"OOWW!"*—he takes a chunk out of your earlobe. Mercifully,

Tom's was a small triggerfish, maybe a foot long, and it took a chunk commensurate with his mouth size. Tom's ear was bleeding, but he'd heal quickly. His lobe was still there, minus a little skin.

After this he'll learn to associate the distinctive sound of triggerfish teeth popping underwater with the horror of facial mutilation. A shark might lacerate a leg or an arm. You see the pictures all the time. Some poor surfer or abalone diver with a line of black stitches across an arm or torso. Nothing like that from a triggerfish.

Hideous. Simply hideous. Short earlobes are almost the distinguishing mark of a veteran rig-diver. A few nips out of the upper ear are also dead giveaways. At weddings, funerals, graduations, and other such wearying affairs, especially of distant friends or relatives, I always study the male earlobes around me in hopes of finding a kindred spirit. Mutilated ears usually mean an engaging conversation on a topic of mutual interest. Even better, we usually clear out anyone around us in short order. Ear mutilations serve as a badge of honor at dive club gatherings in Louisiana—a Purple Heart of sorts.

After you feel the first bite, the sight of a triggerfish near your face chills the very bowels. It's the most dreaded sight in the Gulf. Forget all that buncombe on Shark Week. Forget all those menacing *Jaws*. With sharks you never see the one that hits you anyway, or so I hear. With triggerfish you see everything, almost in slow motion. It moves in stealthily, in plain view, usually with a gang, like a pack of hyenas surrounding a lame wildebeest. They circle you first, looking you in the eye, sizing you up, looking for any exposed tidbit. Nothing sneaky about them.

Tom was looking at three of them, hovering around his face right now. *Jab!* I poked the closest one away with the point of my gun. But it circled back in seconds, positioning it for another chomp at Tom's ear. Once they get a taste, earlobes are like potato chips to a triggerfish. They can't eat just one.

A triggerfish is about one-third mouth—mouth muscles, actually. His eyes lie almost in the middle of his body. Everything in front of them is mouth muscle. These muscles converge on a little pout of a mouth—a harmless, even ridiculous, little orifice. It compares to a shark's or barracuda's toothy maw about like an armadillo's mouth compares to a wolf's. But the little fangs within are as sharp and cruel as anything sprouting from that shark or barracuda.

Halfway into a keg at a dive club meeting once we speculated that the creators of *Alien* might have used a triggerfish's teeth as a model for their creatures. When that slimy big-headed sucker opened his maw and those teeth jutted out my first reaction was: "Geezum, almost as bad as a triggerfish's!" To scale, a triggerfish's fangs are powered by about five times the muscle as a shark's. A shark bites, then shakes vigorously to shear off a mouthful with his saw-edged teeth. A triggerfish bites, and— *chomp*, that's it. Like pruning shears, off comes a chunk of flesh, an earlobe, a fingertip, a tidbit of thigh, of calf, of shoulder, of cheek and, oh yes . . . of *scrotum*.

I kid you not. Verified by three sources, including the victim. But he was asking for it. A veteran diver already when it happened, and *still* clipping fish around his waist. A fish clip is like a huge safety pin that you attach to your weight belt. You spear fish and stick them on through the gills where they flap around enticingly as you fin around. Do this in the vicinity of triggerfish and you're setting the table for a triggerfish banquet alarmingly close to extremely sensitive anatomical regions. Considering the location of the clip, it's like asking for that brief surgical procedure required of male opera sopranos in Renaissance Italy or harem guards in Ottoman Arabia.

Most of us escape with a few scars on our thighs or buttocks and learn our lesson. Chris wasn't so fortunate. He says he was swatting away at a triggerfish that was shredding a pompano on his clip when he felt the bite and howled.

Bob quickly swam over. He was sure Chris had blown a regulator hose. He said he'd never seen such volume of bubbles from exhaling before. Then he thought Chris might be having an appendicitis attack from the way he was doubled over. Then he saw the culprit dangling between his legs, tugging away.

"I couldn't laugh!" he says. " God, I wanted to—but I just couldn't. It was horrible! Chris was kicking and poking, all doubled over, bubbles everywhere. So I started poking at the damn triggerfish with my gun, but Chris almost strangled me. I though he was gonna shoot me! What happened was, the freaking fish wouldn't let go! Every time I jabbed it he just bit down harder and my jab caused him to pull harder on Chris's balls! Geezum, I didn't know what to do! We finally swam up together. He got out the water with the goddamned thing still hanging from his crotch! Terry and them were going crazy on the boat when they saw it. But when Chris yanked off his mask they saw his face, heard his screams, and stifled the laughter somewhat. We had to pry the fucker's jaw open with a dive knife. It was unbelievable. Turned out Chris was lucky. It was a Main Pass dive. The water's always cool in that area because of the currents, so his balls were shriveled. The triggerfish only grabbed skin, and didn't take much with him."

Nothing like that for Tom—yet. Now he was back to swatting with his spear gun; now he was reaching behind himself and clutching a buttock. I finned closer, jabbing away at the marauders and saw that one somehow was attached to his butt. Yes, of course, here's the one drawback to our bogalee wet-suits (old disco clothes). A trig's teeth can get caught in the fabric. With a normal wetsuit, they bite and rip off a chunk of the foam suit. With ours, their teeth get entangled in the polyester fibers. Then they try to disentangle their teeth, can't, and chomp back down, and again, "OW!" Of course, down here it comes out in a cloud of bubbles as "brulll! brulll!" complete with bucking motion.

What a scene. I was about to jab at the butt-biter, then remembered Chris's ordeal. Did I want Tom to lose a chunk of ass? Then I saw the pants seat bulging out. The triggerfish didn't have his ass now, just his pants. *WHACK!* I poked him with my point and actually impaled him. The bastard *still* wouldn't let go. I grabbed him by the tail and yanked. Nothing. We couldn't shake him loose!

Now Tom was back to tugging at his ear—his other ear this time. Then he jerked his butt inward. The trig on his butt must have bit down again. I grabbed the triggerfish again by the tail and pulled. This way I could at least keep him from biting Tom's buttock again. With a firm grip on the triggerfish with one hand and my spear gun in the other, I motioned for us to go up.

Looking around, I saw Pelayo as a faint bubble-spewing blur on the opposite side of the rig, oblivious to our plight.

We started swimming up with me holding the triggerfish away from Tom's butt. What a scene. Halfway up I dropped the spear gun to dangle at my side and reached for my dive knife. Tom looked back, his eyes bulging in his mask. I nodded, trying to calm him. He nodded back. I started prying the little bastard's mouth open, working the blade between those locked fangs. Incredible, the power of these little suckers' mouths. A piscine version of a pit-bull. Worse, actually. A pit bull's jaws aren't designed to crush mollusks.

I finally sprung his teeth and he immediately turned around and clamped onto my sleeve. I jabbed him twice with the knife near the eyes and he finally let go. He swam off clumsily, sideways. His blood-crazed gang noticed and converged around him. They could tell he was wounded. A little tatter of flesh hung from his eye, and one of his comrades moved in for a bite. Now another joined, and another.

I tapped Tom on the shoulder and pointed, just as two others attacked. They'd rip him to pieces within half a minute, I figured, as I finned towards the surface. Tom looked over, arched his eyebrows jauntily inside his mask, and shook his gloved fist at them.

At a recent Grand Isle rodeo it was the non-diving sightseers gawking at the sharks. It always is. They ooohed and aaahed. They marveled in horror at the teeth, they touched them, they teased their kids about *Jaws*—the whole bit. Bona-fide rig divers were crowding around a fouteen pound triggerfish. The fish was barely two feet long, but it sent shudders of horror through the assembled crowd of divers.

"Hope you got a kill shot." Chris remarked.

"I wouldn't want that sucker on the end of *my* shaft alive!" Pelayo blurted.

A triggerfish is a genuine man-eater. He attacks you in order to rip off chunks of your flesh and swallow them. These little bastards attack divers with more gumption and ferocity than anything else in the Gulf. You'll search the dive and saltwater fish manuals in vain for any mention of the triggerfish's ferocity and appetite for human flesh. Indeed, you'll read about a clumsy, innocuous, goofy-looking member of the wrasse family. But you'll always read about sharks.

I know of exactly two divers bitten by a shark. I can't name a diver who *hasn't* been bitten by triggerfish.

I was afraid we'd never get Tom in the water again. But he laughed off the triggerfish assault as we motored towards some shallower rigs further north where we expected the murk to dissipate. We had about two hours of light left.

Sure enough, as we pulled up to one in about 70-foot depths we saw that the water was gorgeous. "Must be the currents," Pelayo remarked as we strapped on the gear. "There's no figuring them out."

"It's all that south wind," I said, as I waved to two rig workers staring from the railing above.

Tom was actually the first in the water this time. When I plunged in and focused he was halfway to the murk layer, 70 feet below. I admired his pluck. But I was taking my time, looking for cobia. They always hang out near the surface. I had a bird's eye view across the whole rig, but none materialized as I slowly descended towards the upcurrent side of the rig. Some large shadows seemed to hover around the beams in that area.

Finning closer I focused and—*yep*, sow snapper, a school of them. *Big snapper for this shallow water*, I thought, as I cocked an extra band. Thirty feet away I held my breath (no bubbles to spook them) and eased around a beam to ambush the closest and—fortunately—biggest one. When I came around he was staring straight at me from maybe ten feet. But I didn't have my gun up. I started raising it slowly, still holding my breath, and he turned to flee just as I crunched the trigger—*SCHLINK!*

Hit a little low. The dreaded belly shot. I hate that on snapper. That delicate flesh makes for a red snapper's exquisite flavor but doesn't hold up well to a spear point. They start spinning and thrashing, making that hole bigger and bigger, and before you get to him—*flup*, he's gone.

Perfect example here. He swam outside the rig when I hit him, and I followed, looking left, then right, then—*whoom!* a grey streak shot out from my right. What? A shark! Yes, a *real* one this time! A blacktip, about seven feet long. I froze in my—well, not exactly *tracks*—but I froze, just as he chomped into the snapper in a burst of silver scales and shredded flesh. He shook his head twice like a huge bulldog and zoomed off, leaving a cloud of scales and a pathetic little piece of snapper tail slowly drifting with the current.

Well, that takes care of *that*, I thought. Who *was* that masked fish? The shaft dangled below me now, and my pulse rate had definitely edged upward. It had happened so fast, I didn't have the chance to get seriously rattled—I was too stunned. Then I looked around to see if anyone had seen it—nope. Their bubble-lines were on the far side of the rig. Too bad. Dialogue is always more credible than a monologue when recounting these events, especially tonight around the fire.

Forget any more snapper around here, I thought. They shagged ass, along with everything else. For some reason I felt like following suit, so I descended to the very edge of the murk and started swimming upcurrent, towards the rest of the crew. Halfway to them, some grayish-white forms took shape just ahead of me; emerging, then sinking back into the murk. These snapper were bigger. No wonder Pelayo and them were over here. Geezuz, a whole school of sow snapper. And here was one coming around this beam. I lifted the gun and waited . . . *shluunk!*

Perfect. The old quartering away kill-shot: the shaft entered a little behind the gills and exited through the snout. He keeled over on his side motionless. I like this. No hassle fighting him. No chance of losing him as he thrashes against the cable tearing a big hole in his soft delectable flesh *again*—to become another shark or barracuda meal within the hour.

No sir. This one would be *my* meal, tomorrow night. Pelayo had already tied the bag to a beam in the middle of the rig. I grabbed the shaft and started swimming towards it when every-thing around me panicked.

I hate to see this. Schools of them—bluefish, hardtails, mangroves, even the lazy lumbering spadefish and sheepshead blazing by, finning frantically, eyes wide with fear. I started finning a little slower, focusing on a huge shadow I'd just noticed at the other end of the rig.

He was a huge gray blur at first, darting back and forth, nothing smooth or graceful or relaxed about his movements. Each dart would send another school of fish scurrying off. Each jerk sent a jolt of panic through the water and everything in it. I'd never seen a gray blur quite this big, especially at these rigs.

I got to the bag, focused better, and saw that he was a hammerhead. His girth was what alarmed me, as big around as an oil drum. Worse, he was erratic. From what I hear, this is when they're dangerous. But I knew there has never been an "unprovoked" shark attack on divers off our coast. Val Rudolfich, Johnny Bonck—guys with forty years of rig diving experience—all confirmed it. So what did I have to worry about?

For one thing, this was a hammerhead. You don't see these hanging up at dive rodeos—none this big anyway. None *half* this big. But you often see them on A&E's Shark Week. And they're always mentioned along with the great white, tiger, and bull sharks as potential man-eaters. This guy certainly seemed capable.

We'd seen hammerheads before. Sometimes they'd circle the boat while we were fishing. Sometimes they'd circle the rig while we dove. But those were smaller, eight to ten feet. Those seemed like harmless fish who'd had unfortunate accidents involving their heads as children and came out looking like the horrible results of some genetic experiment involving Whoopi Goldberg and E.T. Or maybe they didn't listen to their mothers and got their head caught under the leg of a spud barge while playing or something, I don't know.

But down here this sucker looked huge, burly, vicious, hungry, and positively evil—anything but comical. He didn't seem to want to enter the rig. I kept my eye on him as I fumbled with the bag.

I'd almost finished untying it when something jerked my shoulder. I gasped up a torrent of bubbles and turned around to see Pelayo pointing frantically at the brute, his eyes bulging in his mask, huge clouds of bubbles billowing from his regulator, his arms flailing in a frantic pantomime. I think he was trying to remember all the signals we'd learned during the certification course. But he looked like a traffic cop on fast forward. Above him I could see On-the-Ball and Tom heading up.

Anyway, Pelayo's point was unmistakable.There is a very universal type of signal involving the eyeballs: when the eyeballs are about three inches across and almost plastered to the front of the mask, the signal is quite clear—LET'S GET THE HELL OUTTA HERE!

"YES! YES!" I nodded in urgent agreement. "Certainly! I'm WITH YA! LET'S GO!" My own eyeballs felt like kiwi fruits. My stomach like a deep freeze. My bowels like giving up. We started finning for the surface. Halfway up we met with Tom who had a snapper on his shaft like a shish kebob. I pointed behind us. His eyeballs told me he caught on instantly. When I looked back I saw why. The sucker was following us!

I'd always had dreams about this sort of thing. You know, something's chasing you and you can't go fast enough. Now it was happening. So I decided not to look back anymore. Finally we hit the surface. Oh sure, they're "ambushers," I know all that, and he was now swimming normally, but he'd sure been excited before.

First thing we saw was a crowd of rig workers waving and yelling and pointing at us. We couldn't decipher the yells but had a pretty good idea. Pelayo was yelling, too, in between mouthfuls of Gulf.

"Shoulda seen him!" He gurgled. "Shoulda *seen* that big sucker!" Pelayo's eyes were wild. He was spitting out water, laughing, screaming. "He grabbed a freakin' snapper off my shaft! Right off, man!" Another mouthful of water. "And I was holding it! Right on the corner of the rig, man. Almost took my arm off! Scared the living hell outta me!" Pelayo was coughing and screeching. "I see this huge shadow come flying outta the murk— then I see that BIG UGLY HEAD! Five feet in fronta me, MAN!— then WHOOMM! He grabs the snapper, jerks it off the shaft! Scales, pieces of snapper all over the place! Like to crap in my disco pants, man! Who-wee!

We were all cracking up. "Bullshit, hunh?" Tom took out his regulator and spurted. "That stuff this morning about the hammerheads was all BULLSHIT?" He laughed and spurted. Pelayo's boat had a fantail that sat low to the water. This wasn't always an advantage. Today it was a heavenly sight. We hurled our guns, bags, whatever into the boat and lunged for the fantail, BC's and tanks still on.

Amazing what a little incentive and adrenaline does to the old muscles. A wife asks us to help move a sofa and we whine like it weighs two tons. Here, with almost full tanks on our backs, we sprang out of the water like young seals.

Now we could hear the guys on the rig. "Big shark! Right behind you!" They kept pointing, waving, gesticulating.

"Yeah!" We waved and nodded back. The sucker had followed us all the way up. Now it circled behind the fantail. Its top fin and tail jutted almost two feet out of the water as he lumbered around. We had a twenty foot boat—including fantail. So this sucker was at least fifteen.

Fact is, if he'd been bent on attacking, he had plenty of opportunities. He was obviously after the fish we were hauling up.

"First time, Tom," Paul said, while taking off his weight belt. "First time we've had one come this close. I swear."

Nine

BRETON ISLAND BLAST

"Red sky at night," they say. "Sailor's delight."

Too bad this sky was black and gray and lit up with flashes of lighting. The western horizon was ugly. "We're in for it tonight," Pelayo quipped as we idled into the back cove and prepared to anchor. "Lookit that stuff! Hey, On-the-Ball," he continued. "You *did* fix that rip in the tent, didn't you? Looks like we're in for a soaker tonight."

"With some nice lighting too . . . wow!" Just then the sky lit up and the ugly rumbling followed. BOOM-boom-boom, rumble.

"That low pressure system's just hanging around, I guess. Though it mighta cleared out from the looks of it this afternoon. No such luck."

Tom was silent. He has a fear of lighting that always struck me as irrational. For him, that is. I mean here's a guy who faced down Charlie in the jungles of 'Nam. What's a little lightning? Or so it seemed to me. Anyway, there was no choice but to press on. "Not much high ground on that island either, hunh guys?" I snapped.

"Hell no." Pelayo gasped. "Nothing at all. Not a damn tree or anything out here. We're the tallest things around . . . by a long shot."

"And the rods on our tents are all metal, hunh?"

"Every last one."

Tom caught on and started chuckling, but without much conviction. Then the sound took over, booming from the tent area this time. A '79 spring break classic, "I feel like BUSTIN' LOOSE! BUSTIN' LOOSE! Gimme de bridge—NOW!" Ah, yes, Chuck Brown and the Soul Searchers.

"Talkin' bout BUSTIN' LOOSE," we chimed expertly on the last stanza.

Chris and Don were already in from their dive and feeling festive, from the looks of events near the fire. "Y'all nailed 'em?" I asked, as we shuffled up.

"Talkin' 'bout, Bustin' LOOSE!" was the only reply. Their eyes were intense. Don held up The Perfect Woman by the neck and he and Rick bumped her hip from opposite sides with every "BUSTIN'!"

Then Chris jumped out from behind the tent, pumping his fists in the air with every "bustin'" and squatting down with every "LOOSE!" And sporting a gigantic Rasta wig. The thing was hideous. We burst out laughing. Rick was boogie-ing and bellowing along. I noticed an empty rum bottle in the fire. Rational conversation was pointless for the moment.

"Any fish—any big ones?" Tom asked while rooting for beers in an ice chest. His shorts were riding down in the back. Paul pointed and laughed. "Remember Dan Akroyd?" he gasped. "Remember the refrigerator repairman?"

A dead ringer indeed. But Tom was oblivious. He chucked me a can. I popped it open and drank greedily. "And here . . ." he chucked another over to Pelayo who missed it. The Bud thudded against his shoulder, then rolled in the sand.

"Hey!" he jumped, suddenly clutching his shoulder.

"Sorry, man." Tom smiled. "Hey, On-the-Ball!" Tom shouted to Paul, who was changing his shorts. "Ready?" He held up a Bud.

"Freakin'-Aay!"—and he caught it in mid air.

"We did all right," Chris finally blurted, shaking his dreadlocks. "Got this freakin' thing in Jamaica." he gasped, winded from all that bustin' loose. "When Cindy and I went on that cruise during Easter. It was the only way to get rid of em. Geezuz, those natives drive you crazy over there. Following you around, pawing Cindy, wanting to braid her hair. She was getting scared. Finally I gave the guy twenty dollars for this thing and he ran off . . . well worth it."

I followed him back out to their boat, where he lifted the ice chest lid. "Yep, a nice haul," I nodded. The box was crammed with nice mangroves, triggerfish, a couple of pompano, a beautiful grouper, too.

"Who's the chick?" I asked as we splashed back. I'd seen her on the chair near the fire. At first I'd thought it was the Perfect Woman. Then I saw her moving. She was well-tanned.

"The little quadroon?"

"I guess," I said. "The one the one with the bikini top and shorts over there . . . why? Ya mean there's more than *one*?"

"There's two," Chris chuckled. "They're cooks and clean-up girls on the house barge. They're *not* part of the other group. Boy they stressed *that*. So *don't* forget. They're pretty sensitive about it. That outfit has a full-service operation though," he laughed. "Fish-cleaning, cooking, cleaning—everything. Oughta hear these chicks," and here he imitated a black accent: "Shoot man, we does everythang but wipe their butts."

"Customer focus," I quipped, affecting the lisp of an old sales manager of ours, a flaming bull-fruit who spent all of one month on the street actually selling, but who mouthed all the thrice-hyphenated buzzwords with true conviction, loved paperwork, and was perky at all meetings.

"Yeah-yeah," Chris smirked. "Anyway, they've been out here about an hour. We saw 'em fishing when we pulled up after the dive. We invited them over for a drink, maybe a dance. Real nice chicks. Already tidying up the campsite. Oughta look inside the tent. Looks like an army barracks. We're gonna pitch in with a few bucks for 'em, give 'em some fish, too." Chris's eyes shifted over my head for a second.

"Woooh!" something cold on my bare back. I turned around and there she was. The little quadroon, bikini-topped, her red fingernails around a tall, sweat-beaded plastic cup. She was smiling away. A genuine smile, too.

Here was a doll, her wavy black hair in a ponytail, green eyes, caramel skin. An orange bikini top straining against two coconuts. She was short but curvy, big hips and ass. She pointed with her chin behind me and giggled. "Guy over there says you like these?"

I reached for the cup and turned around to see Don, holding up a bottle of Bacardi. "Ye-AH!" I yelled. "Thanks darling!" and I guzzled. Man, how that rum and coke hits the spot after an afternoon of beer. First on the palate, then three gulps later the buzz starts, with all that caffeine and fizzle.

"The Cuervo Gold!" someone yells from my right. And there's Rick, standing on an ice-chest, taking a chug. He finishes just in time to join the rest of us in the second stanza: "The Fine Co—lombian!"

And yep, there's Bob, right behind him, holding up a doobie. "Make tonight a wonderful thing! Say it again!"

We don't miss a beat. This is the theme song from Chris's two-day bachelor party in 1980. Held right here on Breton Island, by the way.

Gene and Glenn are two buddies that we hang with during the Rodeos. They had passed on the afternoon dive, choosing to stick around the campsite. Glenn fished, with the occasional nip no doubt. Gene, from the looks of it, mostly nipped with an occasional cast. He was never much of a diver anyway, or fisherman, or hunter—more of a "social sportsman." He came along for the ride with his chums. He usually sits around the campsite drinking and cooking and stuff. I think his best spear fishing bag was three triggerfish; never has shot a deer. But he never misses a trip.

Chris snickered as Gene staggered by, enveloped in rum fumes. "*Lit* up," Chris whispered with an eye-roll. Then he turned around, caught Pelayo and Paul's attention with a wave and a whistle, and pointed back to Gene, who was bent over, grabbing a tent cord with one hand while he poured from his half-gallon of Bacardi into a forty four ounce big-gulp cup with the other. His head swayed, his enormous torso jerked spastically every few seconds (hiccups). The man had put on weight massively of late.

Could it be? Was this the same "Gene-Gene the dancing machine?"—or "*Mat-cheen?*" My parents dubbed him thusly at my twentieth birthday party, if memory serves. They came home from their friend's party to find their den and living room a swirling, bumping, gyrating mass of boogie-ers. The very house shook from the feverish disco beat.

Gene, as usual at the time, was stealing the show—his legs a blur, his knees rubber, his hips seemingly hinged with ball-bearings. He spun the lovely dark-eyed Gina like a top, caught her in his arms, jerked her onto his shoulders. Barry White was their favorite music. "Gene Kelly," my parents finally explained. "Your friend's another Gene Kelly!" The name stuck. For a while there, Gina and Gene seemed bound for the altar.

Now look at him. Still single, with the silhouette of Barry White—almost. Also, Barry still has hair. Gene's started thinning during LSU. Now his head looks like Danny DeVito's. We'd been mocking him mercilessly. "Mr. Manatee" we yelled when he hit the water around lunch. Glenn, his fraternity brother while at LSU, attempted to defend him. "He ain't heavy," he'd say draping his arm around Gene's shoulder. "He's my brother!"

Sounds stupid, I know. But after six beers it slayed us every time, especially when Gene's had twelve. Later he'd been laying near the water and we all came up and plopped around him, then started writhing around, snorting, bellowing, covering ourselves with sand, mimicking those elephant seals on the Discovery Channel. He laughed and joined in, moving his arm like a big flipper and bellowing heartily. It was early yet.

Now he was bent over, eclipsing a hefty portion of skyline while pouring his next drink—but vainly. Half the rum spilled on the sand. Hopefully that's where most had gone, because the bottle was half empty—a half-gallon, no less.

A horrible feeling, we knew it well. Gene had probably peaked an hour ago. The buzz was backfiring now. No more giddiness. You close the eyes and the head starts spinning. Too late to cut down now, you went over the hump. You blew it. No more fun. Now eat something, take two aspirin, and zonk out.

But he wasn't having that. He wanted that buzz back, dammit. Another eight ounces of rum or so, mixed with ten of Diet Coke. Now some ice . . . a little more rum . . . ah, yes . . . "Whooh!" he yelled with his first sip. A little more Coke? Hell no! He grabbed the rum bottle again and splashed in another four ounces or so, and about ten on his arm.

"This oughta be good," Pelayo looked around and smirked. Gene didn't hear him. We used to laugh at a friend in this condition, egg him on, spur him to more drinking and lunacy, then stand back for the show. But something about Gene's face stifled us, though none of us was purely sober at the time.

"Hey, Gene!" Paul shouted, holding out a package he'd just pulled from the cooler. "How 'bout some salami?"

"Yeah!" The houseboat gals added. "Eat something . . . you should eat something." Paul had been talking up Missy and Nicole (their names, I finally learned) since we came in from the evening dive, sitting on his cooler, one on each side. Pelayo kept pointing at him and smirking. "Yeah, Gene" Glenn added. "Genoa salami and provolone cheese. It's dynamite. I ate half this afternoon while On-the-Ball was diving."

"You shyster bastard!" Paul snapped while looking in his bag, then around at us with a mock frown. "I thought this felt a little light."

"I *hate* salami!" Gene shrieked. He tried to stand up—but too fast, and staggered back against the tent, which gave. A stake pulled out of the sand and Gene fell backwards, the tent collapsing around him as we exploded in mirth.

"Earthquake!"

"Aw, shit, man!" Gene bellowed from his resting spot. "Salami *sucks!* I *hate* freakin' salami, know that?" He was trying to change the subject and that made it worse. We cackled louder, forcing it now.

He was motionless, just lying on the tent, most of his drink splashed across his chest. "Wee!" He threw the cup towards us. "Drink up you buncha wussies! Yeah, I hate that salami—freakin' dago food! I hate dagos. They're oily and stupid. But they sure got nice asses. I like to use 'em for a pillow."

"Heeere we go," Chris sighed. (His wife's maiden name was Di Giovanni. Her first name Gina—yes, the *same* Gina. These inbred friendships have their drawbacks, too. No hiding the wild and wooly past.) Chris wasn't smiling. "Here comes Mr. *Under Control*," he sighed. His face was creased with a bitter smile. "The beast is emerging."

"What?" Gene jerked his head up. "The beast is emerging?" he looked straight at Chris, then around at us. *"The beast is emerging? What the fuck is that supposed to mean?"* He finally rolled over on his side, then jerked himself to a sitting position with a massive groan. "Hunh? What's that beast is emerging bullshit? Hunh? You see, Chris, that's the problem with you, buddy. Nobody ever knows what the hell you're talking about. *The beast is emerging . . . the beast is emerging . . .* see this?" He suddenly grabbed a spear gun point from his pocket and held it in the air, "See this?" he said, with a stupid look on his face. "This is *THIS!* This is *THIS!* What the hell's *that* supposed to mean?"

To paraphrase Maxwell Smart: "Ah yes, the old *Deerhunter* routine." Gene's favorite movie. We all saw it together the first time, then he went back three more times. Hunters ourselves, longtime friends ourselves, quite fond of removing our clothing and sprinting down the street stark naked during lengthy wedding receptions ourselves, the movie struck a chord. Actually, we were more prone to streaking at parties. God knows our wedding receptions were wild enough, and every bit as long as the one in *Deerhunter*. But, hell, there were family and "grown-ups" at wedding receptions. No, we'd wait for our parties or picnics for the streaking bit. Gina, a psychology major at LSU, always tried to read something into it: "latent homosexuality." All kinds of bullshit.

Anyway, we always cackled at that scene with Cazale and De Niro—"This is *THIS!* This is *THIS!*" Gene had Cazale's monologue down perfect, even the very facial expressions. He was getting into it now, big-time. Strange, Gene seemed halfway coherent now. He seemed to sober up a bit. Always seems to happen during a psychic crisis. Like when you see those flashing red lights in the rear-view.

"See, Mikey," Gene continued. "Nobody ever knows what the hell you're talking about. This is *THIS!* This is *THIS!*" Then he held up the spear gun point just like De Niro shook the bullet. "One shot! One shot!"

Then his face hardened. "Mau!" Gene was on his feet now, squinting. "MAU!" Geez, I thought. He's going into the full routine. The russian Roulette scene and everything. "MAU!" He lumbered over to where Chris was sitting on the ice-chest and bent down to get, in his face.

We were helpless with laughter, but Chris's smile was bent. He looked around, sighing, nodding, trying to smile. "Gene, you crazy fuck."

"MAU!" Gene yelled, inches from his face. "MAU!" And he pointed in front of him just like the Viet Cong pointed at the revolver in the movie.

"Mau!" Chris replied. "Heh-heh." But he wasn't smiling. He looked tense, beet red.

"MAU!" Gene screamed.

"MAU! MAU! MAU!" We all joined the chorus, Pelayo standing, looking around, waving his arms, getting everyone involved, trying to inject some levity into the scene. It was getting too tense.

Chris looked around at us, snickering, nodding, pointing at Gene. But Gene was having none of it. He kept at it, right in Chris' face. "MAU!"

"MAU! MAU!" Chris finally replied.

Then, *SMACK!* Gene whacked him across the head, knocking his cap into the fire.

Chris jumped up—Gene had his chin high, inches in front of Chris's face.

"Awl-right *guys*." Tom, not knowing the history or chemistry involved here, tried to intervene.

"Gu-*uys!*" Naturally the gals were upset. "Come *on*, guys. None of that stuff now . . . come on . . . be nice . . . y'all came out here to have fun."

The scene around the campfire reminded me of how I first met Chris. It was in the sixth grade. We were both new to St. Christopher's School that year and were the last ones picked for the football games during recess. We were picked for opposite teams and Chris ended up covering me as I went out for a pass. We were going all out, too, zealous rookies, anxious to prove our worth to the schoolyard veterans. He was on me like white on rice and batted down the ball just as I clutched it.

I was furious and smacked him. He smacked me back, and in seconds we were tumbling through the grass in double chokeholds. A crowd gathered. The prefects showed up, the assistant principals arrived, and we were hauled off by our ears.

First day in a new school and we're already in Principal Fontaine's office. But this was 1967. Fighting in the schoolyard was considered normal for boys. No need for sedation or therapy. This principal had a novel way of handling fights. He ordered us to report back to his office after school. And so we did, already colleagues of sorts. The principal walked us over to the gym, gave us boxing gloves and said to go at it. We laughed and batted at each other for a few minutes.

Shirley and I were recently called to our son's school for a grave and solemn talking to by the principal over an almost identical issue. When I suggested Mr. Fontaine's approach I was regarded like Benito Mussolini.

The Saturday after our introduction, Chris came over to the house, and along with Pelayo (who was over every weekend) we went popping rabbits and robins with our pellet guns. We've been at it ever since. Bonding, as males always have, first by fighting, then by killing things together.

Chris and Pelayo "The Prof" Pelaez went on to room together the first year at LSU. That was enough for the Prof—and that's how he got his nickname. He didn't really take to academia. We all worked offshore for oilfield service companies those mid-'70s summers, making a bundle. Pelayo was mechanically inclined and got himself promoted to where he'd be making more in those three months than most of the people we knew who'd actually graduated from college.

Chris and I went on to earn those invaluable Liberal Arts degrees while Pelayo became a certified electrician. Years later we all got our scuba certifications together, as usual. Here was another excuse to get together on a weeknight without the ole ladies and party afterwards. Well, Pelayo—the only one without a college degree—was the only one who could figure out the decompression tables. Thank God, too. We all copied from his paper.

The point is, however, that Chris was no chump. We'd all seen him tangle with bouncers in his day, the ones who look like the Rock. He had a great routine. He'd always catch the disco babes as they emerged (in groups of course) from the ladies' room. "See that person over there?" he'd say with a straight face while pointing to either Pelayo or me. "He's not a Puerto Rican girl. He's a Cuban guy. But he's still *dyyyy-yiiin' to meet-choo!*"

If (amazingly) this failed to charm their metalflake stockings off, Pelayo and I pressed home the attack. And using the same album. We wore "Some Girls" out that summer of '78. We'd totter over, medallions flashing, bell-bottoms billowing, and block their path. *"You pritty-pritty-pritty, pritty, pritty, pritty girl—pritty, pritty sucha pritty, pritty, pritty,girl . . . come on babe PLEEEASE make love to me . . . "*

A blocked windpipe cut it short one day. Two bouncers, alerted by their friends, burst upon the scene. The gorilla actually *lifted* me by my neck. Another had Pelayo's arm twisted behind his back like a pretzel. These guys didn't mess around. This was a classy disco, 4141, an uptown hot-spot, full of "uptown girls." We looked more like Billy Joel, "backstreet guys."

That Studio 54 bit about some bullfruit standing at the door and picking who could enter caught on in New Orleans, too. And we didn't have a prayer. So we snuck in through the kitchen. A friend who worked there helped with the caper. We were making a late-night delivery, you see, dressed in official Budweiser uniforms, courtesy of another chum who worked at a Bud distributor. We were "commandos." The boxes on our dollies didn't contain beer. They contained our disco clothes, in all their glory. Once inside, we scurried into a storeroom and changed. Then we emerged—*TA-DA!* The blast from a thousand trumpets wouldn't do justice.

Pelayo "El Guapo" Pelaez appeared in his magenta metalflake shirt and tangerine angel-flights that buttoned at the sternum and flopped in magnificent billows below. Mine were fire-apple red, to match the jewel in my medallion. Chris's were lime green, with an orange starburst shirt featuring silver lighting bolts. The whole package tottering on four in heels. We were a sight, wild and crazy guys. Dan Akroyd and Steve Martin had nothing on us, except maybe better taste in clothes. To think that two weekends in a row the doormen had somehow passed over such *magnificoes*.

We lasted about an hour. Then the fracas. In medieval history class I'd just been learning about the *garrotte*. Now I knew what it felt like. No air through my windpipe for about ten seconds. Frantic gasping and wheezing, arms flailing around helplessly like some rag doll. Then *WHACK!* and he dropped me, because *he'd* been smacked. Chris had blindsided the brute with a round-house right to the neck that staggered him. He dropped me and I landed on my knees, choking—almost puking. Since I was knee level as he turned around, I tackled him.

Brilliant move. He collapsed on me. Now I was pinned under his musclebound bulk. And now his partner started on my face with his jackhammer fists. I couldn't duck or dodge or move or anything. Ah, a night to remember. I mostly remember us wheez-ing and rasping at each other for about a week. That wasn't the worst of it. Pelayo started calling me "goldfish." You know, the ones in the aquariums at Chinese restaurants? Those huge black swollen eyes? That was me for about three days.

Tonight, on Breton Island, the more experienced, more mature Chris restrained himself. "That's nine bucks pal," he snapped, while rubbing the sting of Gene's blow from his head. "That's no chickenshit cap," he said, plucking it from the flames. "This damn cap's from the Polo Club in Jamaica. Some classy shit."

He picked it up, and avoided looking at Gene. "Well?" He looked around at us, perched in our chairs and atop the ice-chests. Nobody was laughing now. "Well, we going floundering or what? Who's going floundering? Don? Where's the gigs? And the lantern? No, Pelayo, not *your* lantern . . ."

The man was a pro—a true gentleman. No more ugliness; He didn't want to further screw up the trip with old squabbles. He was melting the tension with a jab at a hilarious incident from a little earlier:

Pelayo's Coleman lantern had already been blazing brightly from a pole. It's an antique. It illuminated the pages of *Playboy* magazines during our junior high–era campouts. Under its gut-tering glare we skinned rabbits popped neatly between their shinning eyes with pellet guns. We took turns shooting the rab-bits and holding the flashlight in mid-night forays away from the campfire and those *Playboy*s we'd snatched from under Chris's big brother's bed.

The lantern used liquid fuel and came with a little funnel to facilitate the pouring process. The little funnel was long gone, probably from about the time "Woolly Bully" was in the Top 40. We'd sing it while fleeing cops. "Whachit, now, WATCHIT! Here he come—here he COME!"

Yeah, some old lady always called the cops about some little punks shooting rabbits in her pea-patch at night. They'd show up and chase us, all right—all of about thirty feet. We'd scurry into the briars and be as safe as any rabbit. But rabbits don't taunt their pursuers. While the cops played their flashlight beams over the brambles and bellowed through their bullhorns, we'd switch to another favorite song at the time. I remember the day Chris bought the 45: Dave Clark Five's "Catch Us if You Can." But Dave Clark didn't add: "You fat assholes!" "You lazy blimps!" or "Come on fatso!" We wouldn't let up. Hey, after tangling with Castro's *milicianos*, these guys were a cinch.

Anyway, it took a steady hand to fill Pelayo's funnel-less lantern—*not* a hand attached to a body that was doing the Bump with a tent pole while David Bowie's "Fame" thundered from a boom-box ten feet away. Fuel had splashed everywhere. "FA—*aame!* Boomp-boomp." Some fuel seemed to make it into the lantern. Then he had to pump the thing with a little handle, back and forth, back and forth, back and forth. And finally, the match—*WHOOM!*

The fireball had probably illuminated Bourbon Street. Pelayo finally extinguished his mustache and eyebrows. But the smell of singed hair had hovered over us all night long.

The storm clobbered us an hour later, it hit fast and hit hard. The wind started, the sand started stung us. Then the icy rain, deafening thunder, and deluge. Aluminum chairs flying around, tarps flapping, making that popping sound, ready to shred. The thing clobbered us, man—no warning. Or maybe it *had* been warning and our campsite scuffle had distracted us. Whatever, not enough time for Missy and Nicole to make it back to their houseboat. No choice but to scurry into our tents.

"Y'all come in here," Chris said, waving from the front of his tent, which was the biggest, the main barrack, and the closest to where they'd been sitting with Paul. But they were scurrying alongside Paul, who was holding a towel over them. They made it to his small two-man tent and slithered inside. Chris pointed, "Lookit at that greedy sucker, with *both* of them. On-the-Ball, all right."

Five minutes later, a gust blew down the poles holding up the wires from the generators, and total darkness set in. And I mean total. A moonless night. The lightning was the only light at times, but not enough to let us see inside Paul's tent. Speculation ran rampant. Chris had the sense to bring in his bottle, and the details became more vivid and aphrodisiacal with each rum and Coke.

At six the next muggy morning I was thigh-deep along the back bay, casting a green beetle amongst the schools of mullet creasing the surface, and digging the terns, the pelicans, the occasional trout smacking my sparkling beetle—four were on my stringer—and especially the solitude, when a boat I didn't recognize entered the cove. Two people were on board, one of them waving frantically. The waver was female.

"Who in the hell?" I'm thinking. I couldn't place them until they got about one hundred yards out. Ah, yes, of course. Buzz and Jenny. I couldn't believe they'd made it. I wished they hadn't. I'd told them about this trip only because I'd bumped into them at Academy Sporting Goods. Never thought they'd show up. One of those "yeah sure, let's do lunch" type of things.

And there they go and show up. Friends of friends, actually, and the last among our crowd to get married—and only three years ago. They were always weird, God knows—raving eccentrics with family fortunes to dip into. Buzzy's new money and Jenny's uptown old. Happens that way in New Orleans a lot. Make that bundle in the suburbs, then start shmoozing for the social cachet in the city.

Old Man McKee, Buzzy's grandad, started an oilfield service company right after World War II, and sold it to a major during the last oil "slump." Buzzy had stayed on for a while as some kind of "manager" or "facilitator," then a "consultant," then left altogether. I'm not sure what he's into these days, but he sure isn't hurting for money. Jenny went to Tulane for about eleven years, if I recall. Finally ended up with some kind of degree—social work, poli-sci, communications, something utterly useless— unless she wants to sell. And she isn't about to soil herself in *that* racket.

Last time most of us saw them was at their bar shower. What a freak show. It was uptown, at some mansion belonging to a friend of Jenny's family. The place was crammed with dizzy, giggling, anorexic "debutantes." Or so they used to call them. Their eyes were uniformly glazed. Half the nostrils were inflamed. These weren't "southern belles." Remember, this is New Orleans. There are no "southern belles" in the usual sense of the term here. These are "uptown chicks." A breed peculiar to New Orleans old money. Two parts Valley girl, three parts Euro-trash and a dash of whoever sang "I'm with the DJ."

That was bad enough. Then our crew of drunkards wheeled in from the suburbs. Uptowners and Bogalees makes for a volatile brew. The place was awash in wine, scotch, tequila, rum, champagne, and God knows what else. Jenny and her friend Babs were the hit of the hot-tub, which was next to the indoor pool. They were the hit with some males, that is.

We heard their hands had roamed feverishly under all those bubbles. Their palms were soft, their fingers nimble, their aim expert—or so I heard. God knows those hands had never done any housework, or yard work. They were nimble nonetheless—so we heard. Rumors—never confirmed—of rampant fellatio also made the rounds. Quite a night and early morning.

In *Modern Manners* P.J. O'Rourke's rules for a "really good" party say that "no friendship or romantic relationship should survive a really *good* party." This one qualified with two dozen bells on. Towards midnight, married couples raved at each other at the slightest provocation. "This beer's hot, you stupid bitch!"

SMACK! "Eat shit, butthead! Then get your own fucking beer!"

"I would, but I wanted to see you take your tongue outta Al's mouth for two minutes."

"Oh yeah? And I suppose Babs really had to sit on your *lap*. That couch's only six feet long! Her tits make a hell of a chin rest, hunh?"

Utter shamelessness . . . rampant groping, co-ed bathrooms, mooning, flashing, sporadic skinny-dipping—and my favorite—women on our shoulders for the water volleyball, which despite our goading only featured occasional—rather than—total, top-lessness. The feeling was that here—for some reason—we could get away with it.

All that banter, all that hinting, all that innuendo from other boozy but more sedate gatherings uncorked here. All that exposed wet flesh stumbling around didn't help matters—or did, depending on your viewpoint. Same for the tequila shots, passed around on trays every ten minutes it seemed.

"Watch it, dude!" Someone would rasp. "That's my wife's face you just stepped on! And *my* ass you grabbed!"

"Hey!" someone else yells after a bite. "Great stuff here! Whaddayya call it?"

"A napkin." his mate answers.

I'll never forget Pelayo. "Hey, toots!" he kept calling to some chick named Meaghen—one of the few sober ones, if I recall. She always kept one of those "wraps" around her waist, so you could-n't see her butt cheeks peeking from under her suit—unless you *really* concentrated. She fancied herself a "management consult-ant" and kept using the words "proactive" and "empower." Words that, considering the tone and rhythm of the evening, seemed fabulously out of place. They always provoked a flurry of hidden snickers. Not so with Pelayo. He was up-front with it.

"Hey, TOOTS!" he'd bellow while hoisting his beer. "How 'bout *empowe-rrrring* yourself to be *PRO-active* and get me another beer! This one's running a *trifle* low," always followed by sucky, kissy noises.

Then he'd try to smile, but his florid face with the glazed, buggy eyes wasn't working right. He always ended up with a demented, psychotic leer that made anyone near him cringe and slink away. He had the poor girl—an out-of-towner from New Jersey, attending Tulane Law School no less—in tears midway through the night.

It was a mess. Too many people who didn't know each other and were in no mood to make friends that night. Everyone had a chip on his or her shoulder. The uptowners all had an attitude. They claimed we did too. So we kept drinking to compensate. And that made it worse. The booze backfired on us. Rather than make us witty and friendly it made us stupid and mean. Modes of communications deteriorated steadily through the evening. No point in trying to scream over the stereo. And hand signals didn't help much with everybody's eyes crossed. The party petered out near dawn and nearly everyone—intra- and inter-couple—parted on exceptionally ugly terms.

And *nary* a cop incident on any ride home. Not odd actually, after *uptown* parties. Then somehow by Mardi Gras everybody had made up. And Jenny and Buzz went through with the wedding two weeks later. And then—good God—that *reception!* But that's another story. Now I'm the lucky one to greet them.

"Hey, Buzz! Hey, Jen! Great to see y'all out here!" I lied as they rumbled up. "Never thought you'd make it."

Buzz was looking dapper in his sun shades. Jenny was all smiles in a killer bikini. "Nice out here this morning," she cooed. "Lovely weather . . . nothing like yesterday. We weren't sure we'd make it. Why don't ya come with us?"

"Where?"

"Out to the shallow rigs." Buzz pointed. "Hear they've been clobbering the cobia out there. Jenny"—he looked at her with a smirk—"wants to fight one . . . come on, we'll have ya back by the time the crew wakes up."

I looked around. Not a soul in sight. "Why not," I said. "But wait . . . lemme get my camera. I could use some good action shots, especially of a chick in a bikini."

The boat ride was delightful—the sun just cresting the eastern horizon, yellow rays peeking through the clouds and sending their shimmering blanket over the calm sound. We were humming along too—47 mph said the speedometer. In minutes Buzz hauled back about a hundred yards from the first rig.

"Humberto?" Jenny was waving a tube of suntan oil from the bow. "Could you?" and she pointed at her back.

"Yeah, sure," I replied gallantly.

"Ummmm," she cooed, shimmying her shoulders seductively as I worked the fragrant oil into her shoulder blades and lower back, even under the straps.

"Quite a thrill for a married man," I glanced at Buzz, Grouchoing my eyebrows as I rubbed away.

He just snorted. Not even a smile.

I went for the rig hook and stood on the bow as Buzz eased closer to the rig. The water was gorgeous. You could see fifty feet down the beams. The murk had vanished with the current. Mangrove, sheepshead, and spadefish everywhere. Then two dark shapes loomed near the surface on the left. "What the? Yep! Over there!" I shouted, pointing with the rig hook. "Cobia! Buzz—gotta be cobia! Two of 'em!"

"I see them!" Jenny shrieked. "Yes, oh my! They're really big! Hurry, Buzzy!"

Buzz was fumbling with the rod holders. "Goddammit Jenny! Didn't I tell ya to . . . " And he finally untangled one and looked up. "Where?" he yelled. "*Where?* Ah! Yeah, big!" and he cast a Magnum Green Cocahoe about twenty feet in front of the first one. Two reel cranks and the front one lunged forward—*WHOOM!* It nailed the lure and almost jerked Buzzy overboard.

"YEEaah!" Buzz reared back and roared as the thing took off like a crazed torpedo—and off, and off. There was no stopping it. It was a still, muggy morning. Buzzy was pumping away, grunting, pouring sweat, gasping. The thing was relentless. For every yard Buzz gained, the fish would strip off three.

"Here, Honey!" he called to Jen after about ten minutes of cranking and huffing. "Fight him for a while! You've always wanted to fight a big one, haven't ya?"

Jenny was stretched on the bow in her pink bikini, slathered in oil and sipping a wine cooler. "No thanks!" she chirped.

"All right, then *dammit!* Crank up the motor and let's follow him!" Buzz snarled. "I'm getting tired—and get the damn gaff ready!"

"I'll get it, Buzz," I offered. "I've gaffed my share of . . . "

"No!" he barked, pointing at me. "*You* get the pictures, Humberto. That's what you came for, *right?* Get some good action shots." Then he pointed at Jenny, his finger trembling and his knuckles white. "*She'll* gaff it. I'm sure she's good for *something.*"

Whoo boy, I thought. Getting edgy already. But she didn't seem annoyed, probably didn't hear him. Buzz lowered his hand, tightened the drag, and started gaining on the fish as Jenny got behind the console and started working the throttle. "Not so *fast,* dammit," Buzz growled. "I can't reel fast enough! And turn a little."

"Whoops," Jenny looked at me, giggling, covering her mouth the way women do when they smile or laugh. She eased back on the gas as Buzz pumped away at the slack. Finally we had the big brown brute lumbering at boat side.

"Gaff him, Jen!" Buzzy barked. "*Get* him, for God's sake!"

Jenny raced for the stern with a happy little whoop, grabbed the gaff, and started leaning over.

"NOT NOW!" he screeched. "Wait for him to get a little CLOSER! Geezuz!"

"Buzzy!" She shot back. "STOP screaming at me, you ASSHOLE! I'm *trying* to HELP!"

I was snapping pictures, thrilled by the show.

"Okay, okay . . . get ready," Buzz sputtered. The fish was coming up again. "Okay—now, now—NOW! GAFF HIM! GAFF the GODDAMN *FISH!!*"

Jenny lunged out, hitting the cobia with the blunt end. He jerked his tail, showering us with spray, and shot off on another spool-screeching run. "What the? WHOA!" Buzzy howled, shaking the water from his face and jamming the rod's butt between his legs. He held on with a two-fisted death-grip, grimacing and pouring sweat as the rod bowed and bucked. Almost looked like he was jerking off.

"DAMMIT, Jenny!" he shouted over the screeching reel. "You're WORTHLESS! Ya know THAT? You're fucking *worthless!*" He wiped his face with his shirt and spit over the side. "I don't know why in the hell I bring your *worthless* ass out here. You *hear* me? This is the last TIME! You hear me! The *LAST!*"

Jenny got up and turned around to face him. She glared for a second and lifted the gaff with a trembling arm while her lips tightened.

Christ, I said to myself. She's gonna gaff him.

But she threw the gaff—*CLANG!* against the metal railing and it bounced back, almost hitting me. I hopped aside just in time.

"*That's* it!" Buzz shouted. "Yeah that's it! GO ahead and gaff him! That's ALL we need! I guess that old woman you knocked down in the parking lot at the Daiquiri Shop wasn't *enough!* Let's get sued *again!* Sure, AGAIN! We can afford it."

"Damn right." I quipped. "I like this boat. Bigger than mine. I could use it. Your new Suburban too. Ha-ha!" But nobody was laughing, or paying attention to me.

Jenny's face was the color of a bad sunburn, and her eyes squinched into little slits of blue rage. Her lips compressed. "You! You ungrateful *pig*, you!" and she broke into sobs, blubbering hysterically. She covered her face with both hands. Her torso jerked and quivered. Then she made a fist and started shaking it towards him. "You're a heartless *bastard!* You *hear* me?"

"Yeah, I hear you." Buzzy snapped. "And so do the guys working on that rig," He pointed with his chin. "And on that rig, and *that* one." An evil sneer creased his sweat-beaded face. "But hey!" his eyes lit up in mock humor. "I bet the ones on THOSE rigs *way over there* can't HEAR YOU!" He let go with one hand so he could point around. "And they probably can't hear us WAY OVER in Venice, EITHER!"

Buzz was rolling his eyes, baring his teeth, and sweeping his free arm in a big circle, "So why don't you *scream* it a little LOUDER, hunh, dar-*ling?* 'I can't HEAR YOU, PYLE! I can't *HEAR YOU!!*'"

Damn if he didn't sound just like Sergeant Carter. But Jenny looked nothing like Gomer Pyle. No idiot grin on *her* face. She looked on the verge of a crack up, her pretty face beet red and contorted, her lips jerking spastically. "Shut UP, Buzzy!" She sputtered. "Just shut up, you miserable PRICK!"

Whooo-boy, I thought. Buzz curled his lips and bared his front teeth like fangs. I was smiling nervously, on the verge of jumping overboard, climbing on a rig and summoning a helicopter.

Jenny was hysterical now, leaning against the rail, sobbing, moaning, nodding her head, wiping the drool from her chin. She looked over at me with red-swollen eyes. "He's so . . . he's SO . . . mean to me, Humberto. So damn MEAN . . . I can't . . ."—then she took a deep breath and looked skyward, clearing her throat.

Christ, I'm thinking. These people are going sideways on me. Why'd I come?

Buzz finally went back to cranking away at the fish and Jenny seemed to calm down. She took another couple of deep breaths and started for the bow—just as a swell from a supply boat hit us. She kept her balance, then stepped on an empty wine-cooler bottle that was rolling around on the floor and went down with a nasty thump. "Aaayyh!" she squealed. "Oh, oh—my arm!"

Her arm twisted awkwardly in the handrail and half her bikini top slipped up to her neck. Suddenly a luscious white tit was jiggling two feet in front of my face, like in a titty-bar, but this was a hundred times more erotic.

"Oh, my!" I reached over. "Here, Jenny . . . you okay? Oh my goodness. Here." My forearm brushed her tit in the process, but she didn't seem to notice . . . or did she? Hmm. I brushed it again while "helping" her up. Then again, but with my nose, as I bent down to pick up the bottle. Man, I love the smell of that piña colada suntan oil she uses. Always reminds me of the beach, of beach bunnies smeared with it, afternoon naps next to them . . .

"There!" I said smiling as I came back up. Buzz had turned back around, nodding and sighing disgustedly. Jenny was adjusting her strap. Her tit was covered now. "You okay?" I asked. "Man, I remember once when I took a spill out here and got snagged on *two* treble hooks from a Magnum Rapala! TWO! Man, shoulda seen that mess."

She was upset. "Buzzy!" she wailed, looking back towards him. "Buzzy, why won't you *help* me! *Look* at me! *Look at me!* You *bastard!* Oh Buzzy, you're so mean to me!" and she broke up again.

I put my arm around her. She was limp, moaning and sobbing

again, rubbing her knee. Buzz just nodded from the other side of the boat, sighing and snorting bitterly.

"Humberto!" Jenny suddenly gasped. Wine fumes pummeled my face as she pointed with her lovely manicured hand. "Will you *look* at him?" She dropped her arm and suddenly seized my leg, pretty high up too. "Just *look* at him. He won't even *help* me. He doesn't care *what* happens to me. He just doesn't *give a shit* . . . DO YOU?" She glared over at him. "DO YOU, you evil PIG!" She tightened her grip as she spat the words.

"Oh, yes I *do!*" Buzz spun around laughing harshly, still cranking away at the fish. "You *bet* I do, my *DARLING!*"

"You're a bastard, Buzzy. And I'm getting *so tired* of your ranting and raving at me for every *little* thing—every LITTLE thing, Buzz. Oh Humberto, I just don't know anymore. I used to—but I just can't take it anymore!" And she collapsed, sobbing on my chest, her hand moving up my thigh.

Whoops, what now? I looked over at Buzz—afraid to look at Jenny—and he was still cranking away at the reel. The soft lovely hand with the gold bracelet gripped right where my shorts ended. And these were pretty short. Was it an accident? My head reeled. I couldn't believe this shit. She gripped tighter and a little higher. The center console blocked Buzzy's view below my chest.

I looked down. The red fingernails stood out against my skin, which—though I tan well—was pretty white this close to my scrotum. Then I looked up at Jenny's face—then back over at Buzz just as I felt a finger slipping under the shorts and start moving, back and forth, inching upward.

"Here, Buzz!" I gasped, and edged towards him. "Let me get the gaff this time. I've got plenty pictures!" I looked at Jenny for a second and she had a weird glazed look I'd never seen before.

The cobia was rolling about ten yards away now and I got ready with a good grip on the gaff. "Huge sucker!" I yelled and looked up at Buzz. "Gotta go fifty, sixty pounds, ya think?"

"I think that crazy bitch behind me needs her white ass spanked red. That's what I think." He chuckled harshly, then turned around and wiggled his tongue at her. "And I think she's gonna get it as soon as we boat this fish."

Oh shit, I thought. Maybe the console *didn't* block everything.

Or maybe I'm out here with raving loons, for God's sake. I haven't seen these people in over a year, had no idea things had gotten like this.

Anyway, did Buzz see Jenny's hand tickling my pubes just now? Does he know she's into this kind of shit? Maybe they're both into it. Maybe they're some kind of swingers or something? I didn't know *what* to think. Then Buzz looked at her with that wicked Nicholson leer of his and chuckled again.

"Ha-ha!" I said, looking over, commenting on the spanking remark. A little jocosity. Just what we need. Maybe the mood is changing. But Jenny just sat on the bow with that glazed look. She didn't say a thing, just sat there, twisting the cap off another wine cooler with the corner of the towel. Then she turned to starboard for a second and guzzled, guzzled a little too fast, actually.

"That's IT! Yeah that's it!" Buzz yelled. "Start puking now, why don't ya! A little early for ya to start puking now, isn't it Ho-*ney?*"

"Almost here, Buzz!" I yelped, trying to defuse the scene. "Get him a little closer." The cobia was at boatside again. "I'll get him." He lumbered up slowly, shaking his head, and I lunged out, under him and up, and *JAB!* hooked him expertly, right under the gills.

Then, with a jerk, he shot straight down, knocking me off my feet and almost overboard. But my chin stopped me as it smacked the gunwhale—*WHACK!* like a jackhammer.

And there goes the fish, with the gaff still impaled in its jaw, the seven dollar lure in its lip and five feet of snapped forty-pound test monofilament.

"You idiot!" Buzz roared. "You fuckin' idiot!"

"Hey, man!" Now I was pissed. *"Fuck you,* all right?" I was sputtering now. "And the horse you rode in on, *all right?* Just chill out, will ya? Geezuz!"

Buzz stood there, lips curled, panting, pouring sweat. Then he wound up like a pitcher and hurled his rod against the console, where it cracked the screen on the depth finder, sending him into a stomping, sputtering, spittle-spewing rage. "We'll NEVER boat one of these goddamn cobia with this crew! NEVER! Christ! Where do I FIND these people!"

I heard a weird little shriek and looked over at Jenny, who was doubled over again, covering her mouth. She seemed to be shaking.

Oh geez, I thought. Here we go again. Then she jerked up and her eyes were bright. She was actually *giggling!* She bent back down, giggling some more. Her sleek little shoulders heaved and shuddered as the giggles turned to guffaws. She had her elbows on her lap, her hands over her mouth, and a lump of white tit peeked from between her forearm and bicep. She finally rolled her head back and started guffawing out loud.

Then I started laughing, looking around at Buzz, who just sat there, glowering—smiling maliciously now. "Ya like that, hunh?"

Jenny was roaring by now, cackling, drooling.

"Yeah, go ahead! *Real* funny." He raced over and grabbed Jenny by the arms.

Good God! I thought. What the hell have I got into now! But she was still laughing, uncontrollably, eyes closed, wrestling playfully with him. "Nah! Nah!" she protested. "Oops! No, no!"

Now he sat on the ice chest, pinned her arms behind her and wrestled her over his lap—like for a spanking. My God, what kind of freaks was I out here with? What now? Laugh along, I guess. They were both cackling now.

She laughed as he pulled down her bikini bottom, exposing that meaty white tail I remembered so well from her diving-board show at the bar shower. Now it shivered and bounced as she kicked and squirmed.

"Yeah! Real *funny*, hunh!" He raged. "Well, how's THIS?" and he smacked her ass.

"OW!" Smack, again. "OW! Oh Buzzy, you're *hurtin'* me!" Smack. But she was laughing—laughing her head off, obviously digging the hell out of it. Her cheeks were red now. Her glute muscles contracted with every whack and her hands tried to reach behind her as he held her down by the neck, her streaked mane bouncing as she cackled and her head jerked around.

A weird scene. Do I laugh along, or jump overboard and swim to something saner like a rig? I looked around for the nearest one. Then I looked back and they're smooching.

I've heard of such things, in *Penthouse Forum*, and actually seen them—on *Sex in the City*. But this was the first live case. And I mean some serious smooching and groping. She still had her bikini bottom around her knees and Buzzy's hand was busy. I was definitely tense now, feeling damn awkward, and a little pissed. I walked to the back of the boat and took a whiz. Then I opened the cooler, grabbed one of Buzzy's O'Doul's and guzzled. "Ahhhhhh!" I gasped. Then belched gloriously, trying to remind them that I *was* around. But they were too engaged to hear me.

"All right, lovebirds," I finally said, clapping my hands. "Almost ten o'clock. I gotta get back to the island. We're going on another dive. I don't wanna miss it."

Nothing to it. They untangled; she jerked up her bikini bottom, shook her mane a bit, wrapped it in a ponytail, and we were roaring back in seconds. Geezuz, what a morning—and early yet.

We had one more dive to go.

Ten

INTO THE BLUE

Paul was in the boat jabbing some ice with an ice pick as I splashed by. He heard me and looked over. "Where the hell where ya? We're gonna hit the *long* ball today!"

"Went out fishing with Buzzy and Jenny," I said, pointing behind me as they roared off through the channel. "Shoulda seen *that*."

"With *who*?" He frowned and shaded his eyes. "Oh, Buzzy? What the hell are *they* doing out here?"

I told him.

We'd be leaving in about fifteen minutes for the South Pass blocs, the deep ones, in order to avoid the murk. I'd just been near there, and told Paul that the water had been green.

"Good," he said. "It'll probably be blue at the SP blocs. If not on top, then it shouldn't be much of a murk layer. Not if it's green this close."

"Actually, you never know with these crazy currents." I replied. "Look at yesterday. That was some of the worst murk we ever dove in."

"Right," Paul said. "That was a helluva day to start Tom on rig diving."

"Shit, man," I said. "He dove like a champ. Helluva lot better than us when we started out. Tom's a trooper."

"I'll give him that, "Paul chuckled. "He's a trooper, all right . . . or nuts.

And then Paul, Pelayo, Tom, and I were roaring over the swells due southeast. Up ahead and a little to the left was Buzzy. It looked like they were trolling now. I leaned close to Pelayo's ear. "That's Buzz and Jenny," I said. "Pass close. We'll moon 'em."

Pelayo swerved to within fifty yards. We bent over and slapped our cheeks while Jenny made biting and grabbing motions. Buzzy shot the bird. He looked pissed that we'd come in that close.

"That's a dizzy chick, boy," Pelayo blurted. He looked at me nodding. "Never forget that bar shower. Toni packed up and moved to her momma's for a week after it. I did all right by myself . . ."

"Right!" I said, remembering the bachelor apartment that he and Chris had maintained for two years before marriage.

"Yeah, man," Pelayo continued. "She came back and the house looked like the inside of a dumpster. Freakin' fungus on the walls. Bathtub was green. Showed *her*."

We roared east toward deep water, fleeing the murk, the Gulf floor sloping away below us. The depth finder went from 300 to 500 feet in twenty minutes. We were approaching the continental slope, where the continental shelf gives way to the perpetual black void of the abyss—the waters over 1,000 feet deep. Helldivers haven't *quite* gotten down there yet. But give them time.

We also hoped to evade the sharks—or at least dive an area where we could see the damn things if they were around. You can't really evade sharks out here. Not completely, and definitely not on this side of the river. They're everywhere—the big ones that is. Their capacity to pop up anywhere and without warning lends a nice edge to every dive.

An hour later we were still roaring east. The water was a darker green now—but not quite blue. A foamy current line loomed ahead. "Is that the rip?" I said, while pointing ahead.

"Yep, looks like it," Pelayo rasped.

It was the rip with bells on. It was dramatic; the water went from dark green to almost purple. We plowed through a mass of sargassum as we hit it—high-fiving around the boat.

"Yeah-you-RIGHT!" Paul howled. WHOO-WHOO!" Cobalt blue water always has that effect on us. It was glorious. A delightful dive was imminent.

"Lookit that wake!" Pelayo boomed. White foam streaked through a backdrop that looked like grape juice. We were pumped. The rigs loomed ahead, another three or four miles away. Scanning around, I saw no menacing cloud patterns on the horizon, but it was early yet. These things pop up out of nowhere this time of year down here.

"*Saw that!*" Tom suddenly screeched. I looked over and his eyes were like saucers, but bright, excited.

"Wow—saw it?" Pelayo yelled a split second later while hauling back on the throttle. They were both wide-eyed, with crazy grins, almost like groupies. What the hell, I thought. Did we drop something? Did something fly out of the boat?

"It was huge!" Tom gasped, while pointing left. His eyes glowed. "Something huge jumped outta the water right over there!"

"Manta ray!" Pelayo said. "Man, that sucker came flying outta the water like a GI-GAN-TIC flying fish! Remember we saw one last year? Maybe he'll jump again. There, lookit!"

This time I saw it. The thing erupted from the base of a swell and sailed for what must have been twenty feet over the Gulf, like some giant bat, then crashed back with a thunderous splash.

"WOW!" I was speechless. It had been years since we'd seen it. "And look!" The monstrosity was airborne again, looking more like a flying grand piano than a bat this time, and then *SPLASH!* Back in, with a huge explosion of water and foam.

"My God! Don't see that very often, Tom, my boy." Pelayo looked around while nudging the throttle up. "Shoot, we've only seen it, what, twice?" he said, looking around. "The whole time we been diving. That's eighteen years."

"That's all I've seen it." I said. "And never on any of those nature shows either, or anything. Remember the first time? We didn't know what the hell to think. We didn't know mantas jumped like that. Who'da thought it? Big thing like that getting airborne? Makes no sense."

Five minutes later I had the rig hook as we approached the immense rumbling platform from down current.

"Lookit that!" Paul whooped. You could see down the beams forever. Fish everywhere. No spooky clouds on the horizon. No murk. No current. No waves—just a gentle swell. The sun, bright and blazing. Two guys waved from the top of the rig, and pointed down at the water, or at us. I clanged the hook on a beam and we commenced another round of high-fives. "We were due for this." Paul smirked. "Been a while since we seen it this pretty."

Tom looked ready to go. He was looking over the railing, smiling, issuing a low whistle, rapt. What a change from yesterday. "Beats Belize," he said finally, looking up, wide-eyed, still smiling. "This water's unbelievable." Then he turned back to the water and his face jerked. "Hey guys!" he yelled. "What's THAT? Another *manta*?"

"Freakin'-aay!" Pelayo said looking over and trying to sound calm. "A freakin' manta ray!"

"Will ya . . . will ya look at the size of the thing!" Paul said with a low whistle.

That's what the guys up above had been pointing at. They had a beautiful view from up there. Not that this was too bad. The mantas finned slowly through their realm about twenty feet below the boat against the deep purple backdrop. They were mostly black, with white near the tips of the wings and on those horns that sweep out from the head. *"Devilfish"* they were nicknamed. Legend had it they wrapped divers in their wings and carried them to their doom. Other legends said they sailed into the air to crash-dive on boats and demolish them.

I guess anything this big and ugly just *had* to be bad. Yet here for the first time we looked at a fish without the urge to spear it. No one was scrambling for the guns and the tanks. We must be slipping, getting soft. An impressive sight nonetheless. The monstrosity was just flying along. His massive wings flapping like a condor on slow motion. From white wing-tip to white wing-tip, he looked three times as wide as our boat.

"Another one! Hey look!" Tom was pointing behind us now—
and sure enough, another one was looming into view, if anything
bigger than the first. Unreal. "Man, I've never seen things like
this," Tom said excitedly while clutching the rail. "Fed the
stingrays in Cayman. And seen eagle rays all over Belize and the
Keys . . . but wow! These things are awesome."

He had it exactly right. "Awesome" was the only way to put it—
not scary. Nothing about them inspired fright. They inspired awe
. . . sheer awe. Then, suddenly, the wing flaps quickened and—
swoosh! They vanished into the blue.

"Geezuz!" Paul chuckled. "Saw that? Those things can turn it
on, hunh?"

Then we saw why. "There he is, gentlemen!" Pelayo said from
the bow while pointing. "There's big boy . . . that's why those
mantas scrammed." The guys on the rig were pointing again,
cupping their mouths and yelling.

We looked up. "YEAH, we see him!" Paul shouted and we all
waved.

He was a huge shark, making a slow pass under the boat. Every
detail visible through the calm, crystalline water, which was 650
feet deep here. Three miles away it dropped to 3,000 feet. So big
ones popped up all the time. Even oceanic whitetips—*bona fide*
oceanic whitetips, the ones who rip into shipwreck survivors and
Cuban rafters, the kind that attacked Cousteau on his first underwater film expedition, the kind my Baton Rouge chum, Clay
Coleman, ran into while snorkeling out here.

Not often you can snorkel in 1,000-foot depths. But Clay was
out here, nailing mangroves and cobia. "I took a deep breath," he
says. "Went down to about twenty feet, leveled out and there he
was! Staring me in the face! Man, his pectoral fins stretched six
feet from tip to tip—I swear . . . looked like wings. He was only
about ten feet away when I saw him, coming head on. I freaked.
Now what? I thought. The big sucker kept coming . . . coming—
finally at five feet he turned. I was getting ready to jab him but
he turned away. Then he turned back, slowly. I started finning
backwards—keeping an eye on him. My gun ready. I finally
bumped the boat with my head—ouch! I clambered aboard raving and stuttering and we decided to try another rig."

But this wasn't a white-tip. This was another great hammer-head. No mistaking these ugly suckers. He came up and circled us once, his top fin slicing over the swells, so tall it actually bent over at the top. His hideous head, spanning almost four feet across, just ten feet away from us. He just cruised by, his gray body almost as long as the boat, wider than the console. He seemed to be warning us. Or daring us—so much for our former enthusiasm.

"There can be no covenant between lions and men," wrote Homer in the Iliad. Sounds like an ancient version of "you can't fool mother nature." And this shark seemed to say that the same applied for sharks. "This is my realm," he glowered. "My 'hood. No trespassing. Violators will be chomped."

Homer was right, of course. The Born Free cubs grew up to kill men. The real life Grizzly Adams was killed and partly devoured by his lovable pet. And though they keep trying for that covenant with sharks on TV, you'll notice the men usually stay in cages.

"Well!" Paul said as the shark faded into the glare. "At least here we can *SEE* 'em right? They won't surprise us *here.*"

"Yeah, boy," Pelayo snorted. "We'll see them charge from a hundred feet away. We'll have plenty of time to crap our disco pants and have a freaking heart attack before they hit us."

"Could be worse," Paul chuckled. "Could be killer whales." He had a point. A local charter captain captured a pod of them on video, rolling, blowing merrily on the surface not five miles from this rig. Now *that* might make for an interesting undersea con-frontation. But what dated and reactionary nomenclature: "killer" whale. Why it's just Willie, the lovable Orca. Just a big dolphin, really.

Yet I remember back in pre-PC days a story in *Outdoor Life* about some guy getting chased over the ice floes by one. The thing would ram them, trying to topple him into the water. I believe it. Makes perfect sense. That's how they snatch seals. Watch in those Time-Life videos. Why wouldn't they grab a human?

Tom was mum. No response. What a shame. He'd been pumped seconds before. Not that *we* were exactly itching to get in the water. I sure as hell wasn't. Then we heard a splash behind us.

The guys on the rig just threw something. We turned around and the shark was heading for it. *Swoosh!*—it bolted towards the splash and we saw a great swirl.

Another splash. Another swirl. We looked up. The rig-workers were throwing snapper carcasses. "Wonderful!" Paul yelled. "They're feeding the goddamned shark!"

"Hey, thanks!" Pelayo screamed. "Thanks a lot!" He shook his head and waved his arm at the rig workers, one was coming down the steel stairway. He leaned on the stairway smiling. He seemed friendly.

"We'll be sandblasting in a minute," he said. "You boys might wanna dive another rig."

"Yeah, sure!" Tom blurted. "Great idea! No problem! None at all! We were just leaving!"

"Yeah, all right." Pelayo smiled and nodded. "Get the hook, On-the-Ball. The guy's right. That silica gets all over the boat when they do that. Once we went down—remember that?" Pelayo turned to me. "When we surfaced that crap was all over the boat, covering the floor, everything. A pain. Let's go." Pelayo leaned on the throttle and we roared off. The next rig was a half-mile away.

The water was equally gorgeous here. But only barracuda—big ones—and mangroves finned under the boat. "Let's get down there before we see something scary." Paul said while jerking up his tank. Look! That another shark? Or a cobia?"

"Cobia," Pelayo blurted.

"Sure about that, hunh?" Tom croaked.

"It's a cobia, Tom." I said. "Hey . . . and there's another. TWO!"

"And I'm getting them," Paul snapped. He bit into his regulator and backflipped off the bow. Pelayo was next to him, spitting into his mask. He jerked it on, looked at his gauge, and plunged backwards.

I went next . . . *splishhh!* The water always feels a little cool when you first hit. The sun had been scorching my body for almost two hours. But the shock lasted mere seconds . . . What a delight to immediately look around and see *everything*—except the cobia . . . where'd they go?

There's the 'cuda, three of them, inside the rig glaring at me
and almost motionless. Damn those things are ugly. Yet they also
look calm and pensive, never in a rush—until you stick one. And
I was in no mood for that. Everything's bright and shimmering
down here today, from the boat's propeller to the amberjacks
blazing past to the bubble-lines from Pelayo and Paul, already
well below, their guns pointed to the fore, their angel-flights bil-
lowed aft. Their flapping collars were visible even from here. I
guess they scared the cobia off. These fish don't see a get-up like
that every day. In this clear water the fish see everything too. No
murk to block the sun today. No gloom for this dive. My mood
was shimmering too.

Splishh! and here comes Tom, tumbling off the bow in a cloud
of silver bubbles. He doesn't even wait for me, doesn't even look
around. He's heading down, cocking his bands. The old boy's taking to this sport with the zeal of a convert. You'd think he'd been
at this for years—instead of a day. Always happens that way.
People either take to this sport immediately or bail out immediately. He was already a hunter, and a diver. So it really wasn't
much of a conversion. Anyway, there was no apprehension for
Tom on this dive.

What a difference the visibility makes. Ten minutes ago we'd
watched a fourteen-foot hammerhead at pissing distance. With
heavy murk around, I dare say we'd have suited up more slowly
for this dive, might have bullshitted longer, might have stalled
further by grabbing a bite or a beer—or even two. No need for
that today.

The panorama was glorious, the entire structure in all its
sprawling, coral-encrusted, fish-surrounded glory. Everything
blue and silver and shimmering. The huge legs stretching into
the deep-blue void below. Two bubble lines *way* down there
already. Pelayo and On-the-Ball were already prowling the
depths, closing on the big AJ's no doubt. They still think they can
beat guys like Gerry and Terry and Stan. Ten years have taught
them nothing.

Tom's on his way, too. I'm savoring the scenery up here for a
minute. No current to fight this time. No "icy-clutch" in the gut
while descending. Hey, it's nice to relax on a dive, *too.*

I always scan the perimeter of the rig first, looking for any big, big shape or shadow, any that stands out, that dwarfs the others. Cobia like it up here, but damned if I can find those two. Only those lazy 'cudas stand out. Mangroves are everywhere. Schools of them fin near the beams. Big jacks, their flanks streaked by sun-lines, flutter around them. They're faster than the snapper, always in a hurry it seems. Bolting this way, now turning, now off in another direction. Now back. They suffer from a piscine version of attention deficit disorder.

I started drifting down and caught up with Tom who'd stopped at around 80 feet. Suddenly he was pointing behind me, jerking his head, pointing with the gun now, but his finger wasn't on the trigger. He looked excited.

Suddenly we were enveloped in a shadow. But Tom still wasn't fleeing, or preparing to shoot. I turned around.

"Holy shit!" I said to myself. The mantas were back—or maybe it was another school. Yes, a *school*. Four of them. Incredible. We'd never seen them underwater before. These things were *huge*, looked wider than my garage. They flapped lazily just outside the rig, slightly above us, showing their white bellies splotched in black with the long gill slits. Long thin tails poked out behind them, like anterior antennae.

They were in no hurry. Their monstrous wings flapped lazily, like giant silver bats on slow motion—actually they looked more like flying saucers from this angle. These twin-horned devilfish things looked pretty weird against a reef or sand backdrop. But next to the rig's surreal structure it's a scene from *Star Wars*. If mantas didn't exist, George Lucas would have to invent them. They're a dead ringer for those half mechanical-half natural creatures he dreams up. Damn, what a sight. I doubt that Timothy Leary or Ken Kesey ever saw anything like this.

And again, we must be slipping. Because I wasn't tempted to shoot. But we definitely wanted a closer look and started finning over, Tom ahead of me. He was eager this time.

I followed him to the edge of the rig and grabbed a beam. He kept going towards the big flapping beasts. Good God, I thought. The boy is in a trance. Now I could see three remoras clinging to the belly of the closest one. Another manta had a chunk of his

wing missing—a rounded chunk, suspiciously similar to the con-
tours of a shark's mouth.

The mantas were probably fifty feet away now, and showed no
alarm. Yet that hammerhead had sent the others zooming off. He
was a natural predator. Us they couldn't figure out. They're not
accustomed to predators in disco suits. Angel-flights and flow-
ered, flapping collars don't register in the manta brain as belonging on anything that'll rip a chunk out of them.

Tom was closing on them. The crazy sucker was almost on
them. I guess he sees this type of stuff in all the yuppie dive magazines; people feeding and riding rays and stuff. Hell, he's done it
himself with the sting rays on Cayman. I guess he was going for
the long ball here. Yep! Looks like he's reaching out. He was over
the nearest one now, over its back. The others sped up and Tom
made a grab for the ridge between those great horns . . . was he
nuts? YES! He grabbed hold.

Then—SWOOOOSH! the manta's wings kicked into fast-for-
ward and it shot off. But without Tom, who was tumbling head
over heels—fins over mask, actually—in a great whirl of backwash, spinning like a toy monkey in the manta's exhaust.

And I was *dying*. Roaring into my regulator. Doubled over in
mirth. Engulfed in a cloud of bubbles. Then I noticed something
sinking below him. Tom's spear gun! In the commotion he
dropped it. Bye-bye, two hundred simoleons, too late to retrieve,
though it'll take a while to sink 650 feet.

Tom finally swam over, adjusting his mask, pointing it up and
blowing to empty it of water. Now he was nodding and hunching
his shoulders as I continued roaring. I poked my face inches
from his and bellowed, showing my appreciation for the show—
a show to shame anything on Animal Planet.

Then I realized I'd used half my damn tank. Enough bullshit.
Time to kill stuff. I pointed down and Tom nodded. He was coming along, for the hell of it, I guess.

Down into that purple void, into that all-embracing vastness.
We were at 100 feet before we knew it. 120 seconds later, Tom
grabbed my shoulder again. He started pointing down, towards
the corner of the rig. Pelayo was down there, about 50 feet below
us, wrestling with something that looked like an AJ.

I nodded at Tom. He nodded back. Looking back, we saw Pelayo with his gun bands up around his shoulder and both hands gripping the fish, on his way up. Nice going. The thing looked huge, maybe sixty, seventy pounds. We swam over toward him. I looked left, outside the rigs, and saw the mantas flapping along again; beautiful, spooky.

Then Tom jerked my shoulder. I looked at him and he pointed more empathically towards Pelayo. His eyes looked wide, tense. I turned my gaze, but Pelayo looked fine. He was about twenty feet below us to our right. He looked all right, finning up slowly, issuing a little line of bubbles, the fish in control. Then I saw something below him. Couldn't make out the shape. At first I though it might be On-the-Ball. But it blew no bubbles. It looked big, but not massive. Maybe another AJ following his stricken mate, I thought. Then I made it out.

A shark, and a massive one. He didn't look big at first because of the angle. He was coming straight up. So I'd only seen his head and forequarters at first. Actually that should have been enough. There's no other way to describe it—that *Jaws* poster. That toothy snout pointing surface-ward. The unsuspecting person above.

But he didn't stay unsuspecting for long. We were swimming over when Pelayo finally looked down. Then over at us. Then he picked up speed, let go with one hand, and pointed down. He was only about thirty feet away from us and we nodded and waved.

No hammerhead this time. Or even a sand tiger. His nose was too wide and blunt. He was either a tiger or a bull. As big around as the beam next to him—a main beam, the kind you can't get the rig hook around. But he wasn't in a hurry. Not jerky or anything. Finally he leveled out six feet below Pelayo, and that's when we saw his true size. Had to be twelve feet long. At least twice as long as a man. But again, no aggression. He finned slowly away from us now.

Pelayo was even with us now, and his eyes said it all. We were pumping for the surface but looking down. I thought for sure Pelayo would let go of the damn amberjack. Give him to the shark, but *nooo*—he held on.

I looked over and here came Paul, pointing down with his gun, moving his other hand like a mouth. Our shark signal. We all nodded back. The monster made another big circle, then drifted outside the rig till we lost sight of him. Must have just eaten. And a manta ray must be filling.

We hit the surface again.

People like Johnny, Terry, and Gerry say the mid-sixties were the heyday of Louisiana dive rodeos—not of Louisiana diving, now—simply of competitive spear fishing. Fact is, there's probably more *spear fishing* now than ever, certainly more certified divers. But the organized clubs and their organized events just don't pack 'em in like they used to. They're no longer chic.

Many still spear fish. Many still enjoy it. But reveling in the slaughter has become un-chic, like trophy hunting in general. Fact: there's more big-game hunting today, even in Africa, than in Hemingway's day. You'd never know it from the mass media. Amazingly, this "shusssssh, let's keep it within the family" attitude has infiltrated even—I'm ashamed to admit it—Louisiana.

The Grand Isle Tarpon rodeo itself—the oldest and biggest in the nation—recently yanked its spear fishing division, "for conservation reasons," according to the Rodeo's president at the time, who happened to be Louisiana's governor's son—a Republican governor no less, big-time hunter himself, NRA supporter, the whole bit. This governor also gave us Louisiana's concealed weapons law. We can pack one down here. This governor (Mike Foster) enjoys enormous support in hunting and fishing circles.

No small feat to become politically incorrect with this bunch. But we managed it.

Every year the Academy of Underwater Arts and Sciences awards something called a NOGI award, a little statuette known as "the Oscar of Diving," in three categories: Sports and Education, Arts and Sciences, Distinguished Service. General do-goodism stuff. Hans Hass and Jacques Cousteau have both won—Hass right here in New Orleans last year. This award has an interesting pedigree, one that might horrify its recent winners. It stands for "New Orleans Grand Isle Invitational."

Remember how Johnny Bonck, Roland Riviere, and their buddies got spear fishing accepted by the Grand Isle Tarpon Rodeo? Well, the NOGI was awarded to the winner. Johnny Bonck first saw the carved wooden statuette in Belize in the 1950s. He brought one over and it became the award for the *Most and Biggest Fish Killed* at the Grand Isle Rodeo—for piling them up, no mercy, no limit, no nothing—at the time.

"I gotta wonder, Hom-boy-da," Johnny laughs. "How many people nowaday *know* that? All these photographers and stuff, they're up there all proud, smiling and everything—wonder if they know we used to get that NOGI for shooting jewfish, barracuda, sharks—and whoever piled up the most, won it. I just gotta wonder. Hell, they might drop it like a snake."

Indeed, Cousteau and Hass didn't win it as spear fishermen. They won well after becoming sanctimonious pests.

The crowd at Westwego City Park drives the point home: we're a hundred people at best; the club divers, their wives, girlfriends, kids.

"Can you believe this?" Pelayo snorted as we crunched into the gravel parking lot. He was nodding pensively, sadly. I was sad too. Same for Tom and On-the-Ball. No escaping that "post-partying depression." You see it at the airport a lot, those glum faces on returning vacationers. I can spot them every time. It's a cinch to tell who's coming and who's going. Three days of heavy boozing, of oblivion towards jobs and bills. Now it all gangs up. Home and its routine tonight. Work tomorrow.

"Geezuz," I said. "Remember when we were little kids? These rodeos packed them in, man."

"Yeah," Pelayo snapped. "I remember, all right. They used to hold these things at West End Park, at the Lakefront. Traffic jams for blocks around. Huge fish hanging up. Unreal."

"Really?" Tom poked his head up from the back seat. "Looks pretty crowded to me."

"*Nothing* like the old days." Pelayo answered while jamming the shift into park. "You wouldn't believe it, Tom. Now I'm talking about the mid-1960s. Parents always took us on "Sunday drives" back then. If it was the Sunday of the rodeo weigh-in, you always wound up at West End Park. Even if nobody in our family was a diver. It was a happening event, that's all."

"Not much happening here," Paul said glumly while getting out. "But—ah!" his face lit up. "I see the keg over there."

"We're right behind." I chimed in.

Actually, we show up at these weigh-ins for the mere hell of it. Our fish never place. We show up, see what's on the board, look at each other, arch the eyebrows, whistle, gasp. Nowadays, the big fish are *way* down, 200 feet plus. Not quite worth it for us. Why embarrass ourselves by even entering our kill? No way. Like I said before, we're in the bush leagues compared to these guys.

Or the fish are way out, forty to fifty miles offshore. Again, not worth it—certainly not in our twenty-two-foot boat. Some of these Sea Tigers, Helldivers, Aqua Aces, Pneumatic Nailers, and Bayou Bandits have been out on chartered trawlers or crew boats close to a week, "bounce-diving" as they call it. They plunge in swim down to 220 feet, look around . . . "Hmm . . . nope. Just little stuff down here. Nothing over 100 pounds." Back up. They might hit fifteen different rigs this way. It's trophy hunting. Take the biggest or nothing.

First guy we ran into on the way to the keg is "Doctor Bruce." Yes sir, Dr. Bruce Thompson, Ph.D. in Marine Biology of LSU's Coastal Wetlands Center. He was hacking and slicing away at a big red snapper. He was covered in slime, spattered with blood, shrouded in flies. He looked ecstatic.

"Whatcha say Dr. Bruce?" I said, waving. He looked up, smiled, nodded, adjusted his glasses with a slime-covered hand, and resumed his butchery. No, he's not cleaning fish in the conventional sense. He's dissecting them. Doctor Bruce likes fresh red snapper as much as anyone, but he's not carving out the white, gorgeous fillets on this one. He won't throw them, lemon and butter drenched, on a grill to sizzle and drizzle over flaming coals. He's more interested in the snapper's ear. Some "earbone" down there somewhere tells Dr. Bruce the fish's age. Next he'll grope for its gonads.

These butcheries and perversions, filtered through Bruce's brain, result in valuable age and spawning information that might be used by the National Marine Fisheries service to set size and harvest quotas. If nothing else they might set size limits for the dive clubs themselves. It happened years ago with jewfish. He determined that these fish didn't spawn until the age at which they weighed around fifty pounds. The Louisiana Council of Dive Clubs promptly disqualified any jewfish under fifty pounds from any competition. Years later, state and federal regulations kicked in. In many ways, on matters of conservation these dive clubs were ahead of the curve by years. Ask Dr. Bruce himself. "No doubt about it," he nods. "These guys have always been helpful."

A sign near the big board commemorated the life of a fallen chum, Warren "Whip" Mermilliod. But with more than just cheap sentiment. The Helldivers' Rodeo has contributed over $5,000 to the Warren J. Mermilliod Memorial Scholarship Fund to date, the only scholarship at LSU offered in the Marine Biology Masters program. Whip himself held an M.S. in Marine Biology from LSU.

Maybe Pelayo and I were contributing right now. "Too much foam, man." Pelayo snorted. "Blow it off."

"Hey whatcha want for seventy-five cents?" Terry Migaud snaps. He was serving at the ever-popular beer booth for now. But he was on the makeshift wooden stage earlier. "Yeah, this keg's gettin' low," he complained while pumping away, draining the last drop.

"See you gotcha a nice barracuda," Paul said, pointing at the board. "Fifty-five pounder, hunh?"

"Stoned him," Terry replied. "Nothin' to it. Hit the trigger and he keeled over. "

Amazingly, Terry's amberjack didn't get first place—after all that. Nor did Gerry Bourgeois's. Joe Michel of the Get-'Em Dive Club edged them out with a 111-pound monster.

Terry's dive mate during the shark escapade, Louis Rossignal, won the Snapper Division with a forty-pounder. And yes, Stan "The Man" Smith took "King Spear Fisherman" with that shark, 490 pounds of it. The steaks will feed another throng at another Helldiver picnic.

We milled around for a while. Tom, still somewhat new to the area, showed the keenest interest in the fish, the divers, and the general ambiance. As usual, the second beer on my empty stomach started clearing things up . . . or maybe just masking the confusion with a mild buzz.

Over by those tables, Gerry Bourgeois and Val Rudolfich, the grand old men of Louisiana rig diving, Sea Tigers, literally and figuratively. "Present at the creation," you might say. It doesn't seem possible. They started in the late 1950s (a *little* after Johnny and Roland) and are still at it. Still plunging deep, sticking monsters and wrestling them up, still making the Board every year, and still chugging beer, but slowly, decorously. They compare to the gang at the other end of the park like a Jagger, McCartney, or Townshend to the stars of today's music awards shows. They watch the current crop of cut-ups from a distance. They nod and smile, shake their heads every now and then.

"Been there," they smirk. "But geezuz! Did we look and act like *that?* Well, we won't begrudge you your fun, kiddies. We sure had ours." They don't *say* it. They don't have to. That wry smile and relaxed look says it. The younger crowd is reveling, indulging, letting off steam. Always happens this way. It suddenly hits you. "Hey, we made it! First off, we're *alive!* And second, check out these fish! And check out these *babes!*"

But the only babes we ogle here are wives, girlfriends, and sisters—and dare I say it . . . *daughters.* But they do bring friends. And when they hear the band crank up and hear the cars piling in, this neighborhood always disgorges a few of its residents for a little fun. But for the most part, over the past ten years these weigh-ins have become inside affairs. The big crowds of gawkers went out with the 1970s—like our disco. Maybe that's why we're here? We can't shake it. Compare this to Johnny and Roland's Rodeos, in a day with a tiny fraction of today's divers. They had international diving stars crowding into Grand Isle, features in every Louisiana newspaper, trophies, TV cameras. Things have changed.

They call this a "young man's sport." In general, it's undeniably true. Just look around this park. After the mid-thirties the passion for this lunacy seems to cool. Look at our own crew. Only a third of us on Breton Island actually dove. Ten years ago we all did. But the same crowd shows up every year. In fact, we got a few more out here this year than last. And *that's* what counts, I think.

Maybe Gene had the right idea all along. Show up. Keep the ties strong. He was fine this morning. Nobody brought up the ugliness. He cooked breakfast, had it ready for everybody when we crawled out of the tents . . . and boy was *that* ever nice, considering how we felt.

"It is our fellows who make life endurable to us," says Mencken. "And give it a purpose and meaning." All the fellows were there, like on our seventeenth birthdays, and our twenty-first birthdays, and our bachelor parties, and our weddings . . . and our (*yikes*) kids' birthdays and christenings! We all partook of the revelry, the good fellowship. And the rest of the gang didn't miss the spearing. They enjoyed loafing around the campsite, a little fishing . . . the boozing.

I expect we're all headed that way. Let's face it—ten, fifteen years ago those manta rays on the last dive would have been dead meat—or maybe *we'd* have been dead meat if they tangled with us. Point is, we'd have shot them.

What would Tata say about that? "*Malditos!*" I'm sure. We'd get our butts switched for sure. But boy, she'd love these amberjack and cobia, and especially the red snapper. "*Pargo,*" for Cubans.

As Tom brings me another draft and a chunk of grilled snapper drenched in lemon butter and seared around the edges, I think, "If Tata could see this . . . if only she could taste it." But, *ouch!* she'd probably wait until it cooled.

I shot a little snapper off Cojimar once, couldn't have been over eight inches long, slightly bigger than the *ronquitos*. But she went crazy. "*Ay! Rubio!* ["Blondie" in Spanish, my nickname] *Mira! Un pargito! Que bueno! Que lindo!*" We spoke with Tata on the phone recently. She had mailed us a stack of uncovered photos from our childhood, and a recent one of her. Amazing, my hair *was* golden at the time, almost the same color as the ronquitos Pelayo and I are holding in the shots.

Some things stick in your mind. The taste of Tata's fried fish is one of them for me. Yes, I was only seven, but I remember it, I don't care what anybody says, *I remember it*. I've never been able to duplicate it. My parents say it's because Tata always fried fish in *manteca* (lard). But I've tried that—not the same.

There's probably 1,200 pounds of fresh fish in the bins around me. Wonder what she'd do if Pelayo and I showed up in a pickup full of cobia, amberjack, and red snapper?

The edge, it always returns to the edge. The Cojimar coast was an edge. Our Mississippi Canyon rigs hug an edge. It is, as Hunter S. Thompson called the edge, "the place where you stretch your luck so far that fear becomes *exhilaration*."

Tata told Mom that her son Evelito hopped on a raft with three friends a few years ago. They did it right off Cojimar, "right where *Rubio* and *Pelayito* used to swim and dive," she said. They told her they'd call when they reached Key West.

Tata still waits for that call. That was the last time anyone saw them. Evelito wasn't seeking any "edge" on this trip. I doubt his fear every "turned to exhileration." That "icy clutch" gripped his guts all right—and never let go. it strangled his gut 'til the end—however it came. When those waves started cresting around him, as the raft started unravelling, when those tigers and whitetips started circling . . . who knows? Evelito would have much preferred to hop a plane like Pelayo and I and our families.

Yes, those who *seek* Thompson's "edge" are the pampered. Evelito had it land in his lap.

Tata still looks nothing like Mami in *Gone With the Wind*. She looks more like Tina Turner now.

We live across the "World's Longest Bridge" from New Orleans, the twenty four-mile causeway over Lake Pontchartrain—the lake where the Helldivers' Rodeo started thirty years ago. For some reason I love hitting that toll booth with my gas gauge needle on "E."

"Wonder if I can make it across?" asks something within me. I get a strange little buzz, especially when I'm dressed in a suit, commuting to a deskbound job. I learned around the campfire last night that several of us do the same thing. "And boy!" Chris added. "Gina *hates* it! Shirley, my wife, hates that "running on empty" bit, too. She's always leaning over to look at the gauge a mile before we hit the booth. "Let's fill up, NOW!" she says.

"Why do you *do* that?" she gasps.

"Why?"